CLEAN HOUSE

Exposing Our Government's Secrets and Lies

TOM FITTON

THRESHOLD EDITIONS

New York London Toronto Sydney New Delhi

Threshold Editions
An Imprint of Simon & Schuster, Inc.
1230 Avenue of the Americas
New York, NY 10020

Copyright © 2016 by Judicial Watch, Inc.

First Threshold Editions hardcover edition August 2016

THRESHOLD EDITIONS and colophon are trademarks of Simon & Schuster, Inc.

For information about special discounts for bulk purchases, please contact Simon & Schuster Special Sales at 1-866-506-1949 or business@simonandschuster.com.

The Simon & Schuster Speakers Bureau can bring authors to your live event. For more information, or to book an event, contact the Simon & Schuster Speakers Bureau at 1-866-248-3049 or visit our website at www.simonspeakers.com.

Interior design by Jaime Putorti

Manufactured in the United States of America

10   9   8   7   6   5   4   3   2   1

Library of Congress Cataloging-in-Publication Data

Names: Fitton, Thomas, author.
Title: Clean house / Tom Fitton.
Description: New York : Threshold Editions, [2016]
Identifiers: LCCN 2016023471
Subjects: LCSH: Political corruption—United States. | Obama, Barack.
Classification: LCC JK2249 .F437 2016 | DDC 973.932—dc23
LC record available at https://lccn.loc.gov/2016023471

ISBN 978-1-5011-3704-4
ISBN 978-1-5011-3706-8 (ebook)

This is dedicated to the hundreds of thousands of patriotic supporters who make all of our work possible.

CONTENTS

CLEAN
HOUSE

INTRODUCTION

WHY JUDICIAL WATCH?

Liberty cannot be preserved without a general knowledge among the people, who have a right, from the frame of their nature, to knowledge, as their great Creator, who does nothing in vain, has given them understandings, and a desire to know; but besides this, they have a right, an indisputable, unalienable, indefeasible, divine right to that most dreaded and envied kind of knowledge; I mean, of the characters and conduct of their rulers.

—JOHN ADAMS, 1765, *DISSERTATION ON THE CANON AND FEUDAL LAW*

John Adams was keenly aware of the relationship between secrecy and corruption in government and the preservation of liberty. Many of the Founding Fathers understood the importance of transparency in a nation's rulers. James Madison wrote that "A popular government without popular information, or the means of acquiring it, is but a prologue to a Farce or a Tragedy, or perhaps both." Thomas Jefferson said that "If we are to guard against ignorance and remain free, it is the responsibility of every American to be informed."

Judicial Watch has always believed that knowing the "characters and conduct" of the individuals who serve in the government and ensuring that the public is "informed" about what its government is doing is crucial to preserving our great republic. That is why for over twenty-two years we have been the most active user of the federal Freedom of Information Act (FOIA) to promote transparency, accountability, and integrity in government, politics, and the law. We are the nation's largest and most effective government watchdog group that works to advance the public interest.

Transparency is all about self-governance. If we don't know what the government is doing, how is that self-governance? How is that even a republic?

When we were founded in 1994, we used the FOIA open records law to root out corruption in the Clinton administration. During the Bush administration, we used it to combat that administration's penchant for improper secrecy. But the Bush administration pales in comparison to the Obama administration. Today, our government is bigger than ever, and also the most secretive in recent memory.

One of the Least Transparent Administrations in History

President Barack Obama promised the most transparent administration in history, but our experience over the eight years of his administration was that the executive branch and its federal agencies were black holes in terms of disclosure. President Obama and his minions made remarkable assertions of secrecy over everything from White House visitor logs to Fannie Mae and Freddie Mac, to Operation Fast and Furious and even the photos of a dead Osama bin Laden and the details of the Islamic burial ceremony used for one of the worst terrorist organizers of the modern age.

Judicial Watch filed well over three thousand FOIA requests with the Obama administration, many of which went unanswered. Our staff attorneys never had a day that wasn't hectic—they were forced to file and litigate more than 250 FOIA lawsuits in federal court. Getting the administration to comply with our requests for information and documents under FOIA was like pulling teeth. Many of these lawsuits were filed just to get a "yes or no" answer from the administration on whether they had any responsive records.

Administratively, federal agencies put up additional hurdles and stonewalled even the most basic FOIA requests. In many cases, we faced tough litigation fights, with Justice Department and administration attorneys and officials fighting hard to resist turning over records they were obligated under the law to disclose. And in many cases, like our fight to get former Secretary of State Hillary Clinton's emails, the administration seems to have misled Judicial Watch and federal judges, claiming that records did not exist that actually did exist or not conducting the legally required searches for the information and documents we were requesting.

Lack of Congressional Oversight

Unfortunately, congressional oversight is also sorely lacking—lacking on all fronts. Congress is like a fire department that shows up after your house burns down and shouts "fire." Even President Obama, flailing for an excuse to cover his own IRS bureaucrats' massively suppressing his political opponents, suggested that the government was too big and he had no way of effectively monitoring his own agencies. Of course, that doesn't explain the misbehavior of the Justice Department under the president's political appointees, Eric Holder and Loretta Lynch, in misleading the courts and resisting disclosure and compliance with federal law. But there have been numerous cases where Judicial Watch, a private citizens' group, has succeeded in uncovering documents that were denied to Congress even when it was trying to conduct oversight.

Judicial Watch has been widely acknowledged to have been performing the oversight function that was the job of Congress. We heard from many members of the House of Representatives who were embarrassed that its committees and oversight had become a joke under former Speaker John Boehner. Judicial Watch had more success investigating the IRS, Benghazi, and the Clinton email scandals than any House Committee under Boehner's direction (or lack of direction). Boehner's willingness to fund rather than oppose Barack Obama's lawlessness was also one of the chief reasons for his forced resignation as the Speaker in September 2015.

Defying the Inspectors General

The cavalier and obstructive attitude of the administration and its Justice Department was also demonstrated by the fact that agencies within the executive branch like the FBI have started refusing to comply with requests from the government's own inspectors general (IGs) to provide requested records, information, and documents the IGs need to conduct their investigations of fraud and abuse by government officials. In 2014, a majority of the IGs signed an unprecedented letter to Congress complaining about the Obama administration's actions. This included IGs from the National Security Agency, the Department of Homeland Security, and even the Justice Department. The IGs asked Congress to use "all available powers" to enforce access to agencies that refuse to comply with the Inspector General Act of 1978, the federal law that requires agencies to provide the IGs with any records the IG deems necessary for their investigations.[1]

In fact, the Obama administration compounded this problem when the Office of Legal Counsel at the Justice Department, which is headed by a political appointee, issued a legal opinion in 2015 justifying this defiance of the law. The opinion told DOJ employees—as well as the employees of other federal agencies—that they could withhold information at their discretion from the IG. To evade audits and investigation of possible misbehavior, the officials only had to claim the information was protected or privileged based on various federal statutes. As the Heritage Foundation explained in a detailed legal analysis, this was a misinterpretation of the straightforward text of the Inspector General Act and the clear legislative intent of Congress in passing it. But it is another sign of how intent the Obama administration was in trying to hide what it was doing from taxpayers, voters, and even our elected representatives in Congress.[2]

Additionally, far too often, the Fourth Estate acts as a public relations representative for big government and fails to do the hard work of keeping watch on government waste, fraud, and abuse. Even under FOIA law, the courts have also deferred to the whims of the executive branch and applied FOIA in a way that makes it more difficult for the American people to find out how their tax dollars are being used or misused.

The Transparency Crisis

All of this has created a transparency crisis in the nation's Capital.

Never in our history has so much money been spent with so little accountability. Frankly, *all* of Congress should focus on government reform and oversight, instead of assigning it to just one or two committees. Americans are rightly worried that they are losing their country. We have the forms of democracy—elections, campaigns, votes, political fund-raising, etc.—but when Congress recently authorized $1.5 trillion in spending after just three days of debate, and the executive branch won't tell you much unless you are willing to make a federal court case out of an issue, that isn't democracy and it isn't self-government.

In the many different scandals of the Obama administration, from Benghazi to Hillary Clinton's emails, how has Judicial Watch succeeded so often in exposing the truth when Congress has failed? Part of it is the hard, focused, and dogged work of our investigators and the skill, professionalism, and tenacity of our lawyers, as well as our other staff who help support and run one of the most effective citizens' groups in the country. But it is also because FOIA is a straightforward tool that quickly gives Judicial Watch access to the federal courts in order to ensure compliance with our record requests to ensure transparency.

Congressional investigations, when committees bother to conduct them, are political by nature. Their effectiveness is often hindered by committee members of the political party whose president is in the White House in order to protect the president, their party, and their political allies. Congress today relies on the Justice Department to enforce subpoenas issued by committees that are intended to force executive branch compliance with requests for information and witnesses.

With a politicized Justice Department, which has been the hallmark of the Obama administration, there is no effective enforcement of such congressional subpoenas. A sorry example of this is the refusal of the Obama Justice Department to enforce the contempt citation against Lois Lerner for refusing to comply with a subpoena for her testimony before the House Committee investigating the IRS scandal. The administration was not about to go to a judge for an order compelling Lerner to testify and reveal what she knew about the administration's targeting of conservative organizations.

Fortunately, Congress has the inherent constitutional power to punish individuals for contempt that is inextricably related to its power to investigate. This power has been recognized by the US Supreme Court, which called it "an essential and appropriate auxiliary to the legislative function."[3] In other words, it does not have to rely on the Justice Department and the courts to enforce its contempt citations against witnesses who refuse to testify or provide sought-after records:

> *The inherent contempt power is not specified in a statute or constitutional provision, but has been deemed implicit in the Constitution's grant to Congress of all legislative powers. In an inherent contempt proceeding, the offender is tried at the bar of the House or Senate and can be held in custody until such time as the*

*contemnor provides the testimony or documents sought, or until
the end of the session.*[4]

Congress first asserted its inherent contempt power in 1795
after three members of the House reported that they had been
offered a bribe by two men. In a House resolution those men
were ordered arrested and detained by the Sergeant at Arms. After
instituting an internal proceeding that was conducted like a trial,
one was found guilty and one was found innocent. The individual
found guilty was held in custody for more than a week before
being released.

Congress exercised its inherent contempt power a number
of times after that, with the last time being in 1935. Obviously,
that power is not limitless. Any individual held in custody by the
Sergeant at Arms or more likely the Capitol Police could challenge
their confinement in a proceeding in federal court. But at least
Congress would not be dependent on a corrupt Justice Department that refuses to enforce a contempt citation against members
of the executive branch. Unfortunately, Congress has not acted
to use this power against defiant witnesses like Lois Lerner in the
modern era. That should change—there is no reason for Congress
not to use that power.

It must be noted that Congress also has another power that it
has rarely used—impeachment. Many people are under the mis-
taken impression that impeachment can only be used to remove
the president or vice president. But the impeachment power given
to Congress in Article II, Section 4 of the Constitution provides
Congress the authority to remove "all civil Officers of the United
States" for "high Crimes and Misdemeanors."

That means, for example, that Congress has the ability to use impeachment to remove individuals who refuse to provide Congress with the information it needs for oversight, or who, like John Koskinen, President Obama's head of the IRS, withheld information from Congress concerning the destruction of records that had been subpoenaed for the Lois Lerner investigation. As James Madison said, impeachment was a necessary power to defend the nation against "the incapacity, negligence or perfidy" of officials within the government.

Of course, if an administration were truly transparent, none of this would matter. Truth fears no inquiry. Crafty, corrupt politicians realize that transparency and accountably go hand in hand. If the Obama administration truly had nothing to hide, it would not have gone to such extraordinary lengths to keep information on what it was doing and its internal machinations from the public. What is needed is a commitment to transparency that cuts across partisan, political lines.

Reforming the Freedom of Information Act

The FOIA law—5 U.S.C. § 552—is a good statute overall. The problem has been in large part the abuse of its exemptions by government officials and its misinterpretation by the courts. For example, the government does not have to produce records that have been classified "under criteria established by an Executive order" as "secret in the interest of national defense or foreign policy and (B) are in fact properly classified pursuant to such Executive order."[5]

Notice the "and" in the middle of this exemption: the record must not only be classified as secret but the classification must have been properly done under the criteria of the applicable executive order. Unfortunately, most courts ignore that second requirement—if the government claims the "classified" exemption to prevent disclosing a document, the courts do not question that exemption. They usually fail to require the government to prove it meets the second part of the exemption and provide evidence that, in fact, the document was *properly* classified. Congress should make it clear that documents that have not been properly classified cannot be withheld.

There is an exemption for "trade secrets and commercial or financial information obtained from a person and privileged or confidential."[6] That should not be an unlimited exemption—it should be tempered by time so that the exemption ends after a reasonable period such as five years. This exemption should not "include the name of a person (individual, institution, corporation, not-for-profit, and similar entities), market data, or information obtained more than 5 years prior."

There is an exemption for "Inter-agency or intra-agency memorandums or letters which would not be available by law to a party other than an agency in litigation with the agency."[7] This somewhat confusing exemption is supposed to protect documents and records that are protected under privileges available to the government in the pretrial discovery context. One of those privileges the government can claim is the deliberative process privilege. However, the government is required to demonstrate that the withheld information is (1) pre-decisional, (2) deliberative, and (3) that the release of the information will harm the agency's decision-making.

Unfortunately, over the years the courts have weakened the deliberative process privilege in the FOIA context. In FOIA cases, the government is only required to show that the information is

(1) pre-decisional and (2) deliberative. The government no longer is required to make a specific showing that release of the records will harm the agency's decision-making—this is just taken for granted by the courts. Congress needs to make clear that if the government is withholding records based on the deliberative process privilege, it must meet all three parts of the test—including showing the harm that will result if the records are released.

Similarly, in the pretrial discovery context, the deliberative process privilege is a qualified privilege, meaning that a party may overcome the privilege being claimed by the other side, in this case the government, upon a sufficient showing of need for the information. But the courts have also weakened this requirement so that they no longer treat it as a qualified privilege in the FOIA context. Judicial Watch believes that any FOIA reform legislation must also reestablish the deliberative process privilege as qualified, so that requestors like Judicial Watch can prove to a court that they have a need for the information being withheld.

Another exemption that has been abused by the government is one for "personnel and medical files and *similar files* the disclosure of which would constitute a clearly unwarranted invasion of personal privacy."[8] Medical and personnel files of individuals should certainly not be subject to disclosure under FOIA. The problem is that bureaucrats have used the "similar files" language in the exemption to cover all sorts of files that were clearly not intended to be protected from disclosure.

Congress should change this language to instead apply only to "personnel and medical files as well as personal information such as contact information." Congress should also make it clear that this exemption does not protect the names of government employees "who make the final decision, sign a contract or agreement on behalf of the agency, or otherwise hold a managerial position or are GS-13 or above."

There is a very broad exemption in FOIA that protects the government from having to disclose "records or information compiled for law enforcement purposes."[9] There are various other requirements for the government to take advantage of this exemption, but the Justice Department and various law enforcement agencies like the FBI have stretched this exemption far beyond what it was intended to do—to prevent disclosure from interfering with ongoing law enforcement investigations and prosecutions, as well as the names of confidential sources. Congress should make clear that this law enforcement exemption does not apply to the "name of an individual who has been arrested, charged, tried, or convicted for committing a felony."

Judicial Watch ran into a great many roadblocks when it tried to get information about Fannie Mae and Freddie Mac, which were so poorly run that they helped precipitate the 2008 financial collapse. There is a FOIA exemption for records "contained in or related to examination, operating, or condition reports prepared by, on behalf of, or for the use of an agency responsible for the regulation or supervision of financial institutions."[10] While Judicial Watch understands the importance of this exemption to prevent premature disclosure of certain reports on banks and other financial institutions that could cause runs or financial collapse, this is another provision where the words "or related to" have been too broadly interpreted. This should be deleted by Congress from the statute to only protect the actual examination, operating, or condition reports themselves.

One of the other big problems in the administration of FOIA

is the failure of government agencies to keep Judicial Watch and other requestors advised of the status of the FOIA request. Agencies should be required to provide an estimate of the amount of time it will take to provide the records. It would be merely advisory and would not be binding, but it would go a long way to averting unnecessary litigation. Congress could also consider putting in a time limit for an agency to provide such an estimate, with a failure to abide by the deadline causing the government to waive all rights to claim any exemptions under the law.

The other problem is agencies' withholding records in a vacuum, with the requestor having no idea of what exactly they are withholding. Agencies should be required to provide a list that individually identifies each document they are withholding and the exemption they are claiming applies to that document.

The path to taking our government back starts with forcing through the Internet Age transparency by which ordinary citizens and watchdog groups can find out what is being done in their name—and stop government abuses before they threaten the foundation of our republic.

1

PEELING BACK THE BENGHAZI COVER-UP

The horror of the 2012 terrorist attack on the US Special Mission Compound in Benghazi was vividly brought home to Americans with the January 2016 release of *13 Hours: The Secret Soldiers of Benghazi*. Directed by Michael Bay (*Pearl Harbor*, *Transformers*), the film is a heartbreaking re-creation of that dark night that left four Americans dead, including Ambassador Christopher Stevens.

"I feel like I'm in a [expletive deleted] horror movie," a soldier in the film confesses as gunfire erupts around him. What follows is a harrowing minute-by-minute tribute to the brave US fighters who kept a horrific situation from turning much worse. The film tells the true story of two former Navy SEALs and their colleagues, who in 2012 were private security contractors charged by the CIA with protecting US intelligence operatives and diplomats in Benghazi.

On the night of September 11, 2012 (the eleventh anniversary of 9/11), Islamic terrorists attacked the US diplomatic compound, penetrating the building's formidable defenses and setting a fire that would ultimately claim the lives of Ambassador Stevens and

Foreign Service Information Management Officer Sean Smith. Meanwhile, at the CIA's annex a mile away, the security contractors are ready to respond but are ordered to wait in their vehicles by the top CIA officer in Benghazi, which almost certainly keeps them from reaching Stevens and Smith in time. Later, two CIA contractors, Tyrone S. Woods and Glen Doherty—former Special Force operators—will perish in a mortar attack on the roof of the CIA annex to the Benghazi diplomatic facility.

Benghazi was essentially a twenty-first century Alamo, but it also may have been a factor in a larger foreign policy scandal involving how the United States allowed the rise of ISIS and our failing war against it.

Judicial Watch has been determined to get to the bottom of what happened. We've learned that the scandals over the attack on the American facility in Benghazi, and the use by Hillary Clinton, while secretary of state, of an illicit email account and server through which classified government information passed are intimately connected.

At issue are the following points: What really happened at Benghazi? Did the State Department know the danger that Ambassador Stevens was in? Who in the Obama administration knew how insecure the compound was? Did the Obama administration abandon the Americans fighting the terrorists that night?

The use of Hillary Clinton's separate email system was unearthed thanks to our litigation and investigations of Benghazi. Here the questions are: What was the server used for? Why was it used? Could foreign intelligence agents have accessed the classified information passed on the server?

At Judicial Watch, we've filed twenty-six lawsuits under the Freedom of Information Act to get the government to release documents about Benghazi and/or Hillary Clinton's emails. We've pried open a great deal of evidence, including a "smoking gun" email that shows the US military was ready to deploy troops to protect the Americans in Benghazi. But no one at the State Department (or in the White House) took any action to deploy those troops in time.

Using the documents we and others have forced out of the government, we can provide a chilling account of what really happened during Benghazi—including what the administration doesn't want you to know.

For example, when it comes to Hillary Clinton we've learned that while people from Sidney Blumenthal, a conspiracy theorist also barred from employment at the Hillary Clinton State Department by the White House, to actor Ben Affleck had Hillary Clinton's personal email, Ambassador Chris Stevens did not. This despite the fact that Libya was one of the most important diplomatic initiatives of Hillary's tenure at State.

Instead, in her testimony before a Senate Committee in October 2015, Clinton had the gall to suggest Ambassador Stevens hadn't taken sufficient security precautions. She said that Stevens "felt comfortable" on the ground, and that he was merely joking when he emailed about whether the Benghazi compound would be closed. "Chris Stevens had . . . a really good sense of humor," Clinton laughed. "And I just see him smiling as he's typing this." Certainly it was no joke though when Stevens's State Department team in Libya sent requests for additional security six hundred times. They were rejected. Some joke on the part of Ambassador Stevens.

She couldn't remember holding a single conversation with Stevens after he was appointed ambassador to Libya. The night of his death she sent an email with the subject line "Chris Smith," mixing up his name with that of fellow diplomat Sean Smith. She spoke to survivors only days later. The night of the attack, she didn't speak with the Secretary of Defense Leon Panetta or the Chairman of the Joint Chiefs of Staff Martin Dempsey.

The "Smoking Gun" Email

After two years of digging, in 2014 Judicial Watch got its big break in opening up the Benghazi scandal. Our efforts led directly to then-Speaker John Boehner appointing a select committee to investigate Benghazi under Rep. Trey Gowdy (R-SC).

The break came in response to one of our FOIA suits and resulted in the release of forty-one new Benghazi-related State Department documents. They included a newly declassified email showing then–White House Deputy National Security Adviser for Strategic Communications Ben Rhodes and other Obama administration public relations officials attempting to orchestrate a campaign to "reinforce" President Obama and to portray the Benghazi consulate terrorist attack as being "rooted in an Internet video, and not a failure of policy." Other documents show that State Department officials initially described the incident as an "attack" and a possible kidnap attempt—all contrary to the White House line that was being peddled for weeks leading up to the 2012 election. As late as September 25, a full two weeks after the Benghazi attacks, President Obama was trying to deflect blame for the attack and pin it on a highly amateur Internet video. "There is no video that justifies an attack on an embassy," Obama told the General Assembly of the United Nations that day.

The documents were released as the result of a June 21, 2013, FOIA lawsuit filed against the Department of State (*Judicial Watch v. U.S. Department of State* [No. 1:13-cv-00951]) to gain access to documents about the controversial talking points used by then–United States Ambassador to the United Nations Susan Rice for a series of appearances on Sunday news programs on September 16, 2012. Judicial Watch had been seeking these documents since October 2012.

The "smoking gun" Rhodes email was sent on sent on Friday, September 14, 2012, at 8:09 p.m. with the subject line: "RE: PREP CALL with Susan, Saturday at 4:00 pm ET." The documents show that the "prep" was for Ambassador Rice's Sunday news show appearances to discuss the Benghazi attack.

The document lists as a "Goal": "To underscore that these protests are rooted in an Internet video, and not a broader failure of policy." The email was sent to a Who's Who of White House communications aides, making it clear that it was establishing the administration's "party line."

Ben Rhodes returned to the "Internet video" scenario later in the email, the first point in a section labeled "Top-lines":

> [W]e've made our views on this video crystal clear. The United States government had nothing to do with it. We reject its message and its contents. We find it disgusting and reprehensible. But there is absolutely no justification at all for responding to this movie with violence. And we are working to make sure that people around the globe hear that message.

The Rhodes email instructs recipients to portray President Obama as "steady and statesmanlike." Another goal, according to Rhodes, is "to reinforce the President and Administration's strength and steadiness in dealing with difficult challenges."

Finally, Rhodes adds this following bit of pure political spin:

I think that people have come to trust that President Obama provides leadership that is steady and statesmanlike. There are always going to be challenges that emerge around the world, and time and again, he has shown that we can meet them.

The brazen deception of the Obama administration's actions on Benghazi started to line up. At 4 p.m. on September 14, 2012, a large teleconference was held on the administration's Secure Video Teleconference System (SVTS). All documents relating to this teleconference have been redacted. But one of the emails unearthed by Judicial Watch, describing the activities of CIA Deputy Director Mike Morell, may reveal the talking points used by US Ambassador Susan Rice, who appeared on five talk shows on Sunday, September 16, to defend the idea that Benghazi was caused by an "Internet video."

"The first draft apparently seemed unsuitable . . . because they seemed to encourage the reader to infer incorrectly that the CIA had warned about a specific attack on our embassy. On the SVTS, Morell noted that these points were not good and he had taken a heavy hand to editing them. He noted that he would be happy to work with Jake Sullivan and Rhodes to develop appropriate talking points."[1]

On September 14 at 10:48 a.m., Hillary Clinton received an email from her adviser, Sidney Blumenthal, in which Blumenthal passes on a piece by his son Max that appeared in *The Guardian*.

Sidney Blumenthal to Hillary Clinton, 10:48 AM, September 14, 2012:

Max knows how to do this and is fearless. Hope it's useful and gets around, especially in the Middle East.

Keep speaking and clarifying. Your statements have been strong. Once through this phase, you might clarify history of US policy on Arab Spring, what has been accomplished, US interests at stake, varying relations with Libya & Egypt, etc.

Romney, of course, is contemptible, but contemptible on a level not seen in past contemptible political figures. His menace comes from his emptiness. His greed is not limited simply to mere filthy lucre. The mixture of greedy ambition and hollowness is combustible. He will do and say anything to get ahead, and while usually self-immolating he is also destructive. Behind his blandness lies boundless ignorance, ignited by constantly wretched judgment. His recent statements are of a piece with everything he has done from naming Ryan on his welfare ads, etc.

Keep speaking . . .

xo

Sid

The Max Blumenthal article forwarded by Sidney, his father, suggests that American conservatives, Zionists, and the Israel government were behind the Internet video that was falsely linked by Clinton and Barack Obama to the Benghazi attack.

Incredibly, Clinton responded with an approving "Your Max is a Mitzvah." Another email shows that Hillary Clinton wanted three copies of the Max Blumenthal article printed out.[2]

We also obtained emails from Hillary Clinton's secret email server showing that a proposed intelligence briefing on September 15, 2012, was cancelled because Hillary Clinton slept through the meeting.

Monica R. Hanley to Hillary Clinton, September 15, 2012, 9:17 AM:

Dan will be at Whitehaven with the PDB (Presidential Daily Brief) at 9:30am this morning.

He has some sensitive items that he would like to personally show you when he arrives.

Hillary Clinton to Monica Hanley, 10:43 AM, September 15, 2012:

I just woke up so I missed Dan. Could he come back after I finish my calls? But I don't have the call schedule yet so I don't know when that would be. Do you?

We obtained a partially declassified transcript of the conversation between Clinton and Turkish foreign minister Ahmet Davutoğlu. The document states that Davutoğlu "called the controversial anti-Islam video 'a clear provocation,' but added that wise people should not be provoked by it." The next line is blacked out and will not be declassified until 2027!

Some parts of the Benghazi cover-up remain secret. These include:

- Communications between Huma Abedin, a senior aide to Hillary Clinton, and Rashid Hussain about how "American Muslim leaders" were tying the Internet video to the Benghazi attack.

- On September 13, 2012, Politico's Mike Allen sent National Security Council spokesman Tommy Vietor an article from Britain's *Independent* titled "America Was Warned of Embassy Attack But Did Nothing." The story reported, "senior officials are increasingly convinced" the Benghazi attack was "not the result of spontaneous anger." Vietor forwarded the story to other top White House and State Department officials, but Vietor's accompanying comments and the comments of other top Obama officials are completely redacted.

- The administration also redacted several emails of top State Department officials discussing a statement by a Mitt Romney campaign spokesman criticizing the "security situation in Libya." It wouldn't surprise anyone if those on the email chain had in mind the fact that just seven weeks after Benghazi was a presidential election in which the future employment of President Obama and his top State Department appointees would be on the line.

US Military Was Prepared to Act in Benghazi

Contrary to what the Obama administration has told the American people, the US military was poised and ready to respond immediately and forcefully against terrorists in Benghazi, Libya.

That's what we learned in December 2015 from an email exchange from then–Department of Defense Chief of Staff Jeremy Bash to State Department leadership immediately offering "forces that could move to Benghazi" during the terrorist attack on Benghazi. In an email sent to top Department of State officials, at 7:19 p.m. ET, only hours after the attack had begun, Bash says, "we have identified the forces that could move to Benghazi. They are spinning up as we speak." The Obama administration redacted the details of the military forces available, oddly citing a Freedom of Information Act (FOIA) exemption that allows the withholding of "deliberative process" information.

The Obama administration and Clinton officials hid this compelling Benghazi email for years. The email makes readily apparent that the military was prepared to launch immediate assistance that could have made a difference, at least at the CIA annex. The fact that the Obama Administration withheld this email for so long only worsens the scandal of Benghazi.

Bash's email seems to directly contradict testimony given by then–Secretary of Defense Leon Panetta before the Senate Armed Services Committee in February 2013. Defending the Obama administration's lack of military response to the nearly six-hour-long attack on the US Consulate in Benghazi, Panetta claimed that "time, distance, the lack of an adequate warning, events that moved very quickly on the ground prevented a more immediate response."

Here is how the *Washington Examiner* reported on these revelations:

> *While parts of the email were redacted, the message indicates the Pentagon was waiting for approval from the State Department to send the forces in. That help never arrived for the Americans under siege at the Benghazi compound. A spokesman for the House Select Committee on Benghazi said investigators had received the unredacted version of the email, which was obtained by Judicial Watch through the Freedom of Information Act and made public Tuesday, last year but had declined to make it public.*[3]

It came out later on the day we released the emails that the House Select Committee on Benghazi had been withholding from the public an unredacted version of the email. Almost immediately upon Judicial Watch's release of the devastating email, a spokesman for the House Select Committee on Benghazi made a snide, sour-grapes announcement to *The Daily Caller* attempting to defend the Committee's decision to keep the email secret for a year by implicitly criticizing Judicial Watch's supposed "rush to release or comment on every document it uncovers." It is hard enough fighting the lawless secrecy of the Obama administration—so it is disappointing to have the unnecessary spitballs from presumed allies for transparency.

The Democrats on the Select Committee thought they helped their cause of defending the indefensible by releasing a complete version of the email. Hardly. The new details show that the military forces that weren't deployed, specifically "a SOF [Special Operations Forces] element that was in Croatia (which can fly to Suda Bay, Crete), and a Marine FAST [Fleet Antiterrorism Security Team] team out of Rota, Spain." The FAST Team arrived well after the attack and the Special Operations Forces never left Croatia. In addition to providing confirming details that forces were ready to go, the Democrats exposed the Obama administration's dishonesty in withholding the information in the first place.

All this goes to underscore the value of Judicial Watch's independent watchdog activities and our leadership in forcing truth and accountability over the Benghazi scandal.

Problems with the Blue Mountain Group

In May 2012, the State Department hired Blue Mountain Group to provide security at the Benghazi compound. Blue Mountain Group subcontracted with the Libyan February 17th Martyrs Brigade to handle a lot of the security.

State Department spokesman Victoria Nuland stated the following at a press conference on September 14, 2012:

> *QUESTION (INAUDIBLE): The claim was made yesterday that a company that is a spinoff of Blackwater, in fact, proposed or contracted the United States Government for this particular kind of eventuality, and it was caught up in some kind of bureaucratic—*
>
> *MS. NULAND: Completely untrue with regard to Libya. I checked that this morning. At no time did we plan to hire a private security company for Libya.*
>
> *QUESTION: Toria, I just want to make sure I understand that, because I didn't understand your first question. You said— your first answer. You said that at no time did you have contracts with private security companies in Libya?*
>
> *MS. NULAND: Correct.*

Three days later, *Wired* broke the story that Nuland had provided false information to her September 14 press conference. The State Department, *Wired* reported, signed a contract for "security guards and patrol services" on May 3 for $287,413.68. An extension option brought the total for protecting the consulate to $783,000. The contract lists only "foreign security awardees" as its recipient.

In her daily press briefing on September 18, 2012, Nuland admitted she made an error concerning the State Department's hiring of foreign security firms in Benghazi. "There was a group called the Blue Mountain Group, which is a private security with permits to operate in Libya," Nuland said. "They were hired to provide local Libyan guards who operated inside the gate, doing things like operating the security access equipment, screening cars, that kind of thing."

But we obtained State Department emails showing that the State Department knew there were problems with the Blue Mountain Group. On June 7, 2012, Tripoli acting security regional officer Jairo Saravia sent the following email to several people, including David Oliviera, another regional security officer assigned to oversee Benghazi security operations.

"Just a quick note in regards [*sic*] to Blue Mountain. The company has lost several security contracts here in Tripoli, including the Corinthian Hotel and Palm City Complex. The latest information is Blue Mountain is not licensed by the GOL (Government of Libya) to provide security services in Libya. I would advise not to use their services to provide security for any of our annexes and/or offices due to the sensitivity this issue has with the current GOL . . ."

Several emails from State Department personnel followed the Saravia email, suggesting that licensing for security firms was a problem, with one email stating, "We have got to get legal to change how licensing is done for contractors."

On June 30, 2012, Blue Mountain Libya sent a "Quality Assurance Compliance Report" to Neal Kern, Department of State contract specialist. The report warned that the number of local security guards leaving their posts had put the mission in Benghazi at risk:

Due to the amount of local guard force members leaving out of fear of their safety and the long process to security check individuals, it makes it very difficult to quickly react to a large drop in staff in quick succession as has been occurring with all the incidents especially when additional staff are requested.

Another section of this report advises that an explosion that blew a hole in the perimeter wall of the Benghazi compound on June 6 had "promoted a fear factor" with a "lasting effect" on the security staff:

> *On the shift 2200–0600 hours on 11.06.12 [REDACTED] emergency staff did not attend for his shift and gave no prior warning of absence, a replacement was not able to be sourced due to the time of evening and the bank staff members not answering their phones. It is believed that the explosive device set off on the compound perimeter wall had a lasting effect on certain members of the staff; this promoted a fear factor when it came to working the nightshift.*

Two further emails uncovered by Judicial Watch discuss the shortages in the number of people assigned to guard the compound. A July 2, 2012, memorandum from David Oliviera included this warning about "manpower issues":

> Per our conversation, the original (Architecture & Engineering) request for guard service was to run from June 6th to June 18th. Unfortunately, due to manpower issues and unforeseen last minute resignations of BMGs guard staff, US Mission Benghazi were only provided the below guards (see email) through the 12th (starting 11th at 2200).

Blue Mountain Group sent a second email to Neal Kern explained how the consistent undermanning of Benghazi security staff caused serious dissension among top security staffers there:

> Between the 18th–30th April a Guard Commander was not provided due to the current Guard Commander [REDACTED] being relieved of his

position due to an altercation with the NTC/QRF [Libyan National Transition Council/Quick Reaction Force] at the US compound. A new Guard Commander has been selected and will begin on the 3rd of May.

On the 22nd April a guard for Shift Charlie [REDACTED] failed to turn up for duty at 2359 hours, we were unable to replace this guard due to [REDACTED] not giving any prior warning that he would not be working. Unfortunately the shift carried out their 8 hour shift with only 4 men.

We obtained further emails showing that the problems with Blue Mountain Group's failure to have a license to operate in Libya continued—incredibly—up to and including the day of the attack on the Benghazi compound. Blue Mountain Libya, the contractor handling the security in Benghazi, was a joint venture between Blue Mountain Group UK (BMUK) and XPAND Corporation. On June 6, 2012, Blue Mountain Group notified State Department Contracting Officer Jan Visintainer that the two companies wanted to dissolve their Libyan partnership. On July 10, 2012, Visintainer responded that the State Department "is not required to mediate any disagreements between the two parties of the Blue Mountain Libya partnership." Visintainer added, "It is in the best interests of both of the 50/50 partners to resolve their differences and successfully complete this contract."

On September 9, 2012, an unidentified partner at Nabulsi & Associates, the law firm representing XPAND, wrote to Visintainer advising the department that XPAND, which owned the security license under which BMG was operating, "hereby bar and prohibit BMUK from utilizing such license . . . Accordingly, we kindly inform you that any use of such license by BMUK in Libya shall be illegal and a clear violation of Libyan laws. We therefore request that the US mission ceases any dealings with BMUK if such dealings are based on any form of reliance on such security license."

In response to XPAND's letter, an unidentified BMG official wrote to Visintainer on September 11, 2012:

> *I have never experienced anything like this in business before. The agreement was signed and we were to operate under the [Blue Mountain Libya] license and confirmation of this was due through from [sic] the partners. However, they have had a change of mind and now this. I will call you very shortly.*

The record shows that the dispute and licensing issue led the State Department to immediately plan to terminate their contract with Blue Mountain Group. On the morning of September 11, 2012, State Department Regional Security Officer David Sparrowgrove wrote to Visintainer and others, "The dissolution of the partnership leaves BMG without a security license to operate in Libya and the Libyan partner has no capacity to manage the guards or the contract. As a result, we feel the best course of action is to terminate the contract in short order."

On September 12, 2012, the day after the attack, the Nabulsi law partner wrote again to Visintainer on behalf of XPAND to express their condolences and to advise the State Department that, in light of the attack, "XPAND shall put its differences with the security operators, Blue Mountain UK, to the side for the moment, and shall allow the use of its security license by BMUK to meet your full needs until a suitable alternative has been arranged."[4] That is how the failure to adequately protect the US compound in Benghazi was bureaucratically buried.

Defense Intelligence Agency Reveals Arms Shipments

While the dispute over the contract for the security compound was occurring, an August 2012 report—one month before Benghazi—was delivered to the Obama administration from the Defense Intelligence Agency (DIA). Judicial Watch was able to obtain release of the eye-opening report in 2015. It warned the Obama administration that the "Islamic State" was gaining strength in the Middle East and was seeking to impose a "caliphate" under the leadership of Syria-based Islamists and al-Qaeda.

The warning of a growing "Islamic State" took on new meaning when DIA in October 2012 reported increased shipments of weapons from the Port of Benghazi to Syrian jihadist rebels. According to the DIA report:

> *During the immediate aftermath of, and following the uncertainty caused by, the downfall of the (Qaddafi) regime in October 2011 and up until early September of 2012, weapons from the former Libya military stockpiles located in Benghazi, Libya were shipped from the port of Benghazi, Libya to the ports of Banias and the Port of Borj Islam, Syria [both under the control of Syrian rebels]. The Syrian ports were chosen due to the small amount of cargo traffic transiting these two ports. The ships used to transport the weapons were medium-sized and able to hold 10 or less shipping containers of cargo.*

The DIA document adds:

> *The weapons shipped from Syria during late-August 2012 were Sniper rifles, RPGs and 125mm and 155mm howitzers missiles.*

The numbers for each weapon were estimated to be: 500 Sniper rifles, 100 RPG launchers with 300 total rounds, and approximately 400 howitzers missiles [200 ea—125mm and 200ea—155 mm].

The publicly available portions of this heavily redacted document do not disclose who was shipping the weapons.[5] The heavily redacted document does not disclose who was shipping the weapons. The level of detail presented suggests that the Obama administration, in the least, was in a position to stop any transfers.

Why is the weapons transfer issue important? Because the Libya fiasco was allowing weapons to move into a jihadist madhouse in the Syria-Iraq region.

Lt. General Michael Flynn, the former head of the Defense Intelligence Agency, told Al Jazeera television in August 2015 that the United States at the time had made a "willful decision" to support a Syrian insurgency that included the Muslim Brotherhood and al-Qaeda: "It was a willful decision to do what they're doing." He also admitted that, in effect, the United States was fully aware of weapons trafficking between the Libyans and the jihadist Syrian insurgency.

Mehdi Hasan, the host of Al Jazeera's *Head to Head* program, zeroed in on this point in his interview with Flynn:

HASAN: In 2012, the U.S. was helping coordinate arms transfers to these same groups (Muslim Brotherhood, al-Qaeda in Iraq). Why did you not stop that if you're worried about the rise of quote-unquote Islamic extremists?

FLYNN: I have to say it's not my job . . . but that . . . my job was to . . . was to ensure that the accuracy of our intelligence that was being present was as good as it could be.

In other words, it was Flynn's pay grade to decide if it was appropriate for the United States to either allow to happen or participate in arms trafficking to the Syrian rebels. Given that the Obama administration had since mid-2011 declared its policy to overthrow Syria's Assad regime, imagine if the revelations of such arms trafficking and possible linkage to the Benghazi attacks had surfaced just seven weeks before the 2012 presidential election? Comparisons to the Iran-Contra scandal that so badly damaged the Reagan administration would have been made, and President Obama's reelection might have been in serious jeopardy. That may provide a motive for the frantic cover-up and the false narrative about Internet videos that was begun on the night of the Benghazi attacks.

The Attack and the Cover-up

The Obama administration took two strategies in dealing with the Benghazi attack. Publicly, it blamed the attack on a video posted by an obscure group in California that allegedly defamed Muhammad. Privately it was well aware the attack was caused by Islamic terrorists out to, in the words of the Defense Intelligence Agency, "kill as many Americans as possible."

On September 12, 2012, the Defense Intelligence Agency sent a report to Secretary of State Hillary Clinton, Defense Secretary Leon Panetta, the Joint Chiefs of Staff, and the National Security Council. The heavily redacted report said the attack on the Benghazi compound "was planned and executed by The Brigades of the Captive Omar Abdul Rahman (BCOAR)." The group, the DIA said, subscribes to "AQ (Al-Qaeda) ideologies."[6]

The DIA noted that "The attack was planned ten or more days

prior on approximately 01 September 2012. The intention was to attack the consulate and kill as many Americans as possible to seek revenge for U.S. killing of Aboyahiye ((ALALIBY)) in Pakistan and in memorial of the 11 September 2001 attack on the World Trade Center buildings." The Associated Press further reported that on September 10, 2011, al-Qaeda leader Ayman al-Zawahiri urged "Libyans . . . to attack Americans to avenge the late militant's death, saying his 'blood is calling, urging and inciting you to fight and kill the Crusaders.' " [7]

"The leader of BCOAR is Abdul Baset ((AZUZ)). AZUZ was sent by ((ZAWARI)) to set up Al Qaeda (AQ) bases in Libya." Abdul Baset, the report states, is "a violent radical." The group's headquarters was set up with the approval of a "member of the Muslim brotherhood movement . . . where they have large caches of weapons. Some of these caches are disguised by feeding troughs for livestock. They have SA-7 and SA-23/4 MANPADS . . . they train almost every day focusing on religious lessons and scriptures including three lessons a day of jihadist ideology." The BOCAR group, according to the DIA, maintained written documents in a "small rectangular room, approximately 12 meters by 6 meters . . . that contain information on all of the AQ activity in Libya."

A second DIA report was sent by the agency to the Department of State Command Center (DSCC) on September 12, 2012. The DSCC then sent it to numerous State Department outlets.

This document, previously classified Secret, includes the following information:

EXECUTIVE SUMMARY. 1. A Salafi group (NFI) is believed to be responsible for the 11 September, 2012, attack on the US Consulate in Benghazi, Libya. The attack was in retaliation for the killing of an al Qaeda operative. The Salafi group attended the [initial] protests and returned at night using overwhelming firepower to overtake security forces of the Consulate.

2. (U) The general atmosphere in Benghazi and Tripoli, Libya relevant to the attack on the US Consulate, on 11 and 12 Sept 12, is that of shock and disbelief. A Salafi group is reported to be behind the attack. The Salafi group responsible for the violent [sic] are believed to be the same group who defaced the Islamic shrines and old historic monuments. Some business owners are siding against the Salafi group, believed to be the culprits, and hoping for international intervention to assure stability and justice. A majority of the local population is reported to hold anti-Salafi views.

3. The attack was an organized operation with specific information that the US Ambassador was present. The Salafi group attended the protest at or near the US Consulate earlier on 11 September 2012, and then returned at 2300 firing small arms weapons and between 25 to 30 RPGs at the Consulate and other unknown targets (NFI).

The local police tried to defend the Consulate but were outmatched by the group's size and their superior firepower.

4. The attack was in [sic] carried out in retaliation for the killing of the Al-Qaeda's number two man, Abu Yah Ya ((AL_LIBI)).

Our lawsuits also unearthed a key piece of information about the lack of a timely US military response during the day of the Benghazi attack. The attack occurred in two phases. The first assault occurred at the main compound at about 9:40 p.m. local time, or 3:40 p.m. Eastern Daylight Time in Washington. The second attack, on a CIA annex 1.2 miles away from the main compound, began three hours later, at about 12 a.m. local time

(6 p.m. in Washington) and ended at around 5:15 a.m. local time (11:15 p.m. Eastern Daylight Time). This second attack ended with a mortar barrage that killed security officers Tyrone Woods and Glen Doherty.

Secretary of Defense Leon Panetta testified before the Senate Armed Services Committee that there was nothing else the administration could do because "time, distance, the lack of an adequate warning, events that moved very quickly on the ground prevented a more immediate response."

However, Gregory Hicks, deputy chief of mission to the US Embassy in Tripoli at the time of the Benghazi attack, testified in 2013 that a show of force by the US military during the siege could have prevented much of the carnage. "If we had been able to scramble a fighter or two over Benghazi as quickly as possible after the attack commenced," Hicks testified, "I believe there would not have been a mortar attack on the annex in the morning because I believe the Libyans would have split. They would have been scared to death that we would have gotten a laser on them and killed them."

Indeed, an email from Department of Defense Chief of Staff Jeremy Bash to Jacob Sullivan, Secretary of State Hillary Clinton's chief of staff, Wendy Sherman, undersecretary of state for political affairs, and Deputy Secretary of State for Management and Resources Thomas Nides, suggests that there were forces that could have been sent in time to prevent some of the loss of life in Benghazi but were not:

> State colleagues:
>
> I just tried you on the phone but you were all in with S (apparent reference to Secretary of State Hillary Clinton).
>
> After consulting with General Dempsey, General Ham, and the Joint

Staff, we have identified the forces that could move to Benghazi. They are spinning up as we speak. They include a [REDACTED].

Assuming Principals agree to deploy these elements, we will ask State to procure the approval from host nation. Please advise how you wish to convey that approval to an [REDACTED]. NOTE TIME? per Tom

Jeremy

It is important to note that the administration has chosen to censor exactly *what* forces were available to be sent to Benghazi. But, as I mentioned above, congressional Democrats helpfully released the details. Certainly, the Bash email shows that the Defense Department knew that—contrary to Secretary Panetta's testimony—forces were available to be sent to Benghazi at the time of the attack.[8]

United States Ambassador to the United Nations Susan Rice was also fully briefed on what was happening in Benghazi.[9]

An email received at the White House at 9:11 p.m. on September 11, 2012, includes the following time line of events, sent by the State Department Bureau of Diplomatic Security, describing events at Benghazi until midnight Libyan time (or 6 p.m. in Washington. (The identity of the person or organization sending the email is redacted.)

At 1549 hrs, DSCC (Diplomatic Security Command Center) was notified that U.S. Mission Benghazi was under attack. At 1600 hrs, DSCC was notified by Regional Security Officer (RSO) Benghazi that armed individuals had entered the compound, and at 1614 hrs RSO Benghazi reported that an armed group had set fire to buildings inside the compound. The US Ambassador was visiting post from Tripoli, and as of 1614 hrs it was suspected that one of the buildings that had been set on fire was the building where the Ambassador was sheltering. [REDACTED] Quick Reaction Force responded from their off-compound Annex, but was turned back due to heavy hostile fire.

As of 1700 hrs, [REDACTED] QRF and host nation militia (17 February Brigade) have redeployed to the compound. One Assistant RSO (ARSO) suffered injuries from smoke inhalation. This agent was in the Principal Officer's Residence with U.S. Ambassador Christopher Stevens and Information Program Officer (IPO) Sean M. Smith. All three moved to the safe haven where the attack began, but had to relocate to the roof as the building caught on fire. The agent reached the rooftop but lost contact with the other two. The agent reentered the residence and found the IPO killed in action (KIA), and was unable to locate the Ambassador. The agent had given his cell phone to the Ambassador.

The QRF and friendly militia forces were unable to locate the Ambassador, and pull back to the off-compound Annex. All classified material on the compound is secured by RSO [REDACTED] personnel. Embassy Tripoli receives a call from the injured ARSO's cell phone (which had been left with the Ambassador) from a male caller saying he is at the hospital with an unresponsive male who matches a physical description of the Ambassador. [REDACTED] Tripoli charters an airplane and sends it to Benghazi with six personnel aboard as a response team.

At 2215 hrs, Benghazi ARSO called DSCC to report that the [REDACTED] response team has been on the ground in Benghazi for approximately 60 minutes, but are waiting for the 17 February Brigade to escort them to [REDACTED]. DS Seniors ask ARSO about the identity of the reported white male in the hospital. [REDACTED MATERIAL] hospital for about two hours. Henderson will call him after this call.

The time line later details that the team did not leave for the airport for another forty-five minutes and did not arrive at the annex until 2313 hours, nearly two hours after the team first arrived. The time line then details the second attack, which takes place only seventeen minutes after the response team arrives:

> At 2332 hrs, ARSO reports they are under mortar attack, with 3 to 4 rounds hitting the Annex. There are [REDACTED] injured and [REDACTED] the need for medical evaluation. The response team is on site and either inside or deployed to the roof. The agents are sheltering in place with 45-minutes to sunrise.
>
> At 2349 hrs, DS Special Agent [REDACTED] was reported hit during the mortar attack, which has since ceased. [REDACTED MATERIAL] All other DS agents are accounted for.

More than six hours after the initial terrorist attack, there is only one plane available to evacuate injured and other personnel from Benghazi. The time line reveals that the plane takes off, leaving some personnel behind, including those killed in action. A Libyan Air Force C-130 airplane transports the survivors and the bodies several hours later.

Documents accompanying this time line also reveal that, at the time of the attack, the Department of Defense apparently had two government contractors in Benghazi working on weapons removal. These contractors apparently operated without the knowledge of the State Department.[10]

State Department Senior Watch Officer Andrew Veprek, at 3:22 a.m. on September 12, 2012, forwarded an email to numerous State Department sources, with the subject line "Death of Ambassador Stevens in Benghazi":

> Embassy Tripoli confirms the death of Ambassador John C. (Chris) Stevens in Benghazi. His body has been recovered and is in the airport in Benghazi.[11]

Obama and Clinton Talk: The Cover-up Speeds Up

At 6 a.m. EDT on September 12, 2012, the State Department's Diplomatic Security Command Center sent out a release to members of a list code-named ALCON, headlined "Benghazi Event Notification":

> *The DS Command Center is sharing the following terrorism event information for your situational awareness . . .*
>
> *As of 0500 EST the US Mission in Benghazi has been evacuated due to ongoing attacks that resulted in the deaths of 4 Chief of Mission personnel including the U.S. Ambassador to Libya and 3 additional COM wounded. At this time everyone has been evacuated to Tripoli and is receiving medical aid and awaiting further movement.*
>
> *This is initial terrorist incident report from the DS Command Center . . .*[12]

In addition, an email sent by Hillary Clinton to her daughter, Chelsea Clinton, at 11:11 p.m. on September 11, 2012, on her unsecured "private" server showed that she knew that evening that Benghazi had been attacked by "an Al Qaeda-like group." Chelsea Clinton used the pseudonym "Diane Reynolds" when emailing her mother over the unsecured server. This email made news in the Select Committee hearing with Hillary Clinton, but it was Judicial Watch that forced the release of the email.

From: H
Sent: Tuesday, September 11, 2012 11:11 PM
To: Diane Reynolds

Subject: RE: I'm in my office

Two of our officers were killed in Benghazi by an al-Qaeda-like group. The Ambassador, whom I handpicked, and a young communications officer on temporary duty with a wife and two young children. Very hard day and I fear more of the same tomorrow.[13]

But while Hillary Clinton was *privately* telling government officials that the Benghazi compound had been hit by terrorists, *publicly* she blamed the attacks not on violent jihadis, but on obscure videos appearing on YouTube.

We obtained some of the emails between State Department spokesperson Victoria Nuland, National Security Council spokesperson Bernadette Meehan, and White House deputy strategic communications adviser Ben Rhodes, a former novelist who admitted to the *New York Times* in May 2016 that he and his colleagues deliberately misled the American people for four years about the extremist nature of the Iranian regime the administration was desperately trying to conclude a nuclear deal with.

The emails that we uncovered include:

6:21 PM, from Nuland: We are holding for Rhodes clearance. BMM (Bernadette M. Meehan), pls advise asap.

6:24 PM, from Meehan: Ben is good with these and is on with Jake now too. ("Jake" was Hillary Clinton's personal aide, Jacob Sullivan.)[14]

So what would the official response to the Benghazi attack be? An email sent at 9:11 p.m. EDT on September 11, 2012, from a sender whose name is redacted to the Department of State Command Center's management and watch teams apparently shows that the White House was initially going to blame a rarely viewed video by Oregon-based pastor Jon Courson titled *God vs. Allah*, a low-key exposition of the Book of Kings.

> Per Ambassador Mull [State Department Executive Secretary Stephen Mull] after SVTS [Secure Video Teleconference System] conference:
>
> DOD is looking at various resources.
>
> [REDACTED MATERIAL]
>
> S (Secretary of State Hillary Clinton) expected to make statements one of which may confirm KIA, notification of next of kin is pending confirmation. Deputy Chief of Mission (DCM) The Hague was to call OPS when completed.
>
> White House is reaching out to U-Tube [*sic*] to advise ramifications of posting of the Pastor Jon video.[15]

Sometime in the next hour, the decision was made to blame an Internet video for the Benghazi attack.

A clue as to what happened surfaced in February 2013. White House press secretary Jay Carney made the grudging admission that: "At about 10 p.m., the president called Secretary Clinton to get an update on the situation." Obviously, it is not a detail Carney was anxious to share. Indeed, it contradicted an earlier White House account that claimed the president had not spoken with Clinton or other top administration officials that night.

Carney's hand was forced by Clinton, who was still Secretary of State when she testified before the Senate Foreign Relations Committee in January 2013. She recounted first learning at about 4 p.m. on September 11 that the State Department facility in Benghazi was under attack. That was very shortly after the siege started. Over the hours that followed, Clinton stated, "we were in continuous meetings and conversations." As part of those discussions, she recalled, "I spoke with President Obama later in the evening to, you know, bring him up to date, to hear his perspective."

We do not have a recording or transcript of this call, and neither Clinton nor the White House has described it beyond noting that it happened. We did obtain an email containing a description of what was said during the call, but the Obama administration blacked out the description. But we do know that at 10:08 p.m., a few minutes after Obama and Clinton spoke, the Washington media began reporting that the State Department had issued a statement by Clinton regarding the Benghazi attack. In it, she asserted:

> *Some have sought to justify this vicious behavior as a response to inflammatory material posted on the Internet. The United States deplores any intentional effort to denigrate the religious beliefs of others. Our commitment to religious tolerance goes back to the very beginning of our nation.*

Many suspect that the subject of Internet videos was part of Obama's conversation with Hillary Clinton. CNS News asked Carney whether, in that 10 p.m. phone call, the president and Secretary Clinton discussed the statement that Clinton was about to issue, and, specifically, whether they discussed "the issue of inflammatory material posted on the Internet." It is significant that Carney declined to answer.

An hour after this discussion mentioning Internet videos, Hillary Clinton sent the private email to her daughter over her secret server admitting that the attack was driven by "an al-Qaeda like group."

At 12:11 a.m., Hillary Clinton's chief of staff, Cheryl Mills, wrote to Nuland, Sullivan, and State Department Senior Communications Adviser Philippe Reines, that even though the press had continued questions about "Chris (Stevens)' whereabouts, they should let Secretary of State Clinton's statement blaming 'inflammatory material on the Internet' stand: 'Can we stop answering emails for the night Toria b/c now the first one (Hillary Clinton's statement) is hanging out there.' " [16]

One more bit of business concerned whether or not to publicly announce the death of Sean Smith, one of the four Americans killed in Benghazi, whom Secretary Clinton mistakenly calls "Chris Smith."

> CLINTON: *Cheryl (Mills) told me the Libyans confirmed his death. Should we announce tonight or wait until morning?*
> NULAND: *We need to ck family's druthers. If they are OK, we should put something out from you tonight.*
> MILLS: *Taking S (Secretary of State Clinton) off.* [17]

On September 12, 2012, the State Department continued to receive accurate intelligence from around the world that many Muslims did not believe that the terrorists in Libya were inspired by an Internet video. Rebecca Brown Thompson, director of the State Department Bureau of Public Affairs' Rapid Response Unit, sent the following email to the State Department's Diplomatic Security Command Center on September 12, 2012:

Nahla Qader, one of our media analysts, found this tweet: Mohammed Fadel Falmy@Repent1 in Egypt says "Threat to kill all Americans in Gaza, after Libya/Egypt due to film insulting prophet Mohamed forces UN staff to bunker in and placed on curfew. Nahla also reports that some Twitter users in Libya and Egypt are spreading reports that the attacks in Libya may not be related to the infamous film but to the killing of Al-Qaeda's second-in-command, who is Libyan." [18]

But by September 12, the disinformation campaign was in full swing. Bernadette Meehan began the process by sending an email to Obama administration officials, announcing that "to ensure we are all in sync on messaging for the rest of the day, Ben Rhodes will have a conference call for USG communicators on this chain at 9:15AM ET today."

The Obama administration engaged domestic and foreign Islamist groups and foreign nationals to push the Internet video narrative. The day after the attack, Rashid Hussain, the Obama administration's special envoy to the Organisation of Islamic Co-operation (OIC), sent an email to OIC's ambassador to the United Nations, Ufuk Gokcen, and OIC official Cenk Uraz, with the subject line "Urgent: Anti-Islamic Film and Violence":

> I am sure you are considering putting a statement on the film and the related violence. In addition to the condemnation of the disgusting depictions, it will be important to emphasize the need to respond in a way that is consistent with Islamic principles, i.e., not engaging in violence and taking innocent life . . .

The OIC agreed, issuing an official statement calling the film "incitement" and stating that the Benghazi attack and a demonstration in Cairo "emanated from emotions aroused by production of a film had hurt (*sic*) the religious sentiments of Muslims. The two incidents demonstrated serious repercussions of abuse of freedom of expression." The OIC noted its previous statements calling for criminalization of criticism of Islam.[19]

The State Department also enthusiastically supported a statement from Rabbi David Saperstein, director of the Religious Action Center of Reform Judaism, which condemned "the video that apparently spurred these incidents. It was clearly crafted to provoke, offend, and evoke outrage. Michael Posner, assistant secretary of state for democracy, human rights, and labor, forwarded this statement to Undersecretary of State Wendy Sherman on September 12, with the note, "This is an excellent statement— our goal should be to get the Conference of Presidents (of Major American Jewish Organizations), the ADL (Anti-Defamation League) etc. to follow suit and use similar language." (In 2014, Rabbi Saperstein became ambassador-at-large for international religious freedom.)

Payton Knopf, deputy spokesman to the US Mission to the United Nations, emailed United States Ambassador to the United Nations Susan Rice at 5:42 p.m. on statements by State Department spokesperson Victoria Nuland's statement that the attack on the consulate had been well planned:

> Responding to a question about whether it was an organized terror attack, Toria said she couldn't speak to the identity of the perpetrators but that it was *clearly a complex* attack.

We also obtained partially declassified information from the military's US Africa Command (AFRICOM) that shows that on September 12, AFRICOM sent a cable, approved by Vice Admiral Charles Joseph Leidig, deputy commander, Africa Command, requesting an "immediate" response from the Joint Chiefs of Staff

for "additional forces" for the mission to "provide limited dura-
tion military and expeditionary antiterrorism and security forces
in support of USAFRICOM commander in order to protect vital
naval and national assets."

The Joint Chiefs approved the request, naming the mission
Operation Jukebox Lotus. Specific details of this mission were
blacked out in the copy of the orders (or EXORD) we received.
The orders detail that several components of the military, includ-
ing Special Operations Forces, were deployed, including "BPT (Be
Prepared To) support for mortuary affairs."

We also received copies of intelligence briefing slides shown
to top Pentagon leaders on September 12, 2012. These slides reported that a June 6, 2012, attack on the Benghazi compound[20]
was tied to a group promoting an Islamic State in Libya, and
"came in response to the 5 June [2012] drone strike on al-Qaeda
senior leader Abu Yahya al-Libi."[21]

On September 13, the State Department issued a document
called "USG Outreach and Engagement Post-Benghazi Attack"
which "captures USG efforts to engage outside voices to encourage
public statements that denounce the attack make it clear that the
anti-Muslim film does not reflect American (*sic*)." The document
highlights "Special Envoy's engagement" with the OIC and the
"Saudi Ambassador."

We still don't have the full story on Benghazi, but thanks to
the dogged efforts of Judicial Watch we know a lot more and are
in a position to continue to crack open the Benghazi cover-up.
Take the email that showed the military was prepared, indeed was
in the process of launching timely assistance that could have made
a difference, at least at the CIA annex where two Americans died.
The *Washington Examiner* correctly noted that the email "casts

doubt on previous testimony from high level officials, several of whom suggested there was never any kind of military unit that could have been in a position to mount a rescue mission during the hours-long attack on Benghazi."

All this goes to underscore the value of Judicial Watch's independent watchdog activities and our leadership in forcing truth and accountability over the Benghazi scandal.

The lies and inaction by President Obama, Hillary Clinton, and Susan Rice (who is now Obama's national security adviser) were monstrous. Rather than tell the truth, and risk political blowback for the Libya mess and the lack of security, the Obama administration abandoned those under fire and pretended that the attack had nothing to do with terrorism.

Judicial Watch saw through the lies and began what has become the most nationally significant investigation ever by a nongovernmental entity. Our Benghazi FOIA requests and subsequent lawsuits changed history. Our disclosure of White House records confirming that top political operatives at the White House concocted the talking points used by Susan Rice to mislead the American people in order save Obama's reelection prospects rocked Washington.

These smoking-gun documents embarrassed all of Congress and forced Speaker John Boehner to appoint the House Select Committee on Benghazi.

And, as you'll see, the pressure from our Benghazi litigation led to the disclosure of the Clinton email scandal, the historical ramifications of which we are now witnessing.

If the American people had known the truth—that Barack Obama, Hillary Clinton, and other top administration officials knew that the Benghazi attack was an al-Qaeda terrorist attack from the get-go—and yet lied and covered this fact up—Mitt Romney might very well be president. Our Benghazi disclosures also show connections between the collapse in Libya and the ISIS war—and confirm that the US knew remarkable details about the transfer of arms from Benghazi to Syrian jihadists.

HILLARY CLINTON'S PRIVATE EMAIL COVER-UP

How desperately did the Obama administration want the existence of Hillary Clinton's "private" email system to remain hidden as long as possible—perhaps until even after the 2016 election?

In April 2016, the Obama State Department admitted it withheld a key Benghazi email of Hillary Clinton's from Judicial Watch since at least September 2014. If the State Department had disclosed the email when first supposedly found, Clinton's email server and her hidden emails would have been disclosed in 2014, before Clinton authorized the alleged deletion of tens of thousands of emails and long before the run-up to the 2016 presidential campaign.

The developments came in a July 2014 Freedom of Information Act (FOIA) lawsuit seeking records related to the drafting and use of the Benghazi talking points (*Judicial Watch v. U.S. Department of State* [No. 1:14-cv-01242]). The lawsuit, which forced the disclosure of the Clinton email records, sought specific records from Clinton and her top State Department staff.

Two years later, the State Department admitted it had found a key email requested by Judicial Watch but withheld it in its entirety: "Upon further review, the Department has determined that one document previously withheld in full in our letter dated November 12, 2014, may now be released in part."

What was in the withheld email?

The September 29, 2012, message to Clinton from then–Deputy Chief of Staff Jake Sullivan concerns talking points for Clinton calls with senators about the Benghazi attack. The email contains Clinton's non-state.gov address.

It is this litigation that prompted US District Court Judge Royce Lamberth to grant limited discovery of the role the State Department played in concealing the evidence. Judge Lamberth ruled that "where there is evidence of government wrong-doing and bad faith, as here, limited discovery is appropriate, even though it is exceedingly rare in FOIA cases." (US District Court Judge Emmet Sullivan also granted Judicial Watch discovery into the Clinton email matter. The discovery plan, agreed to by the State Department, includes the testimony of former and current top State Department officials, such as Clinton aides Cheryl Mills and Huma Abedin.)

Now we know the Obama administration consciously refused to give up key information about Hillary Clinton's email in 2014. It covered up this email both from the court and Judicial Watch. The cover-up provided Hillary Clinton enough time to hide potentially thousands of government records. One aim of our court-ordered discovery will be to get to the bottom of this cover-up.

How Judicial Watch Uncovered the Clinton Emails

Our many lawsuits trying to uncover the story behind the deaths of four Americans in Benghazi took a fascinating turn in 2015 when they helped reveal Hillary Clinton had used a personal email account while Secretary of State. She also had been using a non-state.gov server, supposedly located at a residence in New York. The use of a "private" server left Clinton's emails—including more than two thousand now considered classified—subject to easy hacking from outsider and foreign governments. The Intelligence Community's inspector general concluded in January 2016 that Clinton's server contained information marked "special access program," higher even than Top Secret. In May 2016, the Romanian hacker Guccifer claimed he had hacked into her server. The Senate Committee on Homeland Security and Governmental Affairs concluded that Clinton's server was the subject of hacking attempts from China, South Korea, and Germany after she stepped down in 2013. Even more ominous, Clinton's server may have lacked a threat-detection program for three months, Senate Homeland Security Chairman Ron Johnson says.

The deliberate email secrecy allowed Clinton and her staff to ultimately decide which emails to turn over to the State Department as public records and which they could attempt to destroy. While Clinton claims that only emails of a strictly private nature were held back, the FBI's ability to recover those emails may call into question her judgment of what was public or private. And certainly, the federal courts who granted Judicial Watch discovery may try to force the recovery, review, and potential disclosure of *all* of the emails on Clinton's email system.

It wasn't just Hillary Clinton who tried to conceal the emails. During spring of 2016, a group of federal judges made a set of extraordinary rulings in FOIA cases filed by Judicial Watch that reflected their complete exasperation with how both Hillary Clinton and the State Department email games upended the Freedom of Information Act.

US District Court Judge Lamberth issued an order on March 29, 2016, giving Judicial Watch the ability to take limited discovery of State Department officials on the adequacy of the Department's "search for responsive documents" in a FOIA request filed by Judicial Watch seeking former Secretary of State Hillary Clinton's internal email correspondence. The purpose of the discovery, which, Lamberth admitted, "is exceedingly rare in FOIA cases," is to help the court determine whether the State Department's search "reasonably produced all responsive documents."

Lamberth noted that he has set out the proper standards for limited discovery in a prior FOIA action filed by the Landmark Legal Foundation against the Environmental Protection Agency in which the agency:

> . . . had excluded its Administrator from a search of "senior official" files . . . , did not search personal e-mail accounts where official government business was being conducted, and ultimately disclosed that the Administrator was sending and receiving e-mails in her dog's name—which was not subject to the FOIA search.

As Lamberth said, "where there is evidence of government wrong-doing and bad faith, as here, limited discovery is appropriate."

Lamberth called Clinton's "exclusive" use of "her 'clintonemail .com' account to conduct official government business, as well as other officials' use of this account and their own personal email accounts to conduct official" State Department business "extraordinary."

Lamberth also criticized the State Department's claim that Judicial Watch was relying on "speculation" or "surmise" over the inadequacy of the department's search, noting instead that Judicial Watch was "relying on constantly shifting admissions by the Government and the former government officials."

The State Department claims that it had no obligation to produce Clinton's State Department emails "because it did not 'possess' or 'control' them at the time the FOIA request was made." Lamberth stated, however, that Judicial Watch is "certainly entitled to dispute" this position.

The administration also argued that the fact that it had not actually searched Clinton's emails at the time Judicial Watch asked for all of her emails "was neither a misrepresentation nor material omission"—a dubious claim, to be sure.

In response to the State Department's claim that its non-search and subsequent responses to Judicial Watch did not show "a lack of good faith," Lamberth said, "that is what remains to be seen, and the factual record must be developed appropriately in order for this Court to make that determination."

So now two federal courts have given Judicial Watch the go-ahead to take limited discovery to investigate the State Department's "constantly shifting admissions" over the use of Clinton's home-brewed computer network by Clinton, her aides, and other senior State Department officials and the extent of their knowledge about that unsecured system—a system that would have been a target-rich environment for hackers.

How the Server Scandal Began

Hillary Clinton was obviously hoping to run for president on her record of public service and her appeal to left-wing Democratic

Party circles. But as early as the fall of 2015, a Gallup Poll found that when Americans were asked what they recalled reading or hearing about her, one word—"email"—drowned out everything else.

These findings were collected as part of a Gallup project asking Americans to say what they had read or heard recently about twenty-two major Republican and Democratic candidates.

In the verbatim responses from about 750 US adults familiar enough with Clinton to offer an opinion of her, the word "email" came up 329 times in various forms. Relatedly, there were eighty-three mentions of "server." All of those referred to Hillary Clinton's use of a private, unsecured server for sending and receiving official emails. This revelation has led to an FBI investigation and possible indictments of her and/or her aides on several charges. At Judicial Watch, we've filed more than twenty-six lawsuits seeking the truth about Hillary Clinton and her use of the private "clintonemail.com" server, as well as any warnings that Clinton staffers may have made about the misuse of this private email system.

We at Judicial Watch are proud of the role we played in uncovering the email server scandal. Revelations that then–Secretary of State Clinton conducted all of her official business on a non-state.gov email server dominated national headlines this year and last, and it was Judicial Watch's FOIA lawsuits along with the creation of the House Select Committee on Benghazi that led to the uncovering of a scandal that could have criminal ramifications for Hillary Clinton.

We knew something was up. And we had gotten hints in our litigation that uncovered the smoking-gun documents showing Hillary's top aides at State knew that the Benghazi terrorist attack had nothing to do with "demonstrations" or Internet videos. As *Politico* noted, there is no doubt Justice Watch's litigation was front and center as the seven-year cover-up of Hillary's secret emails was unraveling:

> *The first public sign of the email imbroglio now enveloping Clinton came in late 2014 in an obscure court filing in a lawsuit demanding details of Clinton's response to the attacks on US facilities in Benghazi, Libya. Government lawyers handling the case brought by the conservative group Judicial Watch told a federal judge that the agency had searched its files and had no more records to produce.*
>
> *They changed their tune on February 2.*
>
> *"In the course of preparing additional information to provide to Plaintiff for purposes of settlement discussions, Defendant has discovered that additional searches for documents potentially responsive to the FOIA must be conducted," the attorneys wrote.*

The scandal may impact at least ten Freedom of Information Act lawsuits now active in federal courts as well as about 160 Freedom of Information requests we've filed with the Obama State Department.

Without Judicial Watch forcing the disclosure of the "missing" IRS emails, they would never have been disclosed. Our FOIA lawsuits broke open the Benghazi scandal and first exposed the scandal of Hillary and Bill Clinton raising money illicitly while she was Secretary of State. Judicial Watch also has good reason to suspect that the Obama administration withheld material information while purposefully misleading us, as well as more than one federal court, about these emails.

The State Department's early response to the scandal wasn't encouraging. While new records will be searched in response to future FOIA requests, there are no plans to go back and review the accuracy of what has already been produced in response to FOIA, Marie Harf, a State Department spokeswoman, has said. That's a problem.

Clinton apologists from within and outside of the State Department have made the point that by turning over 55,000 pages of emails to department officials, critics should be placated. So then in order to diffuse the controversy why doesn't Clinton simply release the records she already turned over? To do so "would highlight the fact that Clinton's own aides and lawyers determined which records were work-related," Politico surmises. That is putting it charitably.

There seems to be an assumption that the account(s) at issue are her "personal" accounts. On the contrary, these accounts, which were set up by the secretary of state to conduct government business, are alias government accounts and should be treated as such. No third party reviews, as some are suggesting, are necessary if State follows the law and treats the account(s) as it would any other state.gov account. The State Department is obligated to secure the accounts as soon as possible to protect classified materials, retrieve any lost data, protect other federal records, and search records as required by court orders in our various FOIA lawsuits, and in response to congressional subpoenas, etc.

Rather than her private lawyers/campaign advisers reviewing the accounts and releasing material to the government, the agency should assert its ownership, secure the material, and prohibit private parties from illicitly reviewing potentially classified and other sensitive material.

There's also the question of national security. During a State Department briefing, Harf put off questions from the press asking if the account Clinton used had any kind of encryption as a safeguard against hackers. Moreover, based upon available information there's no way for us to know if Clinton discussed classified material on her unsecured email system.

To be clear, there is potential criminal liability for Mrs. Clinton and others for concealing these government records, stealing these government records, and mishandling any classified information.

Even the Obama White House has tried to avoid accountability by trying to pretend that, ultimately, it was Hillary Clinton's responsibility to ensure she followed the law. This is absurd on its face, and this defense is falling apart even as I am writing.

Reports confirm that the White House supposedly knew in August 2015 about these secret accounts, but covered it up. You can see why this conspiracy is not about Hillary Clinton only, it is about her boss, Barack Obama, and any other top administration officials who knew or should have known that Clinton was breaking the law from the day she became secretary of state.

The email revelations helped prompt the House Select Committee on Benghazi, chaired by Rep. Trey Gowdy (R-SC), to issue subpoenas for "all communications" from Clinton "related to Libya" and to the State Department "for other individuals who have information pertinent to the investigation."

We have no doubt that our Freedom of Information lawsuits against the State Department, one of which led to the creation of the House Select Committee on Benghazi in 2015, forced the State Department to finally admit to Hillary Clinton's illicit concealment of government records.

Judicial Watch Springs into Action

After the news of the Clinton emails broke in March 2015, we immediately acted. We began our lawsuits by submitting a Freedom of Information Act request on March 5, 2015, for the 55,000 pages of emails received by the Department of State from Hillary Clinton since October 1, 2014, all emails sent or received by Hillary Rodham Clinton in her official capacity of secretary of state, and all emails of Hillary Clinton concerning the Benghazi attack of September 11, 2012. We noted that at the time we had filed eighteen lawsuits and 160 Freedom of Information Act requests that could have been compromised by Hillary Clinton's secret email accounts.[1]

Four days later, on March 9, we filed a Freedom of Information Act request for all communications between State Department employees and Hillary Clinton relating to the use of unofficial (i.e., not "state.gov") email addresses since June 1, 2014. We also wanted to know all current and former officials, officers, and employee of the State Department who used unofficial email addresses for government business, as well as any communications concerning whether these emails would be preserved under the Federal Records Act and the Freedom of Information Act.[2]

Hillary Clinton Email Surprise

On March 31, the Associated Press revealed that Hillary Clinton had used an iPad to email members of her staff. This revelation contradicted Clinton's earlier statements that she had used her own email system so that she could conveniently conduct official business on one electronic device. In April, we filed a lawsuit seeking all records by Hillary Clinton or her staff to the State Department office of security technology seeking approval for the use of an iPad or iPhone for official government business.[3]

On May 6, 2015, we filed seven more lawsuits against the State Department, seeking the non-state.gov emails of Hillary Clinton, Huma Abedin, Hillary Clinton's former chief of staff, the names of all State Department employees using unofficial email addresses for official business, all of Hillary Clinton's emails concerning the Benghazi attack, all official State Department records concerning policies designed to prevent conflicts of interest between foreign entities and the Clinton Foundation, and all records concerning Hillary Clinton's resignation as secretary of state.[4]

In July, Judge Colleen Kollar-Kotelly ordered the State Department to produce by August all the documents concerning Hillary Clinton's use of an iPad and iPhone. She denied the State Department's request to delay producing these records until January 2016.[5]

We won another victory on July 20, 2015, when Judge Rudolph Contreras stated that he was "concerned" about the preservation of emails that we requested from the State Department. "If documents are destroyed between now and August 17," he said, "the Hillary email government will have to answer for that, and, you know, if they don't want to do anything out of the ordinary to preserve between now and then, they can make that choice. I will allow them to make that choice, but they will answer for it, if something happens."

Judge Contreras also expressed concerns about the State Department's refusal to provide any information about Hillary Clinton's private emails. "I am a little bit mystified that the government is not more forthcoming in just answering questions that will help this case proceed on a systematic basis, and on a basis that will allow everyone to get the answers that will eventually help resolve these cases."[6]

On August 6, 2015, the State Department, in response to a court order, released the letters the State Department sent to former Hillary Clinton aides Huma Abedin and Cheryl Mills requesting copies of government records in their possession. The letters showed that Cheryl Mills's attorneys acknowledged receipt of the letter on March 24 but by June 25 had turned over a limited amount of records. On June 29, Huma Abedin's attorneys claimed that they did not receive the State Department's request. This request was sent March 11, but was not received until May 19 because a letter sent by mail was returned to the State Department undelivered. An email was sent to two domains (@clinton.senate .gov and @hillaryclinton.com) "that as of March 2015, had not been active for the past several years."[7]

Cheryl Mills's attorney announced to the court that she would destroy all federal records in her possession on August 10. On August 7, Judge Emmet Sullivan ruled that the federal government tell Hillary Clinton, Huma Abedin, and Cheryl Mills not to destroy any federal records that they possessed, and that the government provide the court with all statements that they understood the court's nondestruction orders by August 12.[8]

Hillary Clinton provided, under penalty of perjury, information to the court about 55,000 pages of emails she turned over to State on August 10. Clinton stated that Cheryl Mills did not have an account on "clintonemail.com" but that Huma Abedin did.[9] The statement made public the "clintonemail.com" domain name.

In response to Judge Sullivan's order to the State Department requesting that the department explain the steps it was taking to prevent the destruction of the clintonemail.com emails, the department provided a copy of a letter sent by Hillary Clinton's attorney, David Kendall, which included this statement:

> We have voluntarily provided to the Department of Justice on August 6, 2015, the .pst file containing electronic copies of the 55,000 pages of emails on a thumb drive (along with two copies), which had been securely stored in my possession, after receiving from the Department of Justice an assurance that it would maintain this file in an appropriately secure manner and the Department's opinion that such maintenance would satisfy any preservation obligations I am under. Similarly, Platte River Networks is today providing to the Department of Justice the server and related equipment on which emails to and from Secretary Clinton's clintonemail.com were stored from 2009 to 2013 and which Platte River took possession of in 2013. This is following the Department of Justice's assurances to us and counsel for Platte River that it would maintain the server equipment in an appropriately secure manner. The Department also gave counsel its opinion that such maintenance would satisfy any preservation obligations we have.[10]

This letter revealed that Platte River Networks was the company servicing the clintonemail.com account.

The State Department then claimed on August 18, 2015, that it "did not locate any such devices that may contain records responsive to plaintiff's FOIA request." In addition, the department stated that Huma Abedin and Cheryl Mills were issued BlackBerry devices, but the department couldn't find them.

But if the State Department did not supply Hillary Clinton with the devices she used to access the clintonemail.com account, who did?

On August 25, Judge Sullivan ordered the FBI to work with the State Department about "any information recovered from Mrs. Clinton's server." The judge ordered the State Department to report to the court by September 21 about when searches for information pertinent to our lawsuit would be completed, as well as a statement about how the FBI and the State Department would coordinate efforts to recover the emails. In addition, Judge Sullivan ordered the department to report on the status of any investigation by the department's inspector general "regarding Mrs. Clinton's use of a private server."

David Kendall wrote a letter to Sen. Ron Johnson (R-WI) stating that the FBI did not have any emails that the State Department did not already have.

In addition, another letter by Kendall, this time to the State Department, appeared to state that Hillary Clinton believed that she did not have an obligation to return all emails that exist on devices containing official government records. Nor did Mrs. Clinton believe that she had an obligation to preserve such emails. Kendall states in the letter, "Under the FRA (Federal Records Act) and implementing regulations, she had no obligation to include in that set her personal e-mails, or to retain such personal e-mails." [11]

We filed another lawsuit on September 2, 2015, seeking to determine whether Bryan Pagliano, who served as Hillary Clinton's director of information technology during her 2008 presidential bid, was hired by the State Department in 2009 to maintain the email server and whether the State Department spent taxpayer money to manage the email server. The *Washington Post* reported that Pagliano, while employed at the State Department, "continued to act as the lead specialist responsible for [Clinton's email system] . . . with Pagliano summoned at various times to fix problems. Notably, the system crashed for days after New York was hit by Hurricane Sandy in October 2012, while Hillary Clinton was secretary of state." Our lawsuit sought all records concerning Pagliano's hiring, time sheets, calendars, and similar records, travel records to Clinton's home in Chappaqua, New York, and his records concerning the maintenance of Clinton's email server.[12]

On September 14, 2015, we released several new documents concerning the Hillary Clinton emails. The first was a heavily redacted email from Eric F. Stein, deputy director of State's global information systems, to Margaret P. Grafeld, deputy assistant secretary of state for global information systems. The email reported that the gaps in Hillary Clinton's email messages include:

- Received messages between January 21 and March 17, 2009

- Sent messages between January 21 and April 12, 2009

- Sent messages from December 30, 2012, to February 1, 2013

The same email reveals that Cheryl Mills did not use the clintonemail.com domain because she apparently used cherylmills @gmail.com instead.

Another email, sent by State Department Freedom of Information Act official Margaret Grafeld on October 20, 2014, showed that she did not want to create a written record about issues. Grafeld wrote, "Fyi, I'd prefer to discuss, rather than email. Thx." The State Department redacted details about what caused Grafeld's request for secrecy.

A February 9, 2015, report released at this time, titled Secretary of State Hillary Clinton Email Appraisal Report, describes the emails Clinton returned in December 2014 "as approximately 60,000 to 70,000 pages of email correspondence printed to paper and stored in twelve bankers boxes."

The report shows that the State Department had concerns that Clinton's government email correspondence would not be found:

> *This record series is the only comprehensive set of Hillary Clinton's email correspondence. Some of Secretary Clinton's email correspondence may be available elsewhere in the Department either as duplicate copies or scattered among record-keeping systems and other government officials' email accounts. However, of the sample examined, many of the emails were from Secretary Clinton's personal email account to official Department email accounts of her staff. Emails originating from Secretary Clinton's personal email account would only be captured by Department systems when they came to an official Department email account, i.e., they would be captured only in the email accounts of the recipients. Secretary Clinton's staff no longer work at the Department, and the status of the email accounts of Secretary Clinton's staff (and other Department recipients) is unknown at this time.*

The report confirms Clinton's "personal emails" from her non-state.gov account are government records:

This collection contains instances of personal communications. Nevertheless, the fraction of personal communications is small and does not affect the overriding archival value of this collection. This records series meets all of the relevant considerations for archival retentions under NARA (National Archives and Records Administration) Directive J 441.

The report then confirms that all of Clinton's emails are "Federal records," in a section titled "Record status":

This records series meets the statuary definition for Federal records. Recorded information has record status if 1) "made or received by a Federal agency under Federal law or in connection with the transaction of public business" and 2) "preserved or appropriate for preservation." The sent and received email messages of the Secretary of State used for review, comment, information, or other reason fall under the first part of the definition. As the person holding the highest level job in the Department, any email message maintained by or for the immediate use of the Secretary of State is "appropriate for preservation." This record series cannot be considered personal papers based on the definition of a record in 44 U.S.C. 3301 or Department policy found in 5 FAM 443.

The report also confirms that all of Clinton's emails are subject to "line by line review" for release under the Freedom of Information Act.

State Department rules "specify that personal records of a departing Presidential Appointee may not be removed from the government until the State Department 'records officer . . .' approves of the removal, a process which 'generally requires a hands-on examination of the materials.' "

A final document released on September 14, 2015, revealed that the State Department raised concerns about classified information in Clinton's possession in March 2015. A March 3, 2015, letter to Hillary Clinton's attorney, David Kendall, states:

> We understand that Secretary Clinton would like to continue to retain copies of the documents to assist her in responding to congressional and related inquiries regarding the documents and her tenure as head of the Department. The Department has consulted with the National Archives and Records Administration (NARA) and believes that permitting Secretary Clinton continued access to the documents is in the public interest as it will help promote informed discussion . . . In the event that State Department reviewers determine that any document or documents is/are classified, additional steps will be required to safeguard and protect the information. Please note that if Secretary Clinton wishes to release any document or portion thereof, the Department must approve such release and first review the document for information that may be protected from disclosure for privilege, privacy, or other reasons.[13]

We obtained further correspondence between Patrick F. Kennedy, undersecretary of state for management, and Hillary Clinton's attorney, David Kendall, which we released on September 17. The exchange showed that Kennedy asked Kendall to delete a classified email with possible information about the Benghazi attack.

Patrick Kennedy to David Kendall, May 22, 2015:

I am writing in reference to the following e-mail that is among the approximately 55,000 pages that were identified as potential federal records and produced on behalf of former Secretary Clinton to the Department of State on December 5, 2014: E-mail forwarded by Jacob Sullivan to Secretary Clinton on November 18, 2012 at 8:44 pm (Subject: Fw: FYI—Report of arrests—possible Benghazi connection) . . .

. . . Once you have made the electronic copy of the documents for the Department, please locate any above-referenced classified document in your possession. If you locate any electronic copies, please delete them. Additionally, once you have done that, please empty your "Deleted Items" folder.

David Kendall to Patrick Kennedy:

This will also confirm that, pursuant to your request, we have deleted all electronic copies of this document, with the following exception: I have received document preservation requests pertaining to the 55,000 pages of e-mails from the House of Representatives Select Committee on Benghazi, the Inspector General of the State Department, and the Inspector General of the Intelligence Community (DNI). I have responded to each preservation request by confirming to the requestor that I would take reasonable steps to preserve these 55,000 pages of former Secretary Clinton's e-mails in their present electronic form. I therefore do not believe it would be prudent to delete, as you request, the above-referenced e-mail from the master copies or the PST file that we are preserving . . .

Once the document preservation requests referenced above expire, we will proceed to make the requested deletions. This present arrangement would cover the single document recently classified 'Secret.' Should there be further reclassifications during the Department's FOIA review of former secretary Clinton's e-mails, it also would cover any such additional documents.

However, a letter from Paul M. Wester, Jr. to Margaret P. Grafeld shows that Hillary Clinton never turned over the records as requested:

I would like to reiterate our request that the Department contact the representatives for former Secretary Clinton to secure the native electronic versions with associated metadata of the approximately 55,000 hard-copy pages of emails.

On August 6, 2015, the State Department informed the court that it demanded that Cheryl Mills and Huma Abedin "return copies of all potential federal records in your possession." The State Department did not provide any similar requests for Hillary Clinton.

A September 14, 2015, letter from Kennedy to FBI Director James B. Comey seemingly indicates that the State Department was still trying to obtain the electronic records:

On May 22, 2015, the Department requested from former Secretary Clinton's attorney, David Kendall, that he provide an electronic copy of the approximately 55,000 pages identified as potential federal records and produced on behalf of former Secretary Clinton to the Department of State on December 5, 2014 . . . On June 15, 2015, Mr. Kendall replied that, pursuant to my request, he would "copy onto a disc the electronic version of the emails previously produced in hard copy to the Department on December 5, 2014.". . . Before Mr. Kendall could provide that disc to the Department, however, we understand that the FBI obtained the relevant electronic media. Accordingly, we request from the FBI an electronic copy of the approximately 55,000 pages identified as potential federal records and produced on behalf of former Secretary Clinton to the Department of State on December 5, 2014. This request is in accordance with counsel we have received from the National Archives and Records Administration (NARA).

Additionally, to the extent the FBI recovers any potential federal records that may have existed on the server at various points in the past, we request that you apprise the Department insofar as such records correspond with Secretary Clinton's tenure at the Department of State. Because of the Department's commitment to preserving its federal records, we also ask that any recoverable media and content be preserved by the FBI so that we can determine how best to proceed.[14]

Our next discovery was fifty pages of emails from Huma Abedin, which showed that she used the nonsecure clintonemail .com server to discuss sensitive travel and operations security information that could have placed the personal security of Hillary Clinton and other government officials at risk, such as real-time location information while traveling abroad, and hotel and travel arrangements. The documents also show that State Department officials sent duplicate emails about government business to Abedin's official State Department address and her clintonemail.com account.

On June 27, 2012, Abedin sent this email from huma @clintonemail.com.

> I have no idea about no comms
> of course
> we need secure
> Makes total sense

At Judicial Watch we next learned about how Abedin, formerly Hillary Clinton's chief of staff, became a "special government employee" in 2012, enabling her to work part-time in the private sector, making lucrative consulting fees, Hillary Clinton personally signed the form for Abedin's appointment as a "Special Government Employee/senior adviser" to Clinton on March 23, 2012. The position description form includes a statement by Hillary Clinton that Abedin's "position is necessary to carry out Government functions for which I am responsible." The State Department blacked out Clinton's signature on the form, allegedly to protect her privacy. (Subsequent emails we received suggest that Clinton's then–chief of staff Cheryl Mills may actually have signed the document for Mrs. Clinton.)

The documents include details about Abedin's position, which evidently required a continued Top Secret clearance:

> *As a Senior Adviser (Expert) to the Secretary, the incumbent will provide expert advice and guidance on varying issues related to the planning of logistical arrangements for foreign and domestic missions, and for the coordination of the foreign policy requirements, press, and protocol and security components necessary for a successful and sensitive foreign policy mission.*

The documents raise questions about whether Abedin's new position complied with federal law that prevents special government positions created for work already performed by current employees, On June 4, 2012, Abedin states, "NO, MY NEW POSITION IS IDENTICAL TO MY OLD POSITION."

The records show that there was a rush to appoint Abedin to the position, which was initially set to begin on April 1, 2012.

When Abedin was finally approved in June 2012, she had failed to provide her husband, Anthony Weiner's, financial information, despite repeated requests from the State Department.

In a March 21, 2012, email, State Department Administrative Officer Cynthia Motley writes to Abedin requesting the financial disclosure information:

> Huma, I have been advised to begin the process to convert you from your Non-Career SES (Senior Executive Service) position to Senior Adviser (Expert-SGE) in the Office of the Secretary which is to be effective April 1, 2012. In order to initiate the conversion appointment, I will need the following from you as soon as possible:
>
> The attached SF-278 Financial Disclosure Report must be completed for your termination from the Non-Career SES appointment.

Abedin responded to Motley on April 3, referring to her husband, Rep. Anthony Weiner (D-NY):

> Anthony filed his separate disclosures last June. Nothing has changed. I don't need to include his stuff on mine, right? Just want to confirm. Thanks!

Motley to Abedin, April 4, 2012:

> I have confirmed with the Legal Office that his assets are imputed to you so his assets are reportable on your OGE-278 which should include 2011 and 2012 up to the date.

A month later. Abedin had failed to file the disclosure forms, and received an email (marked "Importance: High") from Sarah Taylor, chief of the Department of State's Financial Disclosure Division:

I have your termination OGE-278 report and the financial disclosure report for the Senior Adviser position. While reviewing your termination OFE-278, I noticed your spouse had several assets that aren't reported on your report. Can you kindly provide an end-of-year summary statement so that I can update your report immediately?

Abedin became a senior adviser on June 4, 2012, without having filed her financial disclosure forms. Sarah Taylor wrote to Marcela Green of the Financial Disclosures Division on June 22, 2012: "Yes, she [Abedin] was supposed to give me some information regarding her spouse's assets and she has not done so."

Another email suggests that as of August 29, 2013, Abedin still hadn't provided the required financial information.

Abedin stated in an email of June 6, 2012, after she had been cleared for her new position, "I really don't know [Weiner's] clients or his work."

Politico reported that, since June 2012, Abedin had been working for outside clients while continuing as a top adviser at the State Department. Abedin's outside clients included Teneo, a strategic consulting firm cofounded by former Bill Clinton counselor Doug Band. According to Fox News, Abedin earned $355,000 as a consultant to Teneo, in addition to her $135,000 State Department compensation.

We filed a new lawsuit on October 28, 2015, requesting all documents on the training Hillary Clinton, Huma Abedin, and Cheryl Mills had in classification, including if they had attended Foreign Service Institute class PK323 on "Classified and Sensitive but Unclassified Information: Identification and Marking." President Obama declared this course mandatory for government employees with "original classification authority" in December

2009,[15] and Congress passed a law requiring this training in October 2010.

In November, we released further emails from Huma Abedin, including this exchange on January 26, 2013, with Clinton aide Monica Hanley:

> ABEDIN TO HANLEY: Have you been going over her calls with her? So she knows that Singh (Indian Prime Minister Manmohan Singh) is at 8?
>
> HANLEY TO ABEDIN: She was in bed for a nap by the time I heard that she had an 8am call. Will go over with her.
>
> ABEDIN TO HANLEY: Very imp to do that. She's often confused.

The Abedin correspondence we obtained includes several instances in which she tried to obtain special treatment from the State Department for business associates and relatives. Abedin apparently worked with Teneo cofounder Doug Band to intercede on behalf of an individual seeking a visa.

On December 11, 2011, Huma Abedin received an email from her mother, Saleha Abedin, founder and dean of Dar Al-Hekma University in Saudi Arabia. In the email, Saleha Abedin seeks the assistance of her daughter to help Dar Al-Hekma president Suhair Al Qurashi attend a State Department "Women in Public Service" ceremony, which included remarks by Hillary Clinton.

(Hillary Clinton spoke at Dar Al-Hekma University in 2010. Qurashi and Saleha Abedin introduced Hillary Clinton's speech and moderated the subsequent discussion.)

We next found emails about the rushed State Department job of vetting Hillary Clinton's memoir, *Hard Choices*. Chapters from the book were delivered to State Department Director of Information Programs and Services John Hackett in February 2014. On

March 7, 2014, Hackett began pressuring his staff for approval. On March 10, senior reviewer Charles Daris urged reviewers at the Bureau of Near Eastern Affairs to "turn these around as quickly as possible to meet the hopes and expectations of the author." That same day, State Department official Neal Silver writes, "The FOIA office is under great pressure to turn this around quickly. If you are tardy in your response, you may get a high-level Department official call."

On March 13, 2014, Daris indicated that the Near East staff was given three working days to respond to the book's chapter on Benghazi. Daris also detailed how former Clinton campaign staffer Ethan Gelber requested that the State Department delay sending the manuscript to the CIA for review. The email traffic from that day also shows "factual comments" on the Iran chapter and that the "Maghreb desk" had a comment on the CIA in Benghazi.

A week later, reviewers were asked to destroy draft copies of the Hillary Clinton manuscript because "revisions were in the works." A March 20, 2014, exchange reads:

> CHARLES DARIS: New marching orders from our Front Office. Will you please suspend our request for clearance and find a way to get back all the copies you sent to EAP (East Asian and Pacific Affairs). Please confirm to me when you have done so.
>
> PAUL BLACKBURN: I have just retrieved the two copies of the chapter portions Neil passed to the China and Japan desks (i.e., pages 53–73 of "Back to Beijing" and 87–119 of "Green Light"). In each case, I was assured that no reproductions were made, so I think we now have "all/all of the copies."
>
> DARIS: Excellent, Paul. Please destroy them. Thank you. C

The documents show a sudden decision to halt all work on the review of Clinton's chapter on Iran, followed by a request that all extant copies be found and destroyed, apparently prompted by the State Department's Iran Desk's concerns about the manuscript.

State Department officials were cautioned to be careful in how they proffered editorial suggestions to Hillary Clinton's staff. In a March 12, 2014, email to Silver, Peter Hemsch [16] suggests, "We may reach out informally to the former Secretary's staff re: the policy issues raised; just a low-key, friendly heads-up to double-check that they have considered a policy angle."

Charles Daris forwarded the email, adding that suggestions should be passed along "reiterating that it is not/not a formal Dept response." (Former government employees who have had to sometimes wage court battles to get their books approved by their former federal agency employers may envy Hillary Clinton's ease of getting approval for her manuscript.)

In December, we launched a new lawsuit against the State Department, seeking the ethics and employment records of Cheryl Mills and Huma Abedin while at the State Department. The forms we are seeking include SF-85s, which all federal government employees must fill out detailing their past work history, education, and references. We had previously requested these forms under the Freedom of Information Act, but the State Department refused to provide them. It appears that Mills might have had an employment arrangement similar to Huma Abedin's after 2012. The *Washington Post* reported that Mills was unpaid during her first few months at the State Department, "officially designated as a temporary expert-consultant—a status that allowed her to continue to collect outside income while serving as chief of staff."

We next obtained emails showing that State Department officials, from the start of Hillary Clinton's tenure as Secretary of State, knew that she was using unsecured devices to transmit sensitive information and hackers or foreign intelligence agents could penetrate such devices.

On March 2, 2009, Eric J. Boswell, assistant secretary of state for diplomatic security, sent an email titled "Use of Blackberries on Mahogany Row." "Mahogany Row" refers to the wood-paneled offices on the seventh floor of the State Department where the Secretary of State and his key assistants work.

INFORMATION MEMO FOR CHERYL D. MILLS—S

FROM: DS—Eric J. Boswell

SUBJECT: Use of Blackberries in Mahogany Row

Our review reaffirms our belief that the vulnerabilities and risks associated with the use of Blackberries in the Mahogany Row [REDACTED] considerably outweigh the convenience their use can add to staff that have access to the classified OpenNet system on their desktops. [REDACTED] We also worry about the example that using Blackberries in Mahogany Row might set as we strive to promote crucial security practices and enforce important security concerns among State Department staff.

I cannot stress too strongly, however, that any unclassified Blackberry is highly vulnerable in any setting to remotely and covertly monitoring conversations, retrieving e-mails, and exploiting calendars.

A March 11, 2009, email reads, "After this morning's A/Secys, Secretary Clinton approached Ambassador Boswell and mentioned that she had read the IM[17] and that she 'gets it.' *Her attention was drawn to the sentence that indicates that we (DS) have intelligence concerning the vulnerability during her recent trip to Asia.*" (Emphasis in original)

The internal State Department debate over the use by Clinton and her staff of "Electronic Devices on the 7th Floor" emerges again

in a February 9, 2011, email from an unidentified source to State Department director of the Office of Physical Security Programs, Gentry
Smith, and Donald Reid, senior coordinator for security infrastructure, Bureau of Diplomatic Security, in which the source advised:
"I wanted to share with you, back channel, a little insight into current
thinking in the Secretary's inner circle on technology issues . . ."

That same day, Reid responded by acknowledging the "vulnerabilities of portable devices" and saying he would expand the
discussion to include Cheryl Mills, who wanted "to correct urban
myths . . . re other agencies." Reid did not clarify what these
"urban myths" were.

On March 2, 2011, Reid wrote: "We have a DS Memo to S
(Secretary of State Clinton) [18] re malicious cyber activity directed
toward Dept seniors that is circulating in final clearance . . ." [19]

We then uncovered a further email exchange about the creation of the unsecured email system. This exchange took place
during Hillary Clinton's first week as secretary of state in January
2009, between Lewis A. Lukens, deputy assistant secretary of state
and executive director of the secretariat, Cheryl Mills, Huma Abedin, and Patrick Kennedy.

From: Cheryl Mills

Sent: Friday, January 23, 2009 6:45 AM

To: Lukens, Lewis A

Subject: Re: Series of questions

Lew—who can I talk to about:

- Can our email be accessed remotely through the web using a non-
DOS computer like my laptop?

- I am traveling to the M-E50[20]—will my DOS bb work there and is there a cell phone attached?
- Spoke to Dan (former Department of State Executive Secretary Daniel B. Smith) re: bb [BlackBerry] for HRC (and reports that POTUS is able to use a super encrypted one which)
- Spoke to Dan re: setting up Counselor office for HRC so she can go across hall regularly to check her email

From: Lukens, Lewis A
To: cmills [REDACTED]
Cc: Habedin [REDACTED]; Kennedy, Patrick F; Smith, Daniel B.
Sent: Saturday, Jan. 24, 19:10:33 2009
Subject: Re: series of questions

We have already started checking into the NSA bb. Will set up the office across the hall as requested. Also, I think we should go ahead (but will await your green light) and set up a stand-alone PC in the Secretary's office, connect to the Internet (but not through our system) to enable her to check her emails from her desk. Lew

From: Kennedy, Patrick F KennedyPF@state.gov
To: Lukens, Lewis A, LukensLA@state.gov; Cheryl Mills
Cc: Huma Abedin; Smith, Daniel B, SmithD2@state.gov
Sent: Sat Jan 24 19:48:25 2009

Cheryl

The stand-alone separate network PC is [a] great idea

Regards

Pat

From: Huma Abedin
To: Kennedy, Patrick F; Lukens, Lewis A; Cheryl Mills

Cc: Huma Abedin; Smith, Daniel B

Sent: Sat Jan 24 19:48:27 2009

Subject: Re: Series of questions

Yes we were hoping for that if possible so she can check her email in her office.

From: Lukens, Lewis A

Sent: Saturday, January 24, 2009 8:26 PM

To: Kennedy, Patrick F

Subject: Re: Series of questions

I talked to Cheryl about this. She says a problem is hrc does not know how to use a computer to do email —only bb. But, I said would not take much training to get her up to speed.[21]

A Judge Grows Impatient

In January 2016, a federal judge ordered the State Department to explain how and when extensive new records from the office of Hillary Clinton were located and why they were not identified previously. The court order came in Judicial Watch's Freedom of Information Act lawsuit seeking records about the State Department vetting of then–Secretary of State Hillary Clinton's potential conflicts of interest.

In January, Judicial Watch learned that the Obama State Department recently found "thousands" of new records from Hillary Clinton's tenure as secretary of state. According to information provided to Judicial Watch by various Justice Department attorneys, the new documents appear be "working" records in electronic format located on both "shared" and "individual" drives accessible to or used by persons identified as being relevant to Judicial Watch's FOIA lawsuits on the Benghazi scandal and controversies from Clinton's term at State. The State Department admitted to Judge Contreras on January 14 that the new records include the files of two of Clinton's top aides:

> *The newly identified files that need to be searched in this case consist of office files that were available to employees within the Office of the Secretary during former Secretary Clinton's tenure as well as individual files belonging to Jake Sullivan and Cheryl Mills.*

Naturally, a trove of emails withheld from a court raises suspicions about what they might contain—especially when we learn that they involve possible conflicts of interest. As we will see, Hillary Clinton's interactions with her staff, family foundation, and her husband, Bill, are part of the FBI investigation now swirling around the former secretary of state.

Bill Clinton: A Traveling Conflict of Interest

Judicial Watch has almost twenty active lawsuits in which the Clinton email system is at issue. In addition to helping break open Hillary Clinton's email scandal, we have pried loose documents that provide a road map of more than two hundred conflict-of-interest rulings by the State Department during Hillary Clinton's tenure. In turn, that led to $48 million for the Clinton Foundation and other Clinton-connected entities during Hillary Clinton's four years in office. Previously disclosed documents in this lawsuit, for example, raise questions about funds Clinton accepted from entities linked to Saudi Arabia, China, and Iran, among others.

One continuing source of controversy concerns Bill Clinton's activities while Hillary Clinton served as secretary of state. Were Bill Clinton's speeches and interactions with foreign entities, either on behalf of the Clinton Foundation or on behalf of Bill Clinton's personal corporation, WJC LLC, either illegal or harmful to America's national interest?

In July 2014, we obtained through the Freedom of Information Act State Department documents (usually called "Request for Conflict of Interest Review of WJC Speaking Engagements") that showed that, during Hillary Clinton's tenure as secretary of state, the Clinton Foundation requested reviews of 223 events, with 311 sponsors. Under established protocols of the State Department, and supplemented by a December 2008 memorandum of understanding between the Clinton Foundation and the Obama presidential transition team, a designated ethics official from the State Department's legal office was assigned to review any "potential or actual conflict of interest" for Hillary Clinton while she was secretary of state. Copies of all decisions were sent to Hillary Clinton's chief of staff, Cheryl Mills, despite her negotiating the underlying ethics agreement!

A joint investigation by the *Washington Examiner* and Judicial Watch found that former president Clinton gave 215 speeches and earned $48 million while his wife presided over US foreign policy, raising questions about whether the Clintons fulfilled the ethics agreements related to the Clinton Foundation during Hillary Clinton's tenure as secretary of state. Among the requests the State Department received for conflict-of-interest review:

- A speech to be held at a "mutually agreeable date" in 2010 at the Mohegan Sun Casino in Connecticut. "This would be a private speech of up to 350 friends and patrons of Mohegan Sun . . . the event will not be open to the public. The event will not be publicly advertised."

- A speech on "Russia and the Commonwealth of Independent States: Going Global," held in Moscow in June 2010 and sponsored by Renaissance Capital, "an investment bank focused on the emerging markets of Russia, Ukraine, Kazakhstan, and sub-Saharan Africa."

- A March 2011 speech at the Ritz-Carlton in Grand Cayman, Cayman Islands, on "the business community in Grand Cayman."

- An October 2011 speech hosted by Wells Fargo in San Francisco, which was "being held by Wells Fargo Private Bank and Wells Fargo Family Wealth Group clients, which are clients that have at least $5 million and $50 million in assets respectively."

- An April 2012 speech to UBS Wealth Management, which would include "approximately 300-400 ultra high net worth clients, prospective clients, and UBS Financial Advisers."

The only proposed speech that the State Department objected to, according to this document, was Bill Clinton's request for a "consultancy arrangement" with Saban Capital Group, Inc. chairman Haim Saban, a major Clinton backer. In February 2009, the State Department ethics adviser noted "an objection" because Saban "is actively involved in foreign affairs issues, particularly with regards [*sic*] to the Middle East, which is a priority area for the Secretary."[22]

Between 2009 and 2011, former President Clinton spoke to more than two dozen leading international investment firms and banking institutions, many of them on more than one occasion. Among these firms were J.P. Morgan, Barclays, Merrill Lynch, PricewaterhouseCoopers, Vista Equity Partners, Goldman Sachs, Vanguard Group, Sweden's ABG Sundal Collier, Brazil's Banco Itaú, Canada's Imperial Bank of Commerce, and Saudi Arabia's SAGIA, the Saudi Arabian General Investment Authority.

Among the fees received for these speeches:

- Barclays Capital Singapore: $325,000.

- Needham Partners South Africa: $350,000.

- Cumbre de Negocios (sponsored by Nacional Financeria and El Banco Fuerte de Mexico)—$275,000 and $125,000[23]

- NTR PLC (which described itself as "developing a new investment portfolio of wind projects in Ireland and the UK"—$125,000

The event sponsored by SAGIA was the 2011 Global Competitiveness Forum, a five-day event held in Riyadh. Another sponsor was Dabbagh Group Holding Company Ltd., which the Clinton Foundation described as "comprising 28 autonomous companies, operating in diversified businesses in 20 countries. Mohammed Husnee Jazeel currently serves as Dabbagh Group's CFO." Bill Clinton was paid $300,000 to speak and attend this event.

We subsequently learned that there might have been further concerns by the State Department about Bill Clinton's foreign travels. A June 2010 message chain addressed to Deputy Chief of Mission in Tanzania Larry E. André and others is labeled "URGENT: RE: Clinton Foundation Issue," and states, "Former POTUS Clinton is on the ground in Tanzania . . . we need guidance fairly urgently to still be relevant."

Another email chain, begun on January 26, 2011, has the subject line "Clinton Foundation Request—Saudi entities," and was sent between several members of the State Department's Legal Affairs Office. The discussion is almost entirely redacted.

One speech that particularly concerned the State Department was a 2009 speech Bill Clinton was to give to the Institute of Scrap Recycling Industries Inc. An April 1, 2009, email from State Department Senior Ethics Counsel Waldo W. "Chip" Brooks notes that the ethics review approval of the speech "was in the hands of Jim (State Department Deputy Legal Adviser Jim Thessin) and Cheryl Mills. They were to discuss with Counsel to the former President. I do not know if either ever did."

A follow-up email to Brooks from a colleague asks, "Was there ever a decision on the Clinton request involving scrap recycling? Below is the last e-mail I have on it—I assume it just died since I don't have an outgoing memo approving the event . . ."

Brooks responds two minutes later:

> I think the decision was a soft call to Clinton's attorney and the talk did not take place. You might want to send an email to Terry (Clinton Foundation Director of Scheduling and Advance Terry Krinvic) and tell her you have a gap in your records because you were gone and wanted to know if the President ever did talk before ISRI?

Bill Clinton spoke to the scrap-recycling group on April 30, 2009, for a reported fee of $250,000.

The documents include a request from Doug Band of the Clinton Foundation for an ethics review of Clinton's proposed consulting arrangement, through WJC LLC, with Laureate Education. The State Department redacted key terms of the attached May 1, 2010, draft agreement, including Clinton's fees and the nature of his services.

Laureate Education is the world's largest for-profit international higher education chain and reportedly uses many of the same practices that spurred a 2012 regulatory crackdown by the Obama administration on American for-profit colleges. In 2010, according to the *Washington Post*, the company hired Bill Clinton to be its honorary chancellor, and since that time the former president has made more than a dozen appearances to such countries as Malaysia, Peru, and Spain on the company's behalf. Since 2010, the former president reportedly has been paid more than $16 million from the company for his services.

The documents show some concern by State Department ethics officials about proposed Clinton speeches to entities linked to the Chinese government. State Department officials had several questions about a proposed 2009 speech to a subsidiary of the Shanghai Sports Development Corporation, a Chinese quasi-governmental organization. Rather than answer the questions, the Clinton Foundation representative emailed, "we are not going to proceed with this." Chip Brooks emailed to Jim Thessin, "Cooler heads have prevailed."

We're still receiving Clinton conflict documents, believe it or not, from the Obama State Department. What we've learned thus far is astonishing. The documents are a bombshell and show how the Clintons turned the State Department into a racket to line their own pockets.

How the Obama State Department waived hundreds of ethical conflicts that allowed the Clintons and their businesses to accept money from foreign entities and corporations seeking influence boggles the mind. That former president Clinton trotted the globe, collecting huge speaking fees while his wife presided over US foreign policy, is an outrage. No wonder it took federal lawsuits to get these documents. One can't imagine what foreign policy issues were mishandled as top State Department officials spent so much time facilitating the Clinton money machine.

The FBI is supposedly investigating the Clinton Foundation and the various conflicts of interest first exposed by Judicial Watch (in addition to the Clinton emails). The FBI should follow the leads. My colleague investigative reporter Micah Morrison, a former reporter for the *Wall Street Journal* editorial page, lays out the scope of the "Clinton machine":

"Machine politics"—today the phrase seems quaint, evoking a bygone Gilded Age of Tammany Hall, cigar smoke and burly ward bosses getting out the vote. But as investigative journalists focus on the torrent of cash generated by "Clinton Inc."—and the growing evidence of the influence obtained by that cash—it's becoming clear that this is something new. Whether by design or happenstance, Bill and Hillary Clinton have created the first truly 21st century political machine.

Partly a philanthropy (the Clinton Foundation), partly a platform for post-presidential private enterprise (Bill's speeches and consulting), at one time a presidential campaign-in-waiting (Hillary at the State Department and after), Clinton Inc. is everywhere and nowhere. It zooms across borders—Bill is in Africa! Hillary is teleconferencing in New York! Chelsea is speaking at the Council on Foreign Relations!—a creature of the digital age and global ambition, powered by celebrity, image and spin, relentlessly raking in money. It includes the Clinton Global Initiative, a glitzy stage for big money pledges to various Clinton endeavors presided over by the Big Dog himself, the Clinton Global Initiative University and the Clinton Presidential Library in Little Rock. Under the auspices of the foundation, there is the Clinton HIV/AIDS Initiative, the Clinton Climate Initiative, the Clinton Giustra Sustainable Growth Initiative, the Clinton Giustra Enterprise Partnership, the Clinton Development Initiative, the Clinton Economic Opportunity Initiative, and the Alliance for a Healthier Generation. Just last week, Chelsea emailed me an update on the foundation's "No Ceilings" initiative. Chelsea urged me to "donate before midnight to help my family's foundation change lives."

Then there is Teneo Holdings, a global consulting firm with deep Clinton connections. Teneo serves as a kind of private-enterprise satellite to Clinton Inc. Doug Band, Mr. Clinton's right-hand man for many years, is a Teneo founder. Huma Abedin, Mrs. Clinton's right-hand woman for many years, was a senior advisor to Teneo at the same time she held a top position as part of Mrs. Clinton's inner circle at the State Department. Bill Clinton was both a paid adviser to Teneo and a client. Secretary of State Clinton's former Economic Envoy to Northern Ireland, Declan Kelly, is a Teneo co-founder and CEO.

Teneo boasts of a vast reach across international arenas, partnering "exclusively with the CEOs and senior leaders of many of the world's largest and most complex companies and organizations." In a Clintonian claim of cosmic proportions, Teneo says the firm addresses a "range of financial, reputational and transformational challenges and opportunities by combining the disciplines of strategic communications, investor relations, investment banking, financial analytics, executive recruiting, digital analytics, corporate governance, government affairs, business intelligence, management consulting and corporate restructuring on an integrated basis."

Got that? In fact, Teneo is rather shadowy, with only a few known corporate clients. It is best known for its relation with the Clintons and the Clinton Foundation. Journalists so far have seemed unwilling or unable to penetrate much further into Teneo. But that appears to have changed with Mrs. Clinton's formal entry into the presidential race and the dawning realization among media types that the Clinton Foundation, Teneo and the disappearing State Dept. emails really do signal that some sort of gigantic sleazy game is afoot.

A Private Little Island

We are also investigating the costs to the taxpayer of trips made by Bill Clinton to the Caribbean island of Little Saint James. In June 2015, we filed a lawsuit against the Department of Homeland Security for any records concerning the costs of Secret Service protection for Bill Clinton to this island, the home of Jeffrey Epstein, a convicted sex offender. According to a flight logbook obtained by Gawker.com, Clinton took more than a dozen trips to the island, and on at least one occasion was accompanied by "4 secret service." The logbooks also show that Clinton flew alongside a woman who are alleged to have procured underage girls to service Epstein and others.

The scandal came to light in December 2014, when Virginia Roberts—now a married thirty-one-year-old mother of three—filed an affidavit in a Florida federal court charging that at age fifteen she was procured by socialite Ghislaine Maxwell to satisfy the sexual needs of Epstein and his friends. The *New York Post* reported:

> *According to Virginia Roberts, who claims to have been one of Epstein's many teenage sex slaves, Clinton also visited Epstein's private Caribbean retreat, known as "Orgy Island."*
>
> *"I remember asking Jeffrey, 'What's Bill Clinton doing here?' " Roberts said in 2011. Four young girls, she added, accompanied the former president, during his stay—two of whom were among Epstein's regular sex partners. "And [Jeffrey] laughed it off and said, 'Well, he owes me a favor.' He never told me what favors they were."[24]*

Flight logs show that Clinton shared Epstein's plane with Maxwell and Sarah Kellen, Epstein's former assistant, on at least eleven flights in 2002 and 2003.

New York magazine reported that in 2002, Clinton recruited Epstein to make his plane available for a weeklong anti-poverty and anti-AIDS tour of Africa with Kevin Spacey, Chris Tucker, billionaire Ron Burkle, and Clinton confidant Gayle Smith (now a member of the National Security Council). The logs from that trip show that Maxwell, Kellen, and a woman names Chauntae Davies joined the entourage for five days. Davies was then a fledgling movie actress who appeared in Epstein's address book under an entry for "massages."

Clinton allegedly severed his connections with Epstein when Epstein was arrested in 2005. Epstein, registered as a "Tier 1" sex offender with the US Virgin Islands Department of Justice, served thirteen months in jail after signing a plea agreement with the US government in 2008. The FBI is said to have identified about forty potential victims of the former investment banker.

3

FAST AND FURIOUS

Imagine if a federal Drug Enforcement Administration (DEA) official let a pound of cocaine onto the streets to try to figure out where it was going, but did not make any efforts to follow it after a drug dealer got his hands on it. When dealing with known criminals, federal law enforcement agents know they are never going to see those drugs again—and those drugs could put someone's life in danger from an overdose or other issues that may arise.

The same concept applies to guns. If federal law enforcement agents allow guns to get into the hands of known criminals, and then don't follow them, those weapons will probably end up being used in the commission of crimes—including murders. As such, federal law enforcement frowns upon and rarely ever lets even a smidgeon of drugs or just one gun walk, never mind a couple of thousand, which is what happened in the Fast and Furious scandal.

Operation Fast and Furious grew out of a toxic mixture of inept bureaucracy and a cadre of politically motivated anti–Second Amendment Obama appointees. Assigning accountability for the scandal has been difficult, but Judicial Watch has already pried out of the Department of Justice records that tell much of the story and may put in motion some needed reforms.

In Fast and Furious, Bureau of Alcohol, Tobacco, Firearms, and Explosives (ATF) agents directed people known as "straw purchasers"—low-level illicit weapons purchasers who work for the Mexican drug cartels' smugglers inside the United States—to buy guns at Phoenix, Arizona–area federally licensed firearms dealers. Those guns were then smuggled into Mexico by cartel operatives, after agents let the weapons get into the hands of those cartel operatives by not tracking them. The smuggled guns continue to turn up in disturbing places. Fast and Furious weaponry was in the arsenal of two terrorists who tried to storm a cartoon convention in Dallas, Texas, in 2015 and was owned by Mexican drug lord Joaquín "El Chapo" Guzmán at the time of his final 2016 arrest.

In October 2009, the ATF Phoenix Field Division created a gun-trafficking division for the purpose of funneling weapons illegally to the Mexican drug cartels. According to Frank Miniter, in a piece titled " 'Fast And Furious' Just Might Be President Obama's Watergate" at Forbes.com:

> Group VII began using the strategy of allowing suspects to walk away with illegally purchased guns, according to a report from the U.S. House Oversight and Government Reform Committee and the staff of Sen. Charles Grassley (R-Iowa), then ranking member of the U.S. Senate Judiciary Committee. The report says, "The purpose was to wait and watch, in hope that law enforcement could identify other members of a trafficking network and build a large, complex conspiracy case. . . . Group VII initially began

using the new gunwalking tactics in one of its investigations to further the Department's strategy. The case was soon renamed 'Operation Fast and Furious.' "[1]

There was one significant issue with Fast and Furious: it didn't catch anybody the Feds wouldn't have caught without allowing the guns to flow through to the Mexican cartels. The so-called straw purchasers—the group of buyers who were funneling the weapons to the cartels—were already known to the ATF. So were the gun shops selling the guns. So why allow them to get to the cartels at all? Miniter explains: "As these guns wouldn't be seen again until they resurfaced in crimes (there were no tracking devices installed or other means to trace these guns), the only purpose for letting these guns 'walk' seems to be to back up the president's position that guns used in Mexican crimes mostly come from the U.S." As I wrote in our first book, *Corruption Chronicles*, in essence, the government was playing politics with the Second Amendment, trying to undercut it by linking guns to crimes.

Again, only one problem: the crimes had to be committed for the guns to show up at the crime scenes. Well, they did, such as the crime scene of the murdered Border Patrol Agent Brian Terry—and countless others in Mexico. Where is the accountability for this reckless insanity?

Once Fast and Furious splashed into the news, the man at the head of ATF, Kenneth Melson, reportedly told Rep. Darrell Issa (R-CA) that the senior officials at the Justice Department were trying to suppress information about the scandal—an admission that surely earned Melson a transfer to a make-work position at Justice. The US Attorney in Phoenix who helped run the operation was forced to resign. And the *Los Angeles Times* reported that two additional high-ranking ATF officials have been demoted as the Justice Department attempts to clean up the mess.

But Eric Holder, the supervisor of all these men, managed to keep his job thanks to an audacious cover-up. But not before Judicial Watch lawsuits peeled back many of the layers of this incredible scandal.

Rep. Issa, then chairman of the House Oversight and Government Reform Committee, subpoenaed Attorney General Holder. "Top Justice Department officials, including Attorney General Holder, know more about Operation Fast and Furious than they have publicly acknowledged," Issa stated. "It's time we know the whole truth."

Why would Rep. Issa have reason to believe Holder and his minions at Justice have been less than truthful? After Holder denied knowledge of the Fast and Furious issue, new allegations emerged that Holder lied to Congress about what he knew and when he knew it concerning the operation, prompting calls for a special counsel to investigate.

How Holder Got into Trouble

On May 3, 2011, in a House Judiciary Committee hearing chaired by Rep. Lamar Smith (R-TX), Holder testified: "I'm not sure of the exact date, but I probably heard about Fast and Furious for the first time over the last few weeks." But documents showed he was receiving weekly briefings on Fast and Furious as far back as July 5, 2010![2]

Holder subsequently said he misunderstood the question. Not many are buying that excuse. How could Holder's Justice

Department credibly investigate him and his underlings (who for months denied the truth about Fast and Furious) for possibly lying to Congress.

Judicial Watch has tried to obtain correspondence between the ATF and some *Washington Post* reporters who wrote glowing pieces about the ATF gun-busting campaign. We think it is important to find out if the Obama ATF ran the Fast and Furious operation as part of a press effort to advance their anti–Second Amendment agenda through a liberal media outlet.

And one would suspect that the Obama administration was desperate to blame "American guns" for the Mexican violence. Not to mention that it all distracts from the fact that one of the key reasons for the drug-gang-fueled violence in Mexico is the unsecured border that allows the drug/human trafficking trade to thrive.

But don't take our word on the human carnage caused by Obama's Fast and Furious guns: the Justice Department's latest admission of crimes associated with Fast and Furious crimes is sickening.

Fast and Furious weapons were likely used to murder US Border Patrol Agent Brian Terry in Peck Canyon, Arizona, in mid-December 2010. The guns—assault weapons known as AK-47s—were traced through their serial numbers to a Glendale, Arizona, dealer. That dealer information in turn led to a Phoenix man the Feds repeatedly allowed to smuggle firearms into Mexico.

But details like these have surfaced slowly as the administration scrambles to decide what version of facts it chooses to give Americans. The nation's assistant attorney general for legislative affairs, Ronald Weich, finally admitted that Fast and Furious weapons had been used in at least three violent crimes in the United States and eight others in Mexico.

The crimes were outlined by Weich in a letter, obtained by Judicial Watch to Senate Judiciary Committee Chairman Patrick Leahy. It was a response to the Vermont Democrat's months-old request for details of crimes associated with guns from the now infamous operation. Besides the Border Patrol agent's murder, a Fast and Furious firearm (7.62mm Romarm/Cugir) was involved in aggravated assault against a police officer in Arizona, Weich tells Leahy in the letter.

In Mexico, the ATF has reported eight events in which guns purchased under Fast and Furious have been recovered in violent crimes, Weich writes. Among them were four firearms used for "kidnap/ransom," two in homicides, and one used during a violent exchange between cartels. A separate stash of Fast and Furious weapons was recovered in various parts of Mexico after being involved in "non-violent crimes," according to Weich's assessment.

For instance, ten guns were retrieved in Atoyac de Álvarez after the Mexican military rescued a kidnap victim. Another ten Fast and Furious weapons were also identified in Durango following a confrontation between Mexico's military and an "armed group." An additional ten rifles were found in Chihuahua after the kidnapping of two people and the murder of a Mexican public official's family member.[3]

We've sued the Justice Department and the ATF to obtain Fast and Furious records. Our first lawsuit was filed on October 11, 2011, when we sued Justice and the ATF to obtain all Fast and Furious records submitted to the House Committee on Oversight and Government Reform.

On June 6, 2012, we filed another lawsuit seeking ATF records detailing communications between ATF officials and Kevin

O'Reilly, former Obama White House Director of North American Affairs at the US National Security Council.

Then in September 2012, we filed a FOIA lawsuit demanding access to Fast and Furious records that had been withheld from Congress due to President Obama's claims of executive privilege. But executive privilege generally is reserved to "protect" White House records, not the records of federal agencies, which must be available, subject to specific exceptions, under FOIA.

In June 2012 the House Committee on Oversight and Government Reform voted to hold Attorney General Holder in contempt of Congress for failing to respond to congressional subpoenas for Fast and Furious records. The full House voted 255 to 67 to hold Holder in contempt, with seventeen Democrats voting in favor. (A number of Democrats walked out in protest, refusing to vote.) A second vote, 258 to 95 (with twenty-one Democrats in favor), authorized the pursuit of records through civil litigation in the courts. A week before the contempt finding, to protect Holder from criminal prosecution and stave off the contempt vote, President Obama asserted executive privilege over the Fast and Furious records that the House Oversight Committee had subpoenaed eight months earlier.

While Justice was holding Congress's records' request at bay, it was also stonewalling Judicial Watch. In January 2013, Justice filed an outrageous motion to indefinitely delay consideration of our FOIA lawsuit for records on the grounds that the lawsuit was "ancillary" to the House's separate lawsuit. Judicial Watch responded immediately and countered that the FOIA law demands a response and that its lawsuit was even more viable than the House lawsuit and ripe for consideration on the merits.

Justice also argued that Judicial Watch's lawsuit might somehow interfere with negotiations between the president and Congress. We countered that our lawsuit "does not vanish if and when the House Committee suit is resolved." We concluded that Justice had only disparaged the public's right to know. Judicial Watch "has a statutory right to request records of the government."

Judicial Watch filed a separate lawsuit against Justice in September 2013, seeking access to all records of communication between Justice and the House Oversight Committee relating to settlement discussions in the Committee's 2012 contempt of Congress lawsuit against Holder. That lawsuit is ongoing.

It took two years, but in October 2014, Judicial Watch finally received from Justice a Vaughn Index describing controversial Operation Fast and Furious records. The document was produced in response to Judicial Watch's September 2012 Freedom of Information Act (FOIA) lawsuit.

Typically, a Vaughn Index must: (1) identify each record withheld; (2) state the statutory exemption claimed; and (3) explain how disclosure would damage the interests protected by the claimed exemption. A federal court had ordered the production over the objections of the Obama DOJ. The document detailed the Attorney General Holder's personal involvement in managing the Justice Department's strategy on media and Congressional investigations into the Fast and Furious scandal. Notably, the document disclosed that emails between Attorney General Holder and his wife, Sharon Malone—and his mother—are being withheld under claims of executive privilege and the deliberative process privilege.

This is the first time that the Obama administration had provided a detailed listing of all records being withheld from Congress and the American people about the deadly Fast and Furious gunrunning scandal. In its cover letter, the DOJ asserted that all of the responsive records described in the index are "subject to the assertion of executive privilege." The Vaughn Index is 1,307 pages in length and explains 15,662 documents.

Based on a preliminary review of the massive document, Judicial Watch found that the Vaughn Index reveals:

- Numerous emails that detail Attorney General Holder's direct involvement in crafting talking points, the timing of public disclosures, and handling Congressional inquiries in the Fast and Furious matter.

- President Obama has asserted executive privilege over nearly twenty email communications between Holder and his spouse, Sharon Malone. The administration also claims that the records are also subject to withholding under the "deliberative process" exemption. This exemption ordinarily exempts from public disclosure records that could chill internal government deliberations.

- Numerous entries detail Justice's communications (including those of Eric Holder) concerning the White House about Fast and Furious.

- The scandal required the attention of virtually every top official of Justice and the Bureau of Alcohol, Tobacco, Firearms, and Explosives. Communications to and from the US ambassador to Mexico about the Fast and Furious matter are also described.

Many of the records were already publicly available such as letters from Congress, press clips, and typical agency communications. Ordinarily, these records would, in whole or part, be subject to disclosure under the Freedom of Information Act. Few of the records seem to even implicate presidential decision-making and advice that might be subject to President Obama's broad and unprecedented executive privilege claim.

The release of Justice's Vaughn Index wasn't the only victory over release of Fast and Furious records that we won in 2014.

In December, Judicial Watch disclosed that, based on information uncovered through a Judicial Watch public records lawsuit against the City of Phoenix, an AK-47 rifle used in a July 29, 2013, gang-style assault on an apartment building that left two people wounded was part of the Obama Department of Justice (DOJ) Operation Fast and Furious gunrunning program. An October 16 letter sent from Sen. Charles Grassley (R-IA) and Rep. Darrell Issa (R-CA) to Deputy Attorney General James Cole discloses that "we have learned of another crime gun connected to Fast and Furious. The [Justice] Department did not provide any notice to the Congress or the public about this gun. . . . This lack of transparency about the consequences of Fast and Furious undermines public confidence in law enforcement and gives the impression that the Department is seeking to suppress information and limit its exposure to public scrutiny."[4]

A Sordid Tale: How Fast and Furious Began

Make no mistake: Fast and Furious is one of the most egregious examples of corruption and malfeasance inside the Obama administration that we've seen yet. The cycle of gunwalking continued despite protests from street agents for more than a year after it began in late 2009, until US Border Patrol Agent Brian Terry was murdered on December 15, 2010, in Peck Canyon, Arizona, by Mexican cartel operatives running a rip crew. A rip crew is a group of bandits who clear corridors in the desert for drug smugglers coming from Mexico into the United States. They are used to eliminate potential competition from other cartels trying to steal drugs en route to a US destination, and from law enforcement officials who may attempt to arrest smugglers.

Two Fast and Furious guns were found at Terry's murder scene, after they had been previously trafficked into Mexico. The revelation sparked what became one of President Obama's first major scandals, one with deadly repercussions that continue to this day. Perhaps even more shocking is that along with Benghazi, the targeting of conservative organizations by the IRS, and a whole consortium of other scandals that the Obama administration is responsible for, Fast and Furious remains the only one in which President Barack Obama has asserted an official executive privilege claim, to withhold documents about the Justice Department operation that were subpoenaed by the House of Representatives.

The origins of the Fast and Furious scandal date back to the George W. Bush Justice Department, which launched the Project Gunrunner initiative through the ATF in 2006. The goal of the initiative was to decrease drug and gun trafficking along the US border, crime trades largely driven by the Mexican drug cartels.

In and of itself, Project Gunrunner was not problematic, but incompetent bureaucrats in Arizona's ATF who launched specific investigations as part of it badly mishandled it. Also in 2006, as part of the larger Project Gunrunner, Tucson, Arizona, ATF officials—including Phoenix-based Special Agent in Charge Bill

Newell, who ran ATF operations in the state and was viewed as a rising star in the agency by officials in Washington—launched an investigation named Operation Wide Receiver.

In Wide Receiver, the beginnings of the gunwalking tactics later employed in a more dramatic and fast-paced way in Fast and Furious were tested. Agents, at Newell's direction, allowed 275 weapons to "walk" in Wide Receiver. According to Sharyl Attkisson's CBS News reports, during Wide Receiver "the vast majority of guns were not tracked and Mexico's government was not fully informed of the case."

"Apparently worried that the gun walking tactics could be viewed as inappropriate, federal prosecutors in Arizona abandoned the case," Attkisson reported. "Then, in the fall of 2009, Justice Department officials decided to go ahead and prosecute the case."

When President Obama first took office in January 2009, he and his new administration stepped up the activity of the Project Gunrunner program started under the Bush administration. Essentially, they were taking it to the next level—beefing up and expanding tactics used in the past.

Hillary Clinton even got into the act. At the end of March 2009, Clinton visited Mexico's capital, Mexico City, more than a thousand miles south of the US border. While there, Clinton gave speeches bashing American gun stores and gun owners for the violence. In one particularly notable interview with MSNBC's Andrea Mitchell, Clinton said: "We're going to start tracing these guns, we're going to start cracking down on illegal gun sales, we're going to go after the straw men and women who go in and buy these guns. We're going to use every tool at our disposal."[5]

The nation's top diplomat's trip was much heralded in the press and was an obvious attempt by the political figures at the top of the Obama administration to mislead people into agreeing with her claim that "90 percent" of the "guns that are used by the drug cartels against the police and the military" actually "come from America."

"Our inability to prevent weapons from being illegally smuggled across the border to arm these criminals causes the deaths of police, of soldiers and civilians," Clinton said.

Clinton's claim is actually false. A diplomatic cable uncovered by WikiLeaks shows that 90 percent of the weapons the cartels get come from Central America or from corrupt Mexican military officials. Oftentimes cartels will raid armories in Guatemala. Or crooked Mexican military officials will split up a shipment of new rifles among their troops and the cartels. For instance, if two hundred new fully automatic AK-47s came in, a dirty military leader might give a hundred to his troops and sell the other hundred to his buddies in the cartel. Then he'll report the missing one hundred weapons as an oversight or as stolen—and nobody will ask any questions.

For organized crime purposes, the guns the cartels get from Central America or from corrupt military leaders are better than what cartels could get from America. They're usually fully automatic, military-grade weapons. Weapons they'd be able to traffic into Mexico via straw purchasing rings from Federal Firearms Licensees gun dealers in the United States aren't fully automatic and aren't military grade—they're semiautomatic at best.[6] The ATF's own figures show that only 17 percent of the guns found at Mexican crime scenes have been traced back to the United States.

Despite the inaccuracy of her claim, that political worldview from Clinton, that gun dealers and owners in the United States are responsible for guns getting into criminals' hands in Mexico—

a view shared by most of the rest of the Obama administration—dominated Fast and Furious, making its dangerous tactics even more deadly than during Wide Receiver in the previous administration. Essentially the administration needed to find evidence to justify its claims that American gun dealers were chiefly responsible for Mexico's cartel violence.

The president himself visited Mexico City on April 16, 2009, a couple of weeks after a visit by Attorney General Eric Holder promoting a new anti–arms trafficking program. There he and Mexican President José Calderón made the same argument Holder and Clinton had made before about weapons trafficking and American gun owners. "In fact, I've asked Eric Holder to do a complete review of how our current enforcement operations are working and make sure we are cutting down on the loopholes that are causing some of these drug trafficking problems," Obama said.

Each of these political direction changes in law enforcement, and more, led to what Republicans on the House Committee on Oversight and Government Reform would later describe as the DOJ's development of "a risky new strategy to combat gun trafficking along the Southwest Border."

"The new strategy directed federal law enforcement to shift its focus away from seizing firearms from criminals as soon as possible—and to focus instead on identifying members of trafficking networks," a House Oversight Committee report on Fast and Furious reads. "The Bureau of Alcohol, Tobacco, Firearms and Explosives (ATF) implemented that strategy using a reckless investigative technique that street agents call 'gunwalking.' ATF's Phoenix Field Division began allowing suspects to walk away with illegally purchased guns. The purpose was to wait and watch, in the hope that law enforcement could identify other members of a trafficking network and build a large, complex conspiracy case."

Those gunwalking tactics had begun as early as November 2009, when agents in the Phoenix ATF office began preliminary work on Fast and Furious. The agents' supervisors were attempting to turn what would later be named Fast and Furious, based on early research about it, into what is called an Organized Crime Drug Enforcement Task Force (OCDETF) case.

As ATF Special Agent John Dodson—an agent who worked on Fast and Furious itself and later became the whistle-blower whose decision to go public with the details of gunwalking is the reason why the American people know about this scandal—revealed in his recent book, *The Unarmed Truth*, an OCDETF case "is a funding program that law enforcement agencies apply for and when approved, it basically gives them an unlimited amount of funds to work a case."

Over the course of the next several months, all the way until Terry's death on December 15, 2010, ATF agents on the ground allowed guns to "walk" into Mexico. Dodson warned his chain of command specifically that a Border Patrol agent would be killed with these weapons. He was ignored. As we now know, several months after Dodson's warning, his fateful prediction turned true: Terry was killed with Fast and Furious guns.

After Dodson learned that ATF was going to at least attempt to cover up what would soon become a massive national scandal, he eventually made contact with investigators in the office of Sen. Charles Grassley (R-IA), the ranking member of the Senate Judiciary Committee.

Over the next few weeks, Dodson provided those investigators with the information they needed to make an official inquiry of the ATF about the matter. Grassley, who did not have subpoena power because he was in the minority in the Senate, sent a document request about Fast and Furious to the ATF leadership in Washington.

On January 27, 2011, Grassley wrote to acting ATF director Ken Melson. "Members of the Judiciary Committee have received numerous allegations that the ATF sanctioned the sale of hundreds of assault weapons to suspected straw purchasers, who then allegedly transported these weapons throughout the southwestern border area and into Mexico," he wrote in part, detailing gunwalking that had—at that point, allegedly—taken place.[7]

Dodson was almost immediately retaliated against by one of his supervisors for speaking out, so Grassley followed up again in a January 31, 2011, letter to Melson to say in part that such retaliation is "exactly the wrong sort of reaction for the ATF." It is also a violation of the Whistleblower Protection Act of 1989, which protects federal employees who report misconduct by federal agencies such as the ATF and the Justice Department.

On February 4, 2011, the DOJ's Assistant Attorney General for Legislative Affairs, Ron Weich, responded on Melson's behalf and categorically denied that the ATF let guns walk in Fast and Furious or any other operation. Weich wrote to Grassley that "the allegation described in your January 27 letter—that ATF 'sanctioned' or otherwise knowingly allowed the sale of assault weapons to a straw purchaser who then transported them into Mexico—is false.

"ATF makes every effort to interdict weapons that have been purchased illegally and prevent their transportation to Mexico," Weich added.

After DOJ's denial of gunwalking on behalf of ATF, Dodson eventually decided to go public on CBS News with his allegations that guns were being allowed to walk—and that Terry's murder was connected to the gunwalking.

Ringing Alarm Bells

Dodson recorded an interview with CBS News' Sharyl Attkisson that aired on March 3, 2011.[8]

We now know that Attkisson's report rang alarm bells throughout the Obama administration. Attkisson, who in 2012 won both the Emmy and the Edward R. Murrow awards for investigative reporting, first began reporting on Fast and Furious in February 2011 when she broke the story, "Gunrunning scandal uncovered at the ATF." Since then, she has filed more than a hundred stories relating to the gunrunning debacle, many of which were exclusive reports.

It sure looks as if her reports rattled people high up in the government. In her book, *Stonewalled*, Attkisson reported that she had received inside information that government-related sources had hacked into both her personal and work computers over a lengthy period of time.

Judicial Watch joined with Attkisson in November 2014 to file a Freedom of Information lawsuit against the Department of Justice seeking "any and all records" relating to FBI background checks and other records on the award-winning correspondent. The request includes correspondence between Attkisson and FBI agents.

"I am pleased to once again partner with Judicial Watch,

which is unmatched in terms of success in litigating Freedom of Information claims against the federal government, whether under Bush or Obama," Attkisson said in a statement. "That I've had to sue to get my own FBI file is concerning. This administration has a terrible record in respecting the First Amendment rights of journalists."

Just how terrible, in Attkisson's case, isn't yet known, because the FOIA suit is ongoing, but a separate lawsuit on Fast and Furious has already provided clues on just how far the Obama administration was willing to go to discredit Attkisson. Justice and the White House targeted the former CBS correspondent. In an October 4, 2011, email to White House Deputy Press Secretary Eric Schultz, Attorney General Eric Holder's top press aide, Tracy Schmaler, described Attkisson as "out of control." Schmaler added ominously, "I'm also calling Sharryl's [sic] editor and reaching out to Scheiffer [sic]" (an apparent reference to CBS's Chief Washington Correspondent and *Face the Nation* moderator Bob Schieffer). Schultz responded, "Good. Her piece was really bad for the AG."

Nor was Attkisson the only critic of Fast and Furious targeted by the Obama Administration. Dobson, the ATF whistle-blower suspected that the Justice Department's Director of Public Affairs Tracy Schmaler had leaked negative information about him to *Fortune* magazine writer Katherine Eban, including Dodson's confidential personnel file. Eban's June 2012 *Fortune* magazine article defending the ATF was denounced by the House Oversight Committee, which publicly called for a retraction.

On September 24, 2012, Dodson filed three FOIA requests seeking information on Justice's treatment of him. After a year and a half of stonewalling, Justice had failed to respond to Dodson's request. But in the meantime, the Justice Department Inspector General published a 2013 report confirming that senior officials at DOJ, including Schmaler, discussed discrediting Dodson. Schmaler resigned her position at the DOJ in March 2013 after news broke that she had worked with left-wing advocacy group Media Matters for America to discredit Dodson, other whistle-blowers, and members of Congress and the media who sought to investigate DOJ scandals.

It was clear that Dodson was smeared by DOJ officials for having the courage to be the first whistle-blower in the Fast and Furious scandal. It was equally clear that those who attacked him have gone unpunished, so Judicial Watch stepped in. In May 2014, it joined with Dodson and filed a FOIA lawsuit demanding the records Justice was withholding.

"For almost two years, the Obama Justice Department has stonewalled my efforts to receive information about me," said Dodson. "It is disappointing that I have to sue to receive information about how my employer provided personal and confidential information about me to eager reporters willing to tell the administration's side of the story."

Judicial Watch's FOIA lawsuit is ongoing, but perhaps once we have the complete records of Justice's actions, the Office of Special Counsel will do its job and we will finally see justice prevail.

Fast and Furious Today

The House's criminal contempt resolution was referred to the US Attorney for the District of Columbia, Ron Machen, who declined to prosecute Holder. House Republicans attempted to enforce the civil contempt resolution with an outside legal team that is suing the Obama administration to have the executive privilege claim overturned and compel document production. But it was Judicial Watch who broke the logjam that resulted in Congress's getting the documents.

Again, Judicial Watch filed a FOIA lawsuit on September 12, 2012, for all the records the Obama White House was withholding from the House of Representatives under its June 20, 2012, executive privilege claims. The House had been separately litigating to obtain the records before US District Court Judge Amy Berman Jackson. We figured, correctly, it turns out, that we'd have better success in court than the hapless Congress would.

Initially, the House lawsuit stalled our litigation. On February 15, 2013, US District Court Judge Bates stayed the Judicial Watch case, in part to allow ongoing settlement discussions between the DOJ and the House Committee to continue.

The "mediation" and the House effort to obtain the Fast and Furious documents went nowhere until after Judge Bates in the Judicial Watch litigation ruled that the Obama Justice Department had to disclose directly to Judicial Watch information that Congress was seeking.

After a lengthy sixteenth-month delay of its lawsuit because of this "mediation," Judicial Watch finally obtained a July 18, 2014, ruling from Judge John D. Bates that lifted a stay of our open records lawsuit and ordered the production of a Vaughn Index by October 1, 2014. Judge Bates noted that no court has ever "expressly recognized" President Obama's unprecedented executive privilege claims in the Fast and Furious matter. Typically, a Vaughn Index must: (1) identify each record withheld; (2) state the statutory exemption claimed; and (3) explain how disclosure would damage the interests protected by the claimed exemption.

On September 9, 2014, another court handling Congress's fight for the same records, citing Judicial Watch's separate success, ordered the Justice Department to produce information to Congress by November 3, 2014.

On September 23, Judge Bates then denied the DOJ's request that it be given more than a month, until November 3, to produce the Vaughn Index. As Judge Bates noted: "at best, it means the Department has been slow to react to this Court's previous [July 18, 2014] Order. At worst, it means the Department has ignored that Order until now."

Holder announced his resignation two days after Judge Bates denied a Justice Department request it be given more than an extra month to produce the Fast and Furious information. We took due credit for forcing Holder out of office, noting it was "no coincidence that Holder's resignation comes on the heels of another court ruling that the Justice Department must finally cough up information about how Holder's Justice Department apparently lied to Congress and the American people about the Operation Fast and Furious scandal, for which Holder was held in contempt by the House of Representatives."

Judicial Watch's FOIA litigation also forced President Obama to retreat in our case from his abusive assertions of executive privilege.

The separate House lawsuit made a big step forward in January 2016, when US District Court Judge Amy Berman Jackson, an Obama appointee, ruled that the Obama administration cannot assert executive privilege to deny Congress critical documents about the Fast and Furious scandal because they had already revealed so much.

The decision explained:

> *Furthermore, there is no need to balance the need against the impact that the revelation of any record could have on candor in future executive decision making, since any harm that might flow from the public revelation of the deliberations at issue here has already been self-inflicted: the emails and memoranda that are responsive to the subpoena were described in detail in a report by the Department of Justice Inspector General that has already been released to the public.*

According to court records, the Obama administration completely or partially withheld 10,446 documents, and 5,342 of those were withheld based on claims of executive privilege— meaning they couldn't be turned over because it would harm the president's ability to deliberate privately with his staff.

In quite an ironic twist that is very revealing about the Justice Department, it essentially made the same unsuccessful arguments that Richard Nixon's attorney general, John Mitchell, made during the Watergate scandal, when Nixon asserted executive privilege to prevent incriminating documents from ending up in the hands of the Senate, and claimed the dispute was a "political question" the courts should stay out of. As Jackson pointed out in her order, that issue had been decided against the government in *Senate Select Committee on Presidential Campaign Activities v. M Nixon*.

But then Senate Majority Leader Harry Reid's 2014 decision to invoke the nuclear option to force through confirmation of Obama's nominees potentially jeopardizes what may happen on the D.C. Circuit Court of Appeals no matter Judge Jackson's decision. Part of the reason why Reid invoked the nuclear option, changing long-held Senate rules and precedent, was to get Obama's ideological and political allies whom he nominated for that D.C. appeals court through the Senate.

Like the final resolution of the lawsuit trying to force the Obama administration to turn over the documents, the deadly consequences of Fast and Furious continue to this day. In December 2013, in a gunfight between Mexican authorities and suspected drug cartel gunmen at a Mexico resort, a Fast and Furious gun was used. CNN reported that five cartel gunmen, including possibly a high-level Sinaloa Cartel chief, were killed in the shootout.

Rep. Trey Gowdy (R-SC) has sadly noted: "There will be consequences from Fast and Furious that last for the rest of our lives." While Washington has seen many political scandals over the years, this is the first one directly responsible for the deaths of many individuals.

The true number of people killed with Fast and Furious weapons will never be known. Hundreds of the guns remain unaccounted for. In fact, even the Obama administration admits more people are going to die. In a statement to Fox News in response to the December 2013 gunfight in Mexico and the revelation that Fast and Furious weapons were involved, ATF said it "has accepted responsibility for the mistakes made in the Fast and Furious investigation and at the attorney general's direction we have taken appropriate and decisive action to ensure that these errors will not be repeated. And we acknowledge that, regrettably, firearms related to the Fast and Furious investigation will likely continue to be recovered at future crime scenes."

Darrell Issa, for his part, puts it more bluntly: "Justice has blood on their hands."[9]

This decrepit city may yawn at the deaths of Brian Terry and myriad other innocents (here and in Mexico) caused by this administration's Fast and Furious insanity, but Judicial Watch is still on the case. Our litigation will continue, and I tell you that we're still investigating new leads on the issue.

VOTER FRAUD

Stealing Elections—The Danger of Voter Fraud
and the Fight for Election Integrity

We have all heard about voter fraud and the attempts by liberal media organs like the *New York Times* and Ivory Tower academics to dismiss it as a nonexistent problem. But it is real, widespread, and substantial to the point that it can decide elections. It also drives honest citizens out of the democratic process and breeds distrust of our government.

The danger lies not only in the results of the fraud itself, but also in the reality that voters who fear their legitimate votes will be outweighed by fraudulent ones are likely to feel disenfranchised and may not even show up at the polls to vote. The sad truth is that our nation's recent history consists of far too many elections that have been called into question due to voter fraud.

Many elections, particularly local elections, are decided by slim margins. In January 2014, Ohio Secretary of State Jon Husted released remarkable statistics showing that thirty-five local races and eight local issues were decided in the Buckeye State in 2013 by one vote or by using the state's designated procedure, such as coin-flipping, to break a tie. Often, it doesn't take much fraud to affect an election.

The Election Integrity Project

Because of our concern over election integrity, Judicial Watch organized an Election Integrity Project designed to help ensure clean elections. This is especially important because of the lack of interest of the Obama Justice Department in investigating and prosecuting voter fraud, such as noncitizens registering and voting in elections. The American public certainly agrees that this is a serious problem. A Rasmussen poll from August 2013 reported that only 39 percent of Americans believe elections are fair. In 2012, a Monmouth University Poll reported that more than two-thirds of registered voters thought voter fraud was a problem. In 2008, when a Gallup Poll asked respondents around the world whether they had "confidence in the honesty of election," 53 percent of Americans said that they did not.

There are, unfortunately, numerous examples of voter fraud and even other, admittedly rarer, threats to election integrity, such as intimidation at the polls. We outlined just a few of those examples in *The Corruption Chronicles*, Judicial Watch's 2012 book on corruption in Washington.[1] Former FEC (Federal Election Commission) Commissioner Hans von Spakovsky and *National Review* columnist John Fund detailed numerous cases of voter fraud in their 2012 book, *Who's Counting? How Fraudsters and Bureaucrats Put Your Vote at Risk*.[2] The Heritage Foundation maintains a database listing over four hundred recent cases of convictions for voter fraud, and the Republican National Lawyers Association also catalogues recent cases.[3]

Instead, as our Senior Counsel, Robert Popper, the head of our Election Integrity Project, explained in a commentary in the *Wall Street Journal*, opponents of election integrity like Barack Obama cite faulty statistics to claim there is almost no voter fraud. For example, in a speech to Al Sharpton's National Action Network on April 11, 2014, Obama cited a 2012 report issued by News21, an Arizona State University project. But that project acknowledged significant gaps in the data it had requested from state and federal officials. Several states did not even respond to News21's request for information about voter fraud cases. Election officials and state attorneys general "admitted they did not track voter fraud." The US Justice Department "referred News21 to its 93 local U.S. attorneys" but many of those officers "referred News21 back to the department." Even when News21 received responses, they lacked "important details about each case." As Popper says, "it is hard to believe any valid conclusions about voter fraud can be drawn from this study.[4]

Furthermore, "judging voter fraud by counting criminal proceedings is," according to Popper, "misguided." For any crime, including voter fraud, "convictions are a fraction of prosecutions, which are a fraction of investigations, which are a fraction of known offense, which are, in turn, a fraction of committed crimes." As Popper says, "this is even more likely to be true of voter fraud, which is often a low enforcement priority." Moreover, such "fraud may be all but impossible to investigate or prove if it is carried out successfully."

That includes odd occurrences that seem to defy common sense where it is very hard to determine if they were due to fraud.

Such as Hillary Clinton winning coin tosses in six different precincts in Iowa in the hotly contested 2016 Democratic caucus where the votes for Bernie Sanders and Clinton were otherwise tied.[5] The odds against winning six out of six coin flips are 64 to 1, or 1.56 percent.

A prime example of intimidation at the polls that reveals the Obama administration's disappointing attitude toward election crimes occurred in the 2008 federal election when two members of the New Black Panther Party stood in a doorway of a polling place in Philadelphia. They were in black paramilitary uniforms and one of them carried and brandished a nightstick. They argued with passersby and shouted racial insults at poll watchers. They attempted to block a poll watcher from entering the polling place and were recorded by a poll watcher with his video camera.

At the time, Robert Popper was a deputy chief in the Voting Section of the Civil Rights Division of the US Justice Department. He was assigned to prosecute a civil action against these men for intimidation and attempted intimidation under the relevant federal statute, Section 11(b) of the Voting Rights Act. The case against the defendants was strong, and they subsequently defaulted by refusing even to answer the charges against them.

But the case was abruptly curtailed and all but shut down by the newly appointed officials of the Obama administration. In the end, they ordered Popper to settle the case for a short, limited, and toothless injunction against only one of the four defendants. There was never a convincing explanation from Eric Holder or the administration as to why the case was cut short. Popper believes that it was a partisan abuse of what are supposed to be neutral law enforcement efforts to enforce the Voting Rights Act. This was only the beginning of the Obama administration's abuse of its power over elections. The damage to the reputation of the Justice Department was enormous and enduring, and the damage to the public's perception of the integrity of elections was incalculable.

Popper left the Justice Department in 2013 to come to work for Judicial Watch, where he leads the Election Integrity Project. He says it was a "liberating moment," reminding him of the movie *The Shawshank Redemption*, when the main character finally breaks out of prison. DOJ lawyers like him (what few there were) who did not agree with the Obama administration's radical voting and civil rights agenda and wanted to enforce the law on a nonpartisan, nonpolitical basis "were sidelined and ignored." In fact, other lawyers allied with the administration "would almost talk in code at management meetings to make sure that dissenters like me wouldn't know what the Voting Section was actually doing." Popper says it was like a scene from *Goodfellas*.[6]

Chris Coates, the chief of the Voting Section, before the administration exiled him to South Carolina, was another lawyer who didn't go along with the administration's radical agenda and wanted to enforce voting laws in a racially-neutral, nonpartisan manner.[7] The Obama administration was particularly angry at him because he had approved the filing of the voter intimidation lawsuit against the New Black Panther Party at the end of the Bush administration. Popper says that the Obama administration set up an entire structure to bypass Coates, with left-wing subordinates who were "trusted" by Obama political officials being used to get around him. There was in essence "a shadow Justice Department with subordinates making recommendations regarding Chris Coates and the cases on which Coates should have been consulted." According to Popper, he and Coates were both "treated as if they were wearing a wire" inside a Mob operation and they might as well "have been pieces of furniture" in the way they were ignored even though they were managers of the Voting Section.

Voter ID—Rhetoric vs. Reality

The intimidation by the New Black Panther Party sheds light on another independent electoral issue, whether it is necessary to require photo identification in order to vote. The need for legislation forbidding violence or the threat of violence and intimidation at a polling place is obvious even if evidence shows that it is rare, that few voters actually fail to vote because of it, or that it has not swayed the outcome of a particular, recent election. Similarly, the value of laws against electioneering or partisan displays inside a polling place is clear even if there is proof that such activities did not change anyone's vote. The laws forbidding these activities provide some of the necessary legal safeguards that should protect the electoral process.

Voter ID laws provide the same basic kind of protection. Allegations of fraud are a regular feature of every election cycle, and fraud does sway elections. For those who care to look, there is a steady stream of stories concerning electoral fraud of various kinds. But the justification for voter ID does not depend on establishing the existence of fraud. It is enough that fraud should not be permitted, and that the opportunity to commit such fraud exists.

That there is an opportunity is clear. To begin with, vote fraud is both hard to spot and hard to prove. Particularly where it is successful, vote fraud may never be detected. For example, without an ID requirement the authorities are unlikely to discover that someone has voted on the still-valid registration of his friend who has moved out of state. Even where vote fraud is detected, successful prosecution remains unlikely. There may be no way to track down a perpetrator where, for example, authorities often have nothing but a bogus signature on a poll book or a bogus registration or absentee ballot form. Too many prosecutors are not interested in pursuing these types of cases because they represent a low priority compared to other crimes or will incur political costs.

The typical argument we hear from the Obama administration and other leftists is that voter ID laws discourage minorities, young people, and the elderly from voting. Yet, we know from reputable surveys that the common sense use of photo ID is supported by every demographic group in America. Two-thirds of African Americans support it; two-thirds of Hispanics; two-thirds of liberals; and even two-thirds of those who consider themselves to be Democrats.

There is simply no evidence to support the contention that the requirement to show a photo ID (which are provided for free in every state with such a requirement) discourages legitimate voters from voting. In fact, in states such as Indiana and Georgia where photo ID requirements have been in place for almost a decade, studies show that voter turnout has actually increased. Photo IDs are part and parcel of living in a modern society. We have to show a photo ID to fly on a plane, cash a check, purchase prescription drugs, and to enter federal and private office buildings—including the US Department of Justice in Washington, where the Obama administration has directed its mostly unsuccessful attacks on voter ID laws. South Carolina beat the Justice Department in a court fight, when former Attorney General Eric Holder tried to stop the state from implementing its law.

That is why Judicial Watch has worked hard to defend states

that have implemented voter ID laws. For example, we filed an amicus brief (a "friend of the court" brief) in Pennsylvania on behalf of state legislators like Rep. Daryl Metcalfe, who was the author and driving force behind that state's voter ID bill. Nearly half of the members of the legislature who supported the bill were signed on to the Judicial Watch brief. Pennsylvania's law was typical of the type of law passed by most states. It allowed voters to use a Pennsylvania driver's license or other government-issued photo ID, such as a passport, military ID, or government employee ID. It provided a free ID at no cost and it allowed an individual without identification to cast a "provisional" ballot that would be counted if the identity of the voter could be confirmed within six days of the election. As we argued in our brief, the "legislature did no more than exercise its sound discretion and create a common sense regulatory scheme to secure free and equal elections." Although the law was upheld in the lower state courts, it was overturned in a clearly politically biased decision by a higher court.

The decentralized nature of our electoral laws and enforcement activity, our national mobility, and the nature of our demographics also create opportunities for voter fraud. In 2012, the Pew Research Center on the States released an astonishing report noting that "[a]pproximately 2.75 million people have active registrations in more than one state." That same report observed that "20 million—one of every eight—active voter registrations in the United States are no longer valid or are significantly inaccurate," and that "[m]ore than 1.8 million deceased individuals are listed as active voters."[8] Those extra registrations are the basic resource needed to steal votes.

It is highly likely that election results in recent years were affected by errors, inaccuracies, and outright crimes. What possible explanation can there be for the fact that in many US counties there are more registered voters than there are residents? Judicial Watch found this to be the case all across the country, including in Alabama, California, Colorado, Florida, Indiana, Iowa, Mississippi, Ohio, Pennsylvania, Texas, Virginia, and West Virginia. Perhaps election officials who don't maintain clean voter lists share the viewpoint of the chair of the Illinois Board of Elections, who said, "there's nothing we can do about any of this because we don't have any money to stop the fraud."[9]

Cleaning Up Voter Rolls

The federal government's abuse of federal law has made the problem harder to address. In 1993, the National Voter Registration Act (NVRA) or "Motor Voter" was passed. Section 5 of the law requires driver's license offices to offer voter registration, and Section 7 requires all government offices providing public assistance, include welfare, to register welfare recipients to vote. The Obama administration has been vigilant in forcing states to abide by Section 7, because it believes these efforts are more likely to add core Democratic voters to the voter rolls. And it worked closely with Project Vote and ACORN in pursuing states to force increased registration at welfare offices.

Judicial Watch obtained documents detailing meetings and emails between White House officials, the Justice Department, and Estelle Rogers, the director of advocacy for the ACORN-affiliated organization Project Vote (and a former attorney for ACORN before it declared bankruptcy) to discuss suing states under Section 7. This included a meeting on April 30, 2009, between Rogers, Deputy Assistant Attorney General Sam Hirsch, Deputy Assistant Attorney General Spencer Overton, and two officials from the White House, Cecilia Muñoz, then–Director of Intergovernmental Affairs and subsequently Director of the Domestic Policy Council, and Tino Cuéllar, Special Assistant to the President for Justice and Regulatory Policy.

A February 23, 2011, email showed Rogers saying that she had "received oral assurances from [Assistant Attorney General for Civil Rights Thomas] Perez on several occasions that enforcement action was imminent," suggesting that Rogers was privy to internal discussions inside the Justice Department regarding pending legal action. One month after this email, on March 18, 2011, DOJ filed its first Section 7 lawsuit against Rhode Island. This lawsuit and others filed by DOJ and Project Vote resulted in increased incidents of voter registration errors. For example, a separate Judicial Watch investigation found that the percentage of invalid voter registration forms from Colorado public assistance agencies was four times the national average after Project Vote successfully forced the state to implement new policies on the registration of welfare recipients during the 2008 and 2010 election seasons.

Judicial Watch obtained a whole series of other documents detailing this partnership between the Obama Justice Department and Project Vote, which once employed Barack Obama. Both Project Vote and ACORN have been linked to massive voter registration fraud. A total of seventy ACORN employees in twelve states have been convicted of voter registration fraud. As documented in a July 2009 report by the House Committee on Oversight and Government Reform, of the 1.3 million registrations Project Vote/ACORN submitted in the 2008 election cycle, more than one-third were invalid. Having Project Vote involved in the

Justice Department's voting rights enforcement was like having the Mafia work with the FBI. And it was clear evidence of the politicization of the Justice Department under Eric Holder.

In spite of all this action to enforce Section 7, the Justice Department refused to enforce Section 8 of Motor Voter, which mandates that states make a reasonable effort to clean up the registration rolls by removing those who have moved or died ("list maintenance"). Obviously, the still-active registration of a voter who has moved away or is deceased provides an opportunity to cast a fraudulent vote. Yet former Justice Department lawyer J. Christian Adams reported to Judicial Watch that the Obama-appointed Deputy Assistant Attorney General for Civil Rights, Julie Fernandes, told the Voting Section staff in 2009 that "they would not be enforcing" this provision of the law during the Obama administration.

According to Adams, Fernandes "plainly said in no uncertain terms that Section 8 of the Motor Voter law was not something they had an interest in, because it had nothing to do with increasing minority turnout." The message here was that the Obama Justice Department decided which aspects of existing voting rights law are to be enforced based on what will make fraud easier to commit. Not a single lawsuit was filed under Section 8 during the entire Obama administration.

So Judicial Watch stepped into the breach left by the Justice Department's refusal to go after election officials who refuse to clean up their voter lists. The Motor Voter law has a private right of action that allows voters to sue to enforce the provisions of the law—a provision that was not used for the first two decades that the law was in force. With the cooperation of True the Vote, a Texas-based, nonpartisan grassroots organization dedicated to election integrity, we filed a lawsuit in August 2012 against the Ohio Secretary of State, Jon Husted, because Ohio was not removing dead voters and voters who had moved away from the voter registration rolls. This was the first private enforcement action ever filed to clean up voter rolls.

During eighteen months of litigation, we learned that the voter registration rolls had been seriously neglected under the prior secretary of state, Jennifer Brunner, a Democrat. Secretary Husted was very cooperative; Judicial Watch's Chief Investigator, Chris Farrell, says that "Husted clearly saw the handwriting on the wall" and took the first steps in years to start clearing the rolls of deadwood. In January 2014, Husted entered into a historic settlement agreement with Judicial Watch and True the Vote. Ohio agreed to take a number of actions to clean up and maintain the accuracy of the list. This was the first settlement of such an NVRA lawsuit by a private party since the NVRA was originally passed in 1993.

Ohio started to use the interstate system known as the State and Territorial Exchange of Vital Events (STEVE) database to identify deceased Ohio voters who had moved or died out of state. Ohio agreed to access the Interstate Voter Registration Crosscheck Program administered by the Kansas secretary of state to identify voters registered in Ohio who are also registered to vote in other states. Ohio also agreed to start automatically using its Bureau of Motor Vehicles driver's license database to automatically update its voter registration rolls whenever a voter changes his address. The NVRA specifically requires states to implement this list maintenance action, but as Secretary Husted admitted, Ohio failed to comply with this requirement for twenty years until Judicial Watch filed suit.

Ohio also agreed to ensure that county election officials did monthly checks for duplicate voter registrations and to coordinate with the state's colleges and universities so that students leaving college are reminded to update their voter registration addresses so outdated information can be removed. Prior to Judicial Watch's lawsuit and the settlement agreement, Ohio had no program in place to share information with election officials on college students who graduated and relocated. Finally, Ohio agreed to have its counties send out yearly vote confirmations to all voters who hadn't voted or updated their registration in two years.

Ohio is a key battleground state, and yet it wasn't taking any of the steps necessary to make sure its voter registration roll was accurately maintained. The Obama administration had no interest in doing anything about this, despite the evidence of inflated rolls with duplicate registrations and voters who had died or moved out of state. It was only Judicial Watch's intervention that acted as a catalyst to begin the cleanup of Ohio's voter registration list, which is a key step in securing the election process.

Judicial Watch was similarly concerned about Indiana. The Bush Justice Department had sued Indiana in 2006 and forced the state to take measures to comply with the voter list maintenance requirement under the NVRA. However, those remedies proved to be temporary. Publicly available information for 2010 showed that the number of people listed on voter registration rolls in twelve Indiana counties exceeded 100 percent of the total number of residents of voting age in those counties. That prompted us to file a lawsuit in 2012 against the state, again with the help of True the Vote. It is a good thing we did—when the registration data became available for 2012, Judicial Watch discovered that sixteen counties had more voters than the US Census showed they had voting-age population. So the problem had gotten demonstrably worse in two years.

The injury to our Judicial Watch members in Indiana was real—we heard from dozens of members expressing their concerns and asking us to protect their voting rights against Indiana's neglect and refusal to comply with the NVRA. In fact, according to Chris Farrell, "some of our members independently contacted the secretary of state and local county election officials complaining about their inaction." It was clear to us that Indiana's failure to clean up its voter rolls was undermining the confidence of our Indiana members in the integrity of elections, making it less likely they would vote in upcoming elections.

We finally dismissed this lawsuit in June 2014 after two years of tough litigation with the state, after we successfully caused major changes in the Hoosier state. Early in the litigation, the federal judge refused Indiana's request to dismiss the lawsuit and instead issued a precedent-setting decision when he found that we had established our initial claim that Indiana was violating the voter list maintenance requirement of the NVRA. Through the discovery process, we uncovered evidence showing that the state's failure to maintain the voter rolls' accuracy was deep and systemic. We discovered that:

- At times, the Indiana Election Division improperly discouraged local county officials from conducting list maintenance—a lawyer working for the Division even told a county official that conducting public records research into whether registered voters over a hundred years old were deceased was "discriminatory against the elderly!"

- According to deposition testimony, state election officials prohibited county officials from removing deceased voters from the rolls even if they read a voter's obituary in the newspaper or attended a voter's funeral.

- Other deposition testimony indicated that the two co-directors of the Indiana Election Division were dead-locked about whether the state should undertake even the most ordinary list maintenance activities, like using the National Change of Address database from the US Postal Service or the Social Security Death Index, so for years Indiana used neither resource and didn't remove voters who had died or moved out of state.

The Indiana secretary of state and the attorney general were extremely uncooperative, resisting all efforts to clean up the state's voter rolls. But because of our lawsuit and action by Judicial Watch members in Indiana, the state legislature finally got involved and made a number of changes to fix these problems. Our Chief Investigator, Chris Farrell, says that the federal lawsuit plus the individual calls by Judicial Watch members to state officials "telling them to just do their jobs" clearly "got under their skin and finally spurred action."

The legislature then acted to make changes such as giving the secretary of state the ability to break a deadlock between the two election directors; giving local officials the power to remove dead voters based on obituaries and other such notices; and making it mandatory that officials use the various state and federal databases maintained by agencies such as the US Post Office and the Social Security Administration to remove ineligible voters. The legislature also appropriated several million dollars to help clean up the voter registration list. In essence, the legislature and the governor had to overhaul their election code and restructure Indiana's election administration to ensure that a broken system was repaired and list maintenance was not neglected.

This was a significant achievement for Judicial Watch and explains why its Election Integrity Project is one of the most important the organization has ever initiated. We helped correct a broken system of bipartisan election maladministration in Indiana. Everyone (except perhaps officials in Indiana before our lawsuit) knows how important it is to remove the names of dead people, and people who have moved, from the voter rolls. Leaving outdated registrations on the rolls leaves our elections wide open to fraud. The problem is that not every state wants to roll up its sleeves and do the work necessary to keep their voter rolls accurate and up to date, even though federal law requires them to do so. And the Justice Department during the Obama administration was not interested in making states live up to their legal obligations under federal law to maintain accurate voter rolls.

With the same goal in mind, Judicial Watch filed an amicus brief in 2012 in conjunction with the Allied Educational Foundation in support of Tennessee's attempts to remove ineligible registrations from the state's voter rolls. A lawsuit had been filed by Rep. Lincoln Davis (D-TN) seeking an injunction to stop the state's effort to clean up its voter registration list. As we told the court, the lawsuit had the "potential to worsen an already significant nationwide problem" since voter rolls in many states remained rife with errors and were often highly inaccurate. It was clear from this lawsuit that the political Left was intent on blocking even the most modest attempts to ensure clean and fair elections. The state eventually agreed to settle the lawsuit through a consent decree in which it simply agreed that election officials would review the voter histories of individuals who had been removed to make sure they were ineligible.[10]

Are Aliens Stealing Our Elections?

In 2014, a disturbing study was released by political scientists at Old Dominion University. Their work showed that a significant percentage of foreign nationals residing in the United States, whether lawfully or unlawfully present, were registered to vote in US elections—and that a significant number of them actually have voted in recent years—6.4 percent in 2008 and 2.2 percent in 2010. That is enough to have swayed election outcomes in some states: "there is reason to believe non-citizen voting changed one state's Electoral College votes in 2008, delivering North Carolina to Obama, and that non-citizen votes have also led to Democratic victories in congressional races including a critical 2008 Senate race [in Minnesota] that delivered for Democrats a 60-vote filibuster-proof majority in the Senate." It is, of course, illegal for noncitizens to vote in federal and state elections. But this study suggests that hundreds of thousands of illegal votes may have been cast in the United States in every federal election.[11]

If this study's results are accurate, the implications are startling. We have Obamacare because of election fraud. We have the Dodd-Frank Wall Street Reform and Consumer Protection Act because of election fraud. We have Solyndra—the alternative energy company that collapsed leaving taxpayers liable for $535 million in federal loan guarantees—because of election fraud. Without the election fraud that helped put Obama and his allies in office, there'd be no lawless amnesty for illegal aliens, no Operation Fast and Furious, no Obama IRS assault on Americans. This shows that no American can take his or her vote for granted. There is a real chance that your vote can be cancelled out by an illegal vote cast by legal or illegal aliens.

The Obama administration's attitude toward the problem of noncitizens voting was demonstrated in Florida, when the Justice Department filed a lawsuit in 2012 to stop the state's efforts to comply with the NVRA by removing 53,000 registered voters who were dead—as well as an additional 2,700 noncitizens. Judicial Watch had sent Florida a warning letter about its bloated registration list in February 2012 as part of its Election Integrity Project. When Justice filed its politically motivated lawsuit, Judicial Watch, on behalf of its client, True the Vote, filed a motion to intervene to help defend what Florida was doing. It was particularly shameful that the US Justice Department was trying to stop Florida from fulfilling its legal obligation to remove noncitizens, who are not just ineligible to register and vote, but who violate federal and state law by registering or voting.

Because of the significant problem we now have of noncitizens illegally registering and voting, Judicial Watch filed an amicus brief with the US Supreme Court in 2012 supporting Arizona's law requiring proof of citizenship in order to register to vote. Judicial Watch was representing Arizona State Sen. Russell Pearce, the driving force behind Proposition 200, the law that Arizona voters overwhelmingly approved in 2004. In *Arizona v. Arizona Inter Tribal Council*, the Ninth Circuit Court of Appeals had ruled that such a requirement violated the Motor Voter law, at least with regard to the federal voter registration form, a decision that was unfortunately upheld by the US Supreme Court in 2013. This is one of the worst Supreme Court decisions on election issues, a decision that struck a real blow against election integrity.

It should not come as a surprise that the Obama Justice Department intervened in the lawsuit against Arizona. Or that it defended the refusal of the acting executive director of the US Election Assistance Commission (EAC) to approve a request by Kansas with regard to the federal voter registration form. Kansas had also passed a law requiring anyone who registers to vote to provide proof of citizenship, such as a birth certificate or naturalization papers (among other documents). However, the EAC refused to change the instructions for any Kansas residents using the federal form to register to vote telling them about this state requirement. The EAC had refused a similar request from Arizona in 2005, after voters there overwhelmingly passed a similar requirement in a 2004 referendum.

However, in the *Arizona v. Arizona Inter Tribal Council* decision, the majority opinion written by the late Justice Antonin Scalia gave Arizona and Kansas a roadmap to get around the Supreme Court's ruling. They could ask the EAC to reconsider its decision and sue the EAC if it refused, arguing that the decision was "arbitrary" because the EAC had accepted a similar request from Louisiana to change the instructions for any state resident using the federal form. That instruction told Louisiana residents to attach additional documentation to the registration form if they lacked a driver's license, ID card, or Social Security number.

Fortunately, after a new executive director was hired at the

EAC, the new director reconsidered the prior decision of the EAC in January 2016 and agreed to change the instructions for Kansas. Common sense finally prevailed at this federal agency.

All of the actions of the Justice Department in these types of voting cases (as well as its abusive behavior on immigration) make it clear that the Obama administration was perfectly happy to allow (and encourage) ineligible aliens—both legal and illegal—to vote in our elections.

Obama's Attack on Election Reform

The White House's close alliance with leftist groups was again shown in the fight over North Carolina's election reforms. In 2013, the North Carolina legislature passed the Voter Information Verification Act (HB 589), popularly known as the "voter ID law." This overhauled that state's election laws, requiring photo ID for in-person voting; eliminating same-day registration during early voting; reducing the number of days of early voting; and requiring that provisional ballots be cast in the precinct where a voter resides.

On July 29, 2013, only four days after the bill passed the North Carolina legislature, political activists from the American Civil Liberties Union (ACLU) and the National Association for the Advancement of Colored People (NAACP), along with Rev. Al Sharpton, attended a meeting at the White House with Attorney General Eric Holder, Labor Secretary (and former Assistant Attorney General for Civil Rights) Thomas Perez, and President Barack Obama. Sharpton subsequently told MSNBC that he was told at the meeting that North Carolina would be sued as soon as "this governor signs the bill" and that DOJ would attack other states implementing voter ID laws.[12]

Judicial Watch filed a motion to intervene in the subsequent lawsuit filed by the Justice Department on behalf of Christina Kelley Gallegos-Merrill. In 2012, she had run for county commissioner in Buncombe County and lost a very close election due to improperly cast ballots, including by voters who had used same-day registration during early voting.

Although the court refused to allow Judicial Watch to intervene, it did allow us to file an amicus brief in the case that ended up providing a crucial analysis to the judge. Contrary to the dire predictions of the Obama Justice Department, minority turnout in North Carolina actually increased in the 2014 primary election after the state's contested election reforms had been implemented. As the brief explained, an expert hired by Judicial Watch, Dr. Steven A. Camarota, compared the 2010 primary election to the 2014 primary election.

The result of his analysis showed "that black turnout increased in 2014 by every meaningful measure. Black share of the total electorate increased. The percentage of black registered voters voting increased . . . [there was] an increase in turnout among blacks of voting age. Finally, while turnout increased across the board in May 2014, and while white turnout increased by 13.7%, black turnout increased much faster—by an astonishing 29.5%." Compare this to the Justice Department's wrong prediction that these election law changes would disenfranchise up to two million voters. In fact, the court refused the Justice Department's request to issue an injunction against the law.

The very same thing happened in the November general election in 2014. Through our briefs, we informed the court that

North Carolina Board of Elections data showed that the percentage of age-eligible black residents who turned out to vote rose to 41.1 percent in November 2014, compared to a turnout of black voters of only 38.5 percent in November 2010. Furthermore, the percentage of black registered voters increased to 42.2 percent in 2014 from 40.3 percent in 2010. The black share of all of the votes cast in the election increased to 21.4 percent from 20.1 percent. And the absolute number of black voters increased 16 percent, to 628,004 from 539,646. Again, the Justice Department "experts" who had predicted that North Carolina's election reforms would lower turnout, particularly of African Americans, were completely wrong.

Caging Gerrymandering

Judicial Watch also intervened in another area that affects our election process and our democratic structure in a critical way—redistricting. Gerrymandered districts are a way that elected representatives manipulate the election process to their own benefit at the expense of voters and the public. One of the most gerrymandered states in the entire country is Maryland (see map below). The congressional redistricting plan signed into law in October 2011 by then Governor Martin O'Malley (D) was so bad that even the normally liberal *Washington Post* criticized it, saying that the plan "mocks the idea that voting districts should be compact or easily navigable. The eight districts respect neither jurisdictional boundaries nor communities of interest. To protect incumbents and for partisan advantage, the map has been sliced, diced, shuffled, and shattered, making districts resemble studies in Cubism." [13]

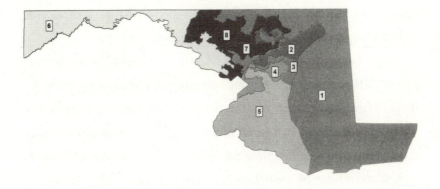

Judicial Watch filed a motion to intervene in the lawsuit against the plan on behalf of MDPetitions.com, which had waged a successful petition drive to place the controversial new congressional redistricting plan on the November 2012 ballot as a referendum. Maryland Democrats has gone to court to stop the referendum from going forward because they did not want voters to have any say in the plan. Not only did the court allow Judicial Watch to intervene, but it ruled against the Democratic attempt to prevent Maryland residents from voting on the redistricting plan.

However, the Maryland secretary of state, in what we believe was an obvious effort to fool voters and help Maryland Democrats, certified misleading ballot language describing the referendum. As we said in a second lawsuit we filed, the ballot language was "a mere 23 words and omits any reference to the fact that Senate Bill 1 makes material changes to existing congressional districts . . . remov[ing] 1.6 million Marylanders from their previous congressional district." Unfortunately, the court ruled in favor of the state. In essence, the people of Maryland were effectively denied their constitutional right to choose their own representation in Congress. Voters were purposefully misled by manipulative ballot language when they voted to approve the gerrymandered redistricting plan in the November election.

When a group of concerned Maryland voters filed a new lawsuit in 2013 against the 2011 congressional redistricting plan, Judicial Watch once again took steps in the litigation to support the Maryland residents. In March 2015, we filed an amicus brief with the US Supreme Court after the Fourth Circuit Court of Appeals upheld a decision by a single federal district court judge dismissing the lawsuit. As we argued, that dismissal violated the Three-Judge Court Act, which requires three-judge panels to hear constitutional challenges to legislative redistricting, and would "allow states to delay judicial review of gerrymandered redistricting plans that disenfranchise voters and violate the Constitution."

Fortunately, the US Supreme Court agreed unanimously with Judicial Watch and issued a decision in December 2015 in *Shapiro v. McManus* overturning the Fourth Circuit and holding that the Maryland voters were entitled to make their case before a three-judge panel. As I said at the time, "no one is above the law, not even the federal courts." This decision would also ensure that a separate lawsuit filed by Judicial Watch contesting the constitutionality of this 2011 congressional redistricting plan as the most distorted and confused plan in the country will have a faster path for relief.

In another redistricting case, *Evenwel v. Abbott*, this time out of Texas, Judicial Watch and the Allied Educational Foundation filed an amicus brief with the US Supreme Court in 2015. The brief supported Sue Evenwel, who challenged the 2013 redistricting plan drawn up by the legislature for state senate districts. The plan was based on total population rather than the number of eligible voters. This gave voters in districts with large numbers of ineligible aliens—legal and illegal—disproportionate power compared to voters in districts with higher numbers of legal residents. As we said in the brief, "Texas is devaluing the votes of certain of its citizens by improperly including noncitizen nonvoters."

Only citizens can vote in federal and state elections and yet "Texas' scheme to give weight to nonvoting noncitizens along with lawful voters is contrary to the principles embodied in citizen voting laws." This policy has resulted in some Texas voters having the equivalent of 1.8 votes while leaving others with only one vote. We argued that the Supreme Court should prevent "state legislators from deliberately disenfranchising their own citizens by . . . strategic placement of noncitizen populations in certain districts in order to dilute the voting power of citizen populations."

This case has national implications. Citing the extraordinary fact that the noncitizen population of the United States has doubled since 1990, the amicus brief of Judicial Watch and the Allied Educational Foundation requested that the Supreme Court finally settle the issue of whether the US Constitution requires that noncitizens be counted when setting up voting districts. This is an important question because out of a total 2012 population of 311 million, roughly 7 percent of the modern US population lacks citizenship—or about one in fourteen people. Accordingly, the opportunity for legislators to resort to the tactical use of noncitizen populations to dilute the voting power of citizens is greater than ever.

Unfortunately, the Supreme Court ruled unanimously that Texas was constitutionally justified in drawing state electoral districts based on total population. The Supreme Court's decision undermines the principle of "one man, one vote." The decision will encourage politicians to fill their legislative districts with more non-citizens and fewer voting Americans. This abuse could lead to unequal voting power for voters in districts with large numbers of alien residents. Under this decision, 100,000 black American voters in one state legislative district would have the same voting power as 10,000 white American voters in another district with 90,000 noncitizens. Even though total population is the same in both districts, voting power is radically different. These types of abuses, already present in Texas, will spread nationally. This is one reason this political decision by the high court won't stand the test of time.

A Jim Crow Election in Hawaii

As these stories attest, Judicial Watch has been involved in crucial election issues all over the country during the past few years, often substituting as the enforcer for work that should have been done by an absent US Justice Department, and often opposing abusive and unjustified lawsuits by that same politicized Justice Department. That politicization was particularly noticeable in an almost unbelievable situation in Hawaii that arose in 2015—a racially discriminatory election reminiscent of the Jim Crow South of fifty years ago. And in this election, which obviously violates the Voting Rights Act and the Constitution, the Obama administration's Justice Department was not only unwilling to enforce the US Voting Rights Act, it actually filed an amicus brief on the side of the discriminators!

What started as an open records request to the state

government of Hawaii to obtain copies of its "Native Hawaiian" voter registration list, became a lawsuit in August 2015 to stop a discriminatory election. Working with the Grassroot Institute of Hawaii, Judicial Watch filed suit on behalf of six residents of Hawaii. Registration for the election was restricted to "Native Hawaiians," who are defined as only those whose ancestors lived on the Hawaiian Island prior to 1778—and only to those willing to confirm a statement affirming "the unrelinquished sovereignty of the Native Hawaiian people." The election was scheduled to run for the entire month of November by absentee ballot, and it would elect delegates to attend a convention to set up a separate Native Hawaiian government.

This is the second time that Hawaii has tried to conduct such a racially restrictive election, which resembles the whites-only elections held in some parts of the South before the Civil Rights Movement began in the 1950s. And the US Supreme Court had already told Hawaii it could not do this the first time it tried.

In *Rice v. Cayetano*, Hawaii allowed only "Native Hawaiians" to register to vote for trustees for the Office of Hawaiian Affairs, a department of the state government, as well as to vote in a special election that asked whether Hawaiians should elect delegates to propose a native Hawaiian government.

This "Native Hawaiian" definition that the state of Hawaii used "implicates the odious 'one drop rule' contained in the racial-segregation codes of the 19th and early 20th centuries," according to Peter Kirsanow, a member of the US Commission on Civil Rights. Or as former US Supreme Court Justice John Paul Stevens ironically pointed out in his dissent in another case, *Fullilove v. Klutznick*, if a government "is to make a serious effort to define racial classes by criteria that can be administered objectively, it must study precedents such as the First Regulation to the Reich's Citizenship Law of November 14, 1935," where the Nazis similarly defined Jews based on their ancestry.

The Supreme Court threw out Hawaii's discriminatory registration and voting scheme in 2000 in the *Rice* case as a fundamental violation of the Constitution. It criticized Hawaii for using ancestry as a proxy for race based on "the demeaning premise that citizens of a particular race are somehow more qualified than others to vote on certain matters." As the Court said, "Race cannot qualify some and disqualify others from full participation in our democracy."

But in 2015 the state government tried to get around this decision by giving a private nonprofit entity, Na'i Aupuni, $2.6 million in public funds to conduct the election of delegates to a convention. It also supplied the nonprofit with the voter registry to be used. That registry was implemented under a state law, Act 195, passed in 2011 and run by a state entity, the Native Hawaiian Roll Commission. All of the commission's members were appointed by the governor of Hawaii.

As Judicial Watch discovered and explained in one of its briefs, there was overwhelming evidence showing "outright collusion" between the state Office of Hawaiian Affairs (OHA) and Na'i Aupuni (NA):

> NA was formed, three years after Act 195 was passed, for no other purpose than to hold the election that OHA could not. NA's bylaws refer to OHA's legislative goals. OHA was, at least for a time, a member of NA. NA's vice-president is married to the CEO of the [Native Hawaiian Roll Commission]. NA was given millions of dollars of public money to hold an election described in a state law, Act 195, in a series of contracts with OHA, wherein OHA

retains all sorts of special rights and privileges. NA "decided" to use the race-based Roll the NHRC had been developing for years, and that OHA is statutorily required to use[.] . . . Indeed, it is particularly telling that NA gave OHA assurances that it would use the race-based Roll to hold a race-based election before the two parties entered into contracts awarding NA millions of dollars to hold that election.

As our Senior Counsel, Bob Popper, said, this was an "outrageous circumvention of the law to try to get around the ban on racist state actions." It was "identity politics to the maximum."

Despite the fact that state action permeated this biased election, however, both a federal judge in Hawaii and the liberal Ninth Circuit Court of Appeals refused to stop the election. The district judge's decision was truly awful, ignoring prior Supreme Court precedent as well as the evidence in the case. He actually compared the left-wing outside group running this racist election to the Kiwanis Club.

What was clearly going on was that the Hawaiian state government, knowing that the Supreme Court has barred it from directly conducting this type of racially discriminatory election, was trying to use a private organization as its proxy to conduct the very same type of election.

Of course, this type of organized misbehavior does not occur in a vacuum. In addition to filing an amicus brief supporting the state, on October 1, 2015, the Obama administration's Department of the Interior published a Notice of Proposed Rulemaking for "reestablishing" a "formal government-to-government relationship" with a new native Hawaiian government if it is established, despite having no legal or constitutional authority for this unilateral action.

But Judicial Watch did not give up. We filed an emergency appeal with the US Supreme Court in November 2015. In a rare move, the Supreme Court overruled the Ninth Circuit, issuing an injunction preventing the defendants from counting the ballots or certifying the results of the election. We were grateful that the Court effectively put a halt to a race-based, state-sponsored, Hawaiians-only election that violates the fundamental constitutional rights of Americans. But it was another prime example of the continuous effort by all too many liberals and the Obama administration to Balkanize America and tear apart the ties that bind us together as one people. In this case, it amounted to a plan to grant secession for certain residents of Hawaii.

You Can Make a Difference

While all of these election cases that Judicial Watch has been involved in could leave Americans depressed about the state of our democracy and the integrity of the election process, they also show the difference that one organization can make. Through the support of our many members and donors, Judicial Watch has been able to mount successful campaigns all over the country to force local governments to clean up their voter rolls, and to support citizens and voters in their efforts to make their voices heard on issues like the rules governing voter registration, common sense voter ID requirements, redistricting, and biased and unfair gerrymandering.

Our Election Integrity Project is an ongoing project that will continue to vigorously fight to secure our most fundamental right—the ability to vote in a fair, nondiscriminatory election without having our votes stolen or diluted.

5

OBAMACARE: CONGRESS EXEMPTS ITSELF

Ever since Obamacare was signed into law in 2010 it has distorted American health care, raised insurance costs, and hurt the economy. It has also been implemented with shameless disregard for the law (having been unilaterally changed by President Obama without the permission of Congress at least twenty-eight times) and with almost no transparency.

We at Judicial Watch started The National Obama Accountability Project to hold Barack Obama and his administration accountable to the American people for its compulsive secrecy and violations of the law. Since then, we have initiated more than 950 open record requests and filed more than 90 lawsuits to protect the people's right to know about what the Obama administration is up to.

Two areas we have focused on are the complete failure of the Obama administration to protect the privacy of your health records and its connivance with Congress to evade the consequences of the Obamacare law and allow its members and staff to receive subsidies under the law that aren't available to millions of taxpayers. In the latter example, we discovered that Republican leaders of Congress are perfectly willing to evade the law and work with the Obama administration if it means allowing Congress to avoid the full consequences of Obamacare.

Congress Claims It's a Small Business

One of the worst examples of the corruption that members of Congress engage in—in this case working in unholy alliance with the District of Columbia government—was the scam Congress pulled to gets its members and staff covered under Obamacare with taxpayer subsidies. The con job engineered by both Democratic and Republican members of Congress would have impressed the two professional conmen played by Paul Newman and Robert Redford in the 1973 movie *The Sting*.

In March 2012, the city council of Washington, D.C., enacted The Health Benefit Exchange Authority Establishment Act of 2011, which implemented an individual health insurance exchange under Obamacare, as well as a Small Business Exchange. The D.C. council appropriated more than 77 million dollars in fiscal years 2013 and 2014 in general fund revenues—taxpayer dollars—to create, administer, and operate the Exchanges. The Small Business Exchange was limited to helping small businesses with fifty full-time employees or fewer.

When Judicial Watch learned that both the US House of Representatives and the Senate had applied to obtain health insurance through the Small Business Exchange for members of Congress, congressional staffers, and their spouses and dependents, despite the fifty-employee limit, we immediately filed a FOIA request for information on the applications. In October 2014, we filed a lawsuit on behalf of D.C. taxpayer Kirby Vining to stop Congress from participating in the Exchange.

Through the FOIA request and the litigation, Judicial Watch discovered that the applications filed with D.C. by the House and Senate each claimed that they only had forty-five employees, an obvious lie and a fairy tale worthy of a Hans Christian Andersen story. Congress employs upward of 20,000 people and at least 12,359 of those employees purchased health insurance through the Small Business Exchange. The applications falsely stated that the House and Senate are "local/state governments" and the "electronic signature" section included the following language:

I've provided true and correct information to all the questions on this form to the best of my knowledge. I know that if I'm not truthful, there may be a penalty.

The actual names of the individuals who signed these applications and fabricated the information on them were blacked out by the D.C. Exchange, which refused to identify them. The D.C. Exchange also conducted outreach to both houses of Congress and even provided weekly support sessions to assist members and their staff with enrollment. The minutes of a November 2013 meeting of the Executive Board running the Small Business Exchange make it clear that the Board and its executive director were well aware that the applications filed by Congress and approved by the Board contained false information and that Congress did not qualify for participation in the Small Business Exchange.

When Judicial Watch was unable to obtain the names of the individuals in Congress who had signed the applications, Senator

David Vitter (R-LA) tried to convince the members of his Small Business Committee to vote to approve a subpoena to obtain those names. According to Vitter, it was "clear that someone in Congress had falsified the document in order to make lawmakers and their staff eligible for taxpayer subsidies provided under the exchange for small-business employees."[1]

The nine Democrats on his committee refused to approve a subpoena; so Vitter needed the vote of all ten Republicans on the committee. But when the vote was held on April 23, 2015, four Senate Republicans voted *not* to approve a subpoena—Mike Enzi (WY), James Risch (ID), Kelly Ayotte (NH), and Deb Fischer (NE). They had apparently promised Vitter early on that they would support the subpoena but changed their minds after being lobbied by Sen. Mitch McConnell (R-KY) and his allies, including Republican Missouri Senator Roy Blunt.

Why would the Republican leadership work to stop the investigation into this scam? As Bob Moffit, a health policy analyst at The Heritage Foundation said, "If there's one thing that absolutely drives Americans fundamentally crazy, it's the idea that Congress can set one set of rules for themselves and another for everybody else. That's political poison and that's why they have been so desperate to avoid the issue."[2]

The 12,359 employees of Congress who signed up for the exchange represented 86 percent of the total number of individuals who enrolled in the Small Business Exchange between October 1, 2013, and September 9, 2014. What was obvious was that every single member of Congress who enrolled in Obamacare obtained their health insurance—and the taxpayer subsidies provided by D.C.—through outright fraud.

Even more amazingly, in the lawsuit, the D.C. government

actually admitted in a motion filed in court that the law passed by the D.C. council did not allow Congress to participate in the Small Business Exchange. But D.C. claimed that the director of the federal Office of Personnel Management, which is the essentially the Human Resources department of the federal government, could override the D.C. law and—implicitly—the Obamacare law.

There is no question that Congress can block or reverse D.C. laws. But it would no doubt come as a surprise to D.C. taxpayers that their own city council believes that a lone federal bureaucrat can rewrite both D.C. and federal law. It wasn't just that Congress was engaging in fraudulent behavior to obtain health insurance, but that D.C. officials were also knowingly participating in a costly and unfair sleight of hand to misuse local tax dollars to help politicians in Congress illegally obtain insurance.

Unfortunately, a local District of Columbia court dismissed the Judicial Watch lawsuit in February 2015 because the court claimed that Kirby Vining, the D.C. taxpayer, did not have "standing" to file this lawsuit. This was a terrible, shortsighted decision because if a D.C. taxpayer whose taxes are being illegally diverted to Congressional employees doesn't have the right to raise this claim, who does? Judicial Watch has appealed the case, but once again, there was no remedy for the corruption that is so often present in so much that happens in Washington, and so far Congress has gotten away with this con job.

Is Your Privacy Safe under Obamacare?

One of the many problems with Obamacare is the issue of how secure your information will be in the Obamacare government computer system. Our lawsuits have uncovered many examples of how easily hackers can access the Obamacare computers and how trustworthy the people are who are hired to help consumers to navigate the Obamacare system. The Department of Health and Human Services reportedly has hired fifty thousand navigators at a cost to taxpayers of $67 million.

We first worried about the people hired to be navigators to assist individuals obtaining health insurance under Obamacare. According to an article in the November 11, 2013, *National Review* Online, among the organizations providing Obamacare navigators is Local 100 United Labor Unions, a New Orleans group run by ACORN founder Wade Rathke. According to the article, "Local 100 is a 'sub-grantee' providing navigators for the Southern United Neighborhoods group, which received a $600,678 grant to promote Obamacare enrollment, as well as $270,193 for similar work in Arkansas and a $486,123 grant for Louisiana." The National Urban League was paid $376,000 for Obamacare outreach in Texas, and Planned Parenthood and the Virginia Poverty Law Center have also received navigator grants.

At a November 6, 2013, Senate Finance Committee hearing, Health and Human Services Secretary Kathleen Sebelius admitted to Sen. John Cornyn (R-TX) that the federal government conducts no background checks on Obamacare navigators.

> *SEN. CORNYN: So I want to ask about the navigators . . . Isn't it true that there is no federal requirement for navigators to undergo a criminal background check, even though they will receive sensitive personal information from the individuals they help to sign up for the Affordable Care Act?*
>
> *SEBELIUS: That is true . . .*

SEN. CORNYN: So a convicted felon could be a navigator and could acquire sensitive personal information from an individual unbeknownst to them?
SEBELIUS: That is possible.

In August 2013, thirteen state attorneys general warned Sebelius that training and safeguards in place for the navigators appeared to be inadequate. They wrote in a letter to the HHS secretary that the background check system "pales in comparison" to what is typically required for workers in programs receiving federal health dollars, adding, "It is not enough simply to adopt vague polices against fraud."

In January 2014, *National Review* reported that as many as forty-three convicted criminals were working as Obamacare navigators in California. In March 2014, Breitbart News Network reported that Obamacare navigators were enrolling clients— including Mexican citizens—at Mexican consulates nationwide.[3]

We were also concerned about the lax rules on "hardship exemptions" under the Affordable Care Act. Rules promulgated by the Obama administration in December 2013 would grant broad "hardship exemptions" to anyone who "believes" that Obamacare coverage options "are unaffordable," essentially opening the law to exemptions for almost anyone who finds the law unpalatable. "The shifting legal benchmarks offer an exemption to anyone who conceivably wants one," the *Wall Street Journal* contended.

Our primary concern was the security and safety of information submitted to the HealthCare.gov website. In a November 2013 hearing before the House Committee on Science, Space, and Technology, web expert David Kennedy of TrustedSec testified that the Obama administration had failed to secure the site from its inception and make sure that adequate security protections were built into the system. "Based on our findings," Kennedy testified, "we are confident that the security around the application was not appropriately tested prior to release, that the safeguards to protect sensitive information are not in place, and that there are and will continue to be for a significant amount of time serious security concerns with the website unless direct action is taken to address these concerns."

At a House Science Committee hearing in January 2014, Kennedy said that the Obama administration had done very little to address the web portal security concerns. "Since the November meeting, there has been a half of one issue fixed . . . of the 18 issued identified through passive reconnaissance. Some issues still include critical or high-risk findings to personal information or risk of loss of confidentiality or integrity of the infrastructure itself."[4]

In September 2014, we released documents showing that top officials of the Department of Health and Human Services's Centers for Medicare and Medicaid Services, including CMS's Director Marilyn Tavenner, and CMS's Chief Information Officer Tony Trenkle, were aware of the gaping security flaws in the HealthCare.gov website, yet Tavenner chose to launch the website anyway. Trenkle resigned on November 15, just six weeks after HealthCare.gov was launched.

In a September 3, 2013, "Authorization Decision" memo, Trenkle reveals a flaw involving Excel macros that could risk malicious code being uploaded into the system. "FFM (Federally Facilitated Marketplaces) has an open high finding: Macros enabled on uploaded files allow code to execute automatically."

The memo continues: "An excel [sic] file with a macro which

executes when the spreadsheet is opened was uploaded for review by another user. The macro only opened up a command prompt window on the local user's machine; however, the threat and risk potential is limitless. Keeping macros enabled relied on the local machine of the user who downloads to detect and stop malicious activity."

Among the "recommended corrective actions" to fix the problem, the memo says: "implement a method for scanning uploaded documents for malicious macros." The due date provided for correcting this "limitless" risk problem—May 31, 2014, eight months after the launch of HealthCare.gov.

(The *Wall Street Journal* reported in September 2014 that "A hacker broke into part of the HealthCare.gov insurance enrollment website in July and uploaded malicious software, according to federal officials.")

Another section of the memo details another flaw: "FFM has an open high finding: No evidence of functional testing processes and procedures being adequate to identify functional problems resulting in non-functional code being deployed . . . Software is being deployed in implementation and production that contains fundamental errors. Untested software may produce functional errors that cause unintentional Denial of Service and information errors." The memo promised that this problem would be fixed by February 26, 2015—again, well over a year after the Obamacare exchange site opened.

The memo identified another security flaw: Many FFM controls are described in CFACTS as "Not Satisfied." (CFACTS is the government database used to keep track of security problems and fixes in the agency's information systems.) "There is the possibility that the FFM secure controls are ineffective. Ineffective controls do not appropriately protect the confidentiality, integrity, and availability of data and present a risk to the CMS enterprise." Officials promised to correct this problem by February 7, 2014.

Finally, the memo warned, "FFM appears to have selected an inappropriate E-Authentication level . . . The E-Authentication level of a system determines the security controls and means when connecting to a system over or from an untrusted network. Use of inappropriate controls exposes the enterprise to additional risk." This problem was scheduled to be corrected by February 7, 2014.

On September 6, 2013, Tony Trenkle wrote a memo to CMS Director of Consumer Information and Insurance Systems Group James Kerr advising, "There are no findings in CFACTS for the FY13 Security Control Assessment (SCA) or the recent penetration hearing." This meant that security problems involved in testing the website had not even been entered into the database set up to keep track of security problems. Nonetheless, Trenkle gave his "Authorization to Operate," concluding, "The current risk is deemed acceptable."

We also obtained the August 20, 2013, and December 6, 2013, Security Controls Assessment Test Plans sent by CMS to MITRE Corporation, the vendor tasked with testing the security of the HealthCare.gov portal. The plan provides the following risk ratings:

> *High: Exploitation of the technical or procedural vulnerability will cause substantial harm to CMS business processes. Significant political, financial, and legal damage is likely to result.*
>
> *Moderate: Exploitation of the technical or procedural vulnerability will significantly impact the confidentiality, integrity, and/or availability of the system or data. Exploitation of the*

vulnerability may cause moderate financial loss or public embar-
rassment to CMS.

   Low: Exploitation of the technical or procedural vulnerability
will cause minimal impact to CMS operations. The confidential-
ity, integrity, and availability of sensitive information are not at
risk of compromise. Exploitation of the vulnerability may cause
slight financial loss or public embarrassment.[5]

We next obtained emails showing that the security flaws affecting HealthCare.gov had not been fixed a month after the formal
launch of the website in October 2013. In a heavily redacted November 6, 2013, email, Julie Bataille, CMS director of the office of
communications, informed Marilyn Tavenner and Jeffrey Zients,
HealthCare.gov tech manager, that "the Dept of Homeland Security's public affairs team reached out to ASPA" (apparently referring
to the assistant secretary for public affairs). The outreach originated
with Kevin Greene, program manager—software assurance, Department of Homeland Security (DHS) Cyber Security Division.

   On November 8, 2013, Tavenner forwarded Bataille's email
to David Nelson, the acting CMS chief information officer, and
Trenkle, the departing chief information officer. Tavenner added
the message "For you guys to follow up. I support. Thanks."

   Trenkle was in no position to respond. In November, 2013, he
left the government to take a position in the private sector.

   These emails followed Tavenner's request:

   November 8, 2013, NELSON TO GREENE: As the new Act-
   ing Chief Information Officer for CMS, I would be very interested
   in talking to you about the type of support DHS may be able to
   provide for HealthCare.gov.

December 9, 2013, GREENE TO NELSON: I had a very productive meeting with Kevin Charest [HHS chief information officer] and his team on [sic] last week and would love to meet with you soon. Please let me know a good time to schedule a meeting.

December 11, 2013: LISA MACK (special assistant to David Nelson) TO GREENE AND NELSON: Dave is available in Baltimore on Monday, January 13th between 1:00 –2:00 pm.

Another email exchange on January 14, 2014, suggests that White House pressure helped push "Digital Media Campaign Tagging," which promoted changes to HealthCare.gov privacy policies to allow certain private information of HealthCare.gov users to be shared with advertisers. In the email chain, with the subject line "Call on 8 Tagging Issues," Jon Booth, director of the CMS website and New Media Group, informs Nelson, Bataille, and Mary Wallace, deputy director of the CMS Office of Communications, of White House interest in using HealthCare.gov user information for advertising. "There is a huge push from the White House," Booth writes, "to implement a robust (and more importantly) measureable digital ad campaign."

This email chain includes a link to a website posting by a security expert who details that security was an "afterthought" on the Obamacare website, that seventy thousand HealthCare.gov records were easily viewable using Google, and that "the head of [HealthCare.gov's] security that had to sign off on the security of the website during its launch wouldn't, and was forced out the door."

The Associated Press revealed in January 2015 that HHS was disclosing health and private information of HealthCare.gov users to advertisers.

The government's health insurance website is quietly sending consumers' personal data to private companies that specialize in advertising and analyzing Internet data for performance and marketing, The Associated Press has learned.

The scope of what is disclosed or how it might be used was not immediately clear, but it can include age, income, ZIP code, whether a person smokes, and if a person is pregnant. It can include a computer's Internet address, which can identify a person's name or address when combined with other information collected by sophisticated online marketing or advertising firms.

A few days prior to this article, Marilyn Tavenner resigned[6] after being accused of padding Obamacare enrollment numbers. According to the *New York Times*:

Representative Darrell Issa, Republican of California and former chairman of the House Committee on Oversight and Government Reform, said Ms. Tavenner "had to go." He said that she had "padded the Obamacare enrollment numbers" to make them look larger than they were.

Congressional investigators discovered in November that the administration had overstated enrollment by including about 400,000 dental insurance subscribers in the total of 7.1 million people with coverage purchased through the exchanges.

"The mistake we made is unacceptable," HHS Secretary Sylvia Burwell said in a Twitter post at the time.[7]

We unearthed additional problems with the October 2013 launch of HealthCare.gov in emails we released in January 2016.

We learned that on September 21, 2013, CMS Information Security Officer Tom Schankweiler discussed with Deputy Chief Information Officer Henry Chao seventeen initial "moderate" security issues findings and two "high" security issues. Two high findings and three moderate findings were resolved, according to the documents.

A separate security analysis found seventeen "high" security issues, prompting Chao to ask, "What are we actually signing off on?" Schankweiler responded in CMS Security Officer Teresa Fryer's refusing to approve the "ATO" (Authorization to Operate), something he indicated he found out belatedly.

On September 30, 2013, the day before the HealthCare.gov launch, Blue Canopy, a contractor that was testing the security of the system, reported that the "parsing engine did not properly handle specially crafted messages. . . . As a result, consumption of these messages would cause the service to crash."

In a November 6, 2013, email to colleagues, George Linares, acting chief technology officer of CMS, said that HealthCare.gov "is operating without an ATO . . . Operating without an ATO is a serious issue and it represents a high risk to the agency."

Another November 6, 2013, email, sent by CMS Security Testing Contractor Adam Willard warned CGI Federal programmer Balaji Ramamoorthy, "It is possible for anyone to run a brute force [attack] against HealthCare.gov to obtain the results of their eligibility."

(CGI Federal was the Canadian IT contractor hired by CMS to oversee most of the HealthCare.gov website development. In January 2014, the Obama administration announced it was replacing CGI Federal with Accenture, at a cost of $90 million.)

Further evidence of Tom Schankweiler's misgivings about the security of HealthCare.gov comes from HHS roll call manifests reporting attendance and actions at meetings to discuss whether to proceed with a relaunch of the site. Schankweiler did not attend a November 2013 meeting to discuss deployment of a new version of HealthCare.gov and did not send a representative in his place. As he was not present, Schankweiler, representing "Security," is listed as the only official not voting to approve the HealthCare.gov "promotion" or relaunch.

On November 26, 2013, Schankweiler stressed security issues to CMS official Todd Couts: "I would like to escalate this ticket to high risk on the defect list. I know that a bunch of security risks have recently appeared on the list, but I wanted to let you know this one is considered a high priority."[8]

All these documents show the Obama administration cast aside the rules and knowingly allowed its Obamacare website to put the most private health care information of millions of Americans at risk. The Obama administration is prosecuting private companies for the same security lapses it knowingly allowed with its own Healthcare.gov. Will Justice Department prosecutors now investigate the Obamacare website security scandal? Given what we now know about Obamacare's security, I have little doubt that Healthcare.gov is in danger of being in violation of federal privacy laws. If you share private information on Healthcare.gov or a related Obamacare site, you should assume that your private information is unsecure and at risk of being hacked.

We Will Continue to Fight Obamacare

Obamacare's first years have been fraught with failure, but its future looks even more bleak. Big premium increases are coming this year and next for people who purchased health insurance on the Obamacare exchanges. Millions of others with coverage outside the exchanges lost their previous policies and now are facing double-digit premium hikes. Many Americans say the new policies they are forced to buy don't meet their needs—with excessive benefit requirements and impossibly high deductibles. Congress is continuing to try to evade the law and exempt itself from key provisions, and your privacy is still at risk.

We at Judicial Watch will continue to hold the government to account over this unfair and unworkable health care law and pressure the new president and Congress elected in 2016 to come clean and level with the American people on its deficiencies.

USING THE IRS AS A POLITICAL TOOL

Most people know that "BOLO" is a law enforcement term short for "be on the lookout" for criminals and suspects on the run. But for the Obama administration's Internal Revenue Service, BOLO meant literally "be on the lookout" for any citizens' groups who might be opposed to President Barack Obama's agenda.

In what was an obvious effort to help the president implement his unilateral policies and get reelected in 2012, in 2010 the IRS started stonewalling the nonprofit applications from Tea Party and other conservative groups that were seeking tax-exempt status. IRS officials, led by Lois Lerner, the director of the Exempt Organizations Division, issued a BOLO with the criteria to be used to flag applications. The criteria included: whether "Tea Party," "Patriots," or "9/12" were used in the organization's name; whether the issues outlined in the application included government spending, government debt or taxes; whether the organization was educating the public about how to "make America a better place to live" or about the Constitution and the Bill of Rights; or if there was a statement by the organization criticizing how the country is being run. This unwarranted and illegal scrutiny and delay went on for years.

The initial hint of what had happened was first disclosed by Lois Lerner on May 10, 2013, in response to a planted question during a speech to the American Bar Association. She knew that the Treasury Department's inspector general was releasing a report on May 14 on the political targeting, and was apparently trying to get ahead of the story.[1] Lerner claimed in her presentation that the "improper" targeting was engineered by "low-level" IRS employees in Cincinnati, a claim that emails obtained by Judicial Watch and other disclosures later showed to be completely false—the scrutiny of Tea Party organizations was directed from Washington, D.C. In fact, former Cincinnati Program Manager Cindy Thomas excoriated Lerner for blaming employees in Cincinnati in an email uncovered by Judicial Watch. President Obama also made this false claim, blaming the Cincinnati IRS office for the "boneheaded" targeting of conservative groups.

Going After the IRS

Judicial Watch realized immediately the seriousness of this abuse of the authority granted to one of the most powerful federal agencies in Washington. Within one week of the release of the IG report, we filed FOIA requests with the IRS. We sought all of the records on the number of organizations targeted by the IRS under this BOLO; all communications between the IRS and members of Congress who may have been involved in spurring the actions of the IRS; any communications between the IRS and other federal agencies, including the White House, about the targeting; copies of any of the voluminous "questionnaires" that were sent to applicants asking for irrelevant information, which included names of donors; and any records of communications between Lerner, the IRS, and other groups outside of the government about what was going on.

As has been the case far too often in the Obama administration, which may go down as the *least* transparent administration in history, the IRS refused to respond to our FOIA requests. Judicial Watch was forced to sue the IRS in federal court in October 2013, shortly after Lois Lerner had "retired" to avoid the consequences of her actions.

Judicial Watch's efforts through these FOIA requests and subsequent litigation led to the discovery that in addition to targeting conservatives at the IRS, Lois Lerner sent confidential taxpayer information to attorneys at the Federal Election Commission, which enforces federal campaign finance rules, in violation of federal law. Email communications revealed that Lerner, who formerly worked at the Federal Election Commission (FEC), sent extensive materials on conservative organizations—the American Issues Project and Citizens for the Republic—to the FEC, including detailed confidential information, after inquiries from the FEC attorneys.

She disclosed this information in spite of Section 6103 of the Internal Revenue Code, which bars the IRS from sending such information to anyone, including other federal agencies. It also turned out that the FEC attorneys were acting without authority to make such an inquiry, because the commissioners who run the agency had never approved an investigation. The emails discovered by Judicial Watch provided a disturbing window into the activities of two out-of-control federal agencies, whose employees, because of their political bias, were trying to target conservative organizations.

Lerner and the Obama IRS violated that same statute again. According to other emails obtained by Judicial Watch, she had communicated with the FBI and lawyers at the Department of Justice about whether it was possible for DOJ to criminally prosecute conservative tax-exempt organizations for supposed "political activities." In fact, in October 2010 after a meeting initiated by Richard Pilger, director of the Election Crimes Branch at DOJ, Lerner illegally sent the FBI twenty-one computer disks containing 1.1 *million* pages of confidential information about tax-exempt organizations. The FBI returned the discs in 2014 when this became public, with even the Justice Department finally admitting that the information should never have been sent to the FBI.[2]

As Representatives Darrell Issa (R-CA) and Jim Jordan (R-OH) said in a 2014 letter[3] to the administration, the "IRS apparently considered political speech by nonprofit groups to be so troublesome that it illegally assisted federal law-enforcement officials in assembling a massive database of the lawful political speech of thousands of American citizens, weeks before the 2010 midterm elections, using confidential taxpayer information."

Lerner acknowledged in a March 27, 2013, email that prosecuting organizations for engaging in so-called political activities was "not realistic under current law. Everyone is looking for a magic bullet or scapegoat—there isn't one. The law in this area is just hard." Lerner was complaining about the difficulty of prosecuting organizations for engaging in activity that is at the core of the First Amendment, one of the most outrageous and dangerous attitudes by a government official that Judicial Watch has ever encountered.

The emails and other information obtained by Judicial Watch showed extensive communications between IRS officials and Democratic politicians who were pressuring the IRS to shut down conservative-leaning tax-exempt organizations. Former Deputy IRS Commissioner Steven Miller assured Sen. Carl Levin (D-MI) that IRS regulations were flexible enough for IRS agents to send detailed "individualized questions and requests" to selected 501(c)(4) organizations. The Democrats and IRS officials like Lerner wanted to use existing IRS policies to revoke the nonprofit exemptions of active conservative groups and deny exemptions to new applicants. Levin even told the IRS which conservative organizations he wanted targeted, including the Club for Growth, Americans for Tax Reform, the 60 Plus Association, and the Susan B. Anthony List.

The Dog Ate the Emails

A major development in the FOIA lawsuit against the IRS occurred in June 2014. After months of delay, the IRS finally revealed that it had "lost" emails generated by Lois Lerner because her laptop had crashed and her BlackBerry was "wiped." We learned later that the IRS found out about the lost emails in February when it was putting together its first production of records responsive to Judicial Watch's lawsuit. But the IRS did not notify Congress, Judicial Watch, or the court for four months. In fact, when IRS lawyers filed a status update with the court on April 30, 2014, it made no mention of the lost emails, a material omission of fact. The IRS was obviously in full cover-up mode.

US District Court Judge Emmet G. Sullivan was obviously

angry about what happened. We requested a hearing, where the judge ordered the IRS to submit a written declaration under oath (not the court brief that would typically be filed) about what happened to Lois Lerner's "lost" emails and any other computer records lost by the IRS. This was an extraordinary order to a federal government agency; Sullivan even appointed a federal magistrate to supervise the discussions between Judicial Watch and the IRS about how to obtain all of the missing records.

The IRS response was so lacking in detail and explanation of what had happened that Judge Sullivan launched an independent inquiry into the missing emails. Things got even worse when the DOJ attorneys representing the IRS admitted to Judicial Watch that all of Lois Lerner's emails were backed up in case of government-wide catastrophe, contradicting other IRS officials, including IRS Commissioner John Koskinen, who claimed under oath that some of the backup tapes no longer existed because they had been recycled.

In any event, the DOJ lawyers claimed, the backup system would be too "onerous" to search. However, it turned out later that the Inspector General for Tax Administration, who had issued the initial report on the targeting, obtained hundreds of backup tapes that neither the IRS nor DOJ had bothered to find, search for, or produce. At one point in February 2015, IG officials even testified that hard drives previously reported by the IRS as having been destroyed had not, in fact, been destroyed. Sullivan eventually issued an order on July 1, 2015, requiring the IRS to produce responsive records to Judicial Watch on a weekly basis, including the newly recovered Lerner emails.

What became evident from the IRS's behavior as well as the behavior of its DOJ lawyers in our case, was that it couldn't care less about the federal court's orders to provide full information about the missing emails. Instead, the IRS with the help of a compromised Justice Department was engaging in a series of transparently evasive distractions. Both agencies thought they could game the federal court and Congress to delay any accountability over what the IRS did. In fact, they at first refused to comply with Judge Sullivan's July 1 weekly production order.

At a hearing on July 29, 2015, Sullivan threatened to hold both the IRS Commissioner and the DOJ lawyers in contempt of court for failing to produce the sought-after records. He called their behavior "indefensible, ridiculous, and absurd." He told the DOJ lawyers that he was "not going to tolerate further noncompliance" with his orders and if there were any further delays, he would "haul into court the IRS Commissioner to hold him personally in contempt." He then "encouraged" the DOJ lawyers to read the opinion in *Contempt Findings in United States v. Stevens*, in which "the United States Court of Appeals for this circuit affirmed this Court's decision to hold [former Sen. Ted] Stevens' [DOJ] prosecutors in contempt of court." "You're walking out of court" today and not being held in contempt, Sullivan told the DOJ lawyers, but "that might not always be the case" if they didn't start complying with his orders.

Harassing Conservative Organizations

Judicial Watch finally obtained IRS documents that showed the IRS went to absurd lengths in its efforts to harass organizations applying for tax-exempt status, asking organizations like Tea Party Patriots for copies of all information on its Facebook page and

Twitter account, or asking an Ohio group, American Patriots
Against Government Excess, for all of the books read in their book
club meeting—including a summary or book report for each of
the books! The documents also showed the agency acknowledging
that its demands that applicant organizations provide the names of
their donors were neither needed nor relevant. A May 21, 2012,
internal memo by the IRS deputy associate chief counsel said that
"such information was not needed" and that it was "not used in
making the agency's determination on exempt status."

Another IRS email thread on June 27, 2012, revealed that the
inappropriately obtained donor lists were being used for a "secret
research project" that, because of redactions and blackouts, could
not be identified. Other documents obtained by Judicial Watch
confirmed that the IRS started using donor lists of tax-exempt
organizations in 2010 to target those donors for audits. The House
Ways and Means Committee announced at a May 7, 2014, hearing, after scores of conservative groups provided donor information to the IRS, "nearly one in ten donors were subject to audit."

In February 2011, as many as five donors of the conservative organization Freedom Watch, as well as its former president,
Bradley Blakeman, were targeted for personal audits without justification. The IRS officials were using the supposed applicability
of a gift tax to donations to such organizations as a pretext for the
audit. But a gift tax on donations to 501(c)(4) organizations was
considered by most to be a dead letter since the IRS had never enforced the rule after the US Supreme Court ruled that such taxes
violated the First Amendment. In fact, the documents showed
that the IRS had not enforced the gift tax since 1982. But internal emails showed Lois Lerner supported applying the gift tax,

contradicting an IRS statement to the media that the audits were not part of a "broader effort looking at donations to 501(c)(4)s."

Emails to and from IRS attorney Lorraine Gardner showed a bias against the US Chamber of Commerce, too, with one saying that the Chamber might "find itself under high scrutiny." "One can only hope," added Gardner. Gardner also emailed a donor list of another 501(c)(4) to a former branch chief in the IRS Office of the Chief Counsel; later, this information was shared with the IRS Estate Gift and Policy Program Manager while Gardner sought "information about any of the donors." Crossroads GPS, a non-profit organization associated with Karl Rove, was also so disliked by IRS officials that it was specifically referenced in emails in the context of applying the nonapplicable gift tax to donations made to the organization.

In early May 2011, once the media began reporting on the IRS audits of donors, IRS officials reacted quickly. One official acknowledged the issue was "a biggy" when a reporter from the *New York Times* contacted the IRS on May 9. Two months later in July 2011 the IRS retreated and soon-to-be acting IRS Commissioner Steven Miller directed that all audits of donors related to the gift tax be "closed."

The IRS finally admitted its wrongdoing with respect to at least one conservative organization, the National Organization for Marriage. It settled a lawsuit for $50,000 filed by NOM over the unlawful release of its confidential tax return and donor list by the IRS. The Human Rights Campaign, the chief political rival of NOM, published the tax returns and donor list in March 2012. But the Justice Department refused to prosecute either the IRS employee involved or the individual the information was given to.

A Corrupt Justice Department "Investigation"

Judicial Watch launched another FOIA lawsuit against the Justice Department connected with the IRS scandal. In May 2013, former Attorney General Eric Holder declared that the IRS targeting was "outrageous and unacceptable," and then announced that the Justice Department was opening an "investigation" of the IRS targeting. He assigned oversight of the case to an attorney, Barbara Bosserman, in the Civil Rights Division. Not only was Bosserman heavily invested in President Obama and the Democratic Party as one of its political contributors (almost $7,000), but she is a civil rights lawyer with no experience in the type of issues present in the IRS case. It is the Public Integrity Section of the Criminal Division of the Department of Justice that is responsible for investigating and prosecuting pubic corruption, not the Civil Rights Division, according to Hans von Spakovsky, a lawyer at The Heritage Foundation and a former Counsel to the Assistant Attorney General for Civil Rights.

As House Oversight Committee Chairman Darrell Issa (R-CA) and subcommittee chairman Jim Jordan (R-OH) said, Bosserman had a "startling conflict of interest." It was incredible that "the department would choose such an individual to examine the federal government's systematic targeting and harassment of organizations opposed to the president's policies." Another obvious conflict of interest was the involvement of the DOJ's Election Crimes Branch in the "joint" investigation, given that branch's earlier involvement with Lerner and its facilitation of unlawfully giving the FBI confidential taxpayer information. But Holder apparently wanted to make sure that DOJ would not conduct a serious investigation, and he refused to remove Bosserman from the investigation.

We filed suit in June 2014 to discover how many hours Bosserman had expended in the IRS investigation. As Issa and Jordan said, her involvement was "highly inappropriate" and "compromised the Administration's investigation." The mere fact that Judicial Watch had to file a lawsuit to find out if the lead DOJ investigator was actually spending any time investigating the scandal tells us all we need to know about how much Eric Holder had compromised and politicized the Justice Department. So did the extreme lengths to which DOJ went to avoid having to produce this information, claiming no fewer than four separate exemptions to the FOIA law. The IRS, despite winning in the lower court, settled with Judicial Watch after our lawyers filed their papers with the federal appeals court. This was a nice victory. The IRS, through the Department of Justice, gave us the total number of hours Bosserman worked on the IRS scandal criminal investigation. According to DOJ, "Ms. Bosserman's investigative efforts totaled 1,529.25 hours." Given the massive amount of time, one has to wonder if the Obama donor was the only DOJ prosecutor working on the case.

The IRS Cover-up

The emails Judicial Watch uncovered also proved one other point—the IRS cover-up started long before it became public knowledge. For example, we obtained a November 3, 2011, email in which an IRS manager warned about litigation over the targeting and admitted that she had sent a letter requesting additional information from one conservative group who had been complaining about the long delay in obtaining its tax-exempt status in order "to buy time" so the group would not contact their congressional office. There were hundreds of backlogged application cases open, many of them pending for years.

In February 2012, Rep. Jim Jordan (R-OH) requested information about a Tea Party organization that had been waiting for eighteen months to hear from the IRS. Lois Lerner conducted the briefing of Rep. Jordan, very pointedly omitting to tell him about the backlogs, the Tea Party targeting, or the concerns that had been expressed by the organizations and their lawyers over the inappropriateness of the information being sought by the IRS.

The IRS clearly did not want anyone finding out what it was doing—and it is highly likely that neither Lerner nor anyone else at the IRS would have admitted what was going on if the Treasury Department IG had not released his report in May 2013. Another piece of evidence that demonstrates this point is that it wasn't until August 2015, almost two years after Judicial Watch filed its FOIA lawsuit, that the Justice Department and the IRS suddenly admitted that Lois Lerner had conducted government business on her personal email account, including one using the name "Toby Miles," which was apparently a reference to her dog (Toby is the dog's name and Miles is the surname of Lerner's husband, Michael Miles).[4]

In fact, the documents provided to Judicial Watch in its lengthy, hard, tough court fight with the Justice Department and the IRS showed that despite their public denials, Lois Lerner and other top officials at the IRS closely monitored and approved of the mishandling of tax-exempt applications by Tea Party and other conservative groups. This might not have been discovered except for the work done by Judicial Watch. At a House subcommittee hearing in July 2014, Rep. Jim Jordan (R-OH) said to IRS Commissioner John Koskinen: "My theory is this, Mr. Koskinen, you guys weren't ever gonna tell us until we caught you. And we caught you because Judicial Watch did a FOIA request."

The Political Bias at the IRS

Lerner's motivation was revealed in her official emails. In a November 9, 2012, email to a colleague, she referred to conservatives as "assholes," suggesting that conservatives were ruining the country: "So we don't need to worry about alien teRrorists [*sic*]. It's our own crazies that will take us down." As House Ways and Means Committee Chairman Dave Camp (R-MI) said in a letter to Attorney General Eric Holder, it showed "that Ms. Lerner's mistreatment of conservative groups was driven by her personal hostility toward conservatives."

Refusing to Prosecute Lois Lerner

As you would expect, Lois Lerner asserted her Fifth Amendment right against self-incrimination and twice refused to answer questions from a congressional committee investigating the IRS mistreatment of conservatives. In a rare move, the House of Representatives held her in contempt on May 7, 2014. US Attorney for the District of Columbia Ronald Machen, however, declined to present her contempt citation to a federal grand jury, as he was required to do by federal law, because he claimed Lerner had not waived that right when she appeared before the committees.

But as former Justice Department lawyer Hans von Spakovsky noted, Machen's claim was wrong. He failed entirely to consider what we now know—that Lerner submitted to a secret, twelve-hour interview with DOJ without any immunity or promise of nonprosecution. Applicable case law in the District of Columbia says that once a witness like Lerner gives a voluntary statement to the government, she waives her right to assert the Fifth Amendment. She had no right to refuse to answer questions from Congress and therefore was subject to prosecution under federal law for contempt. It is clear that Machen's refusal to enforce the contempt citation was legally unjustified; the administration obviously did not want her to testify about what she did, and what she knew about the involvement of other administration officials in what happened.

In a further but certainly not surprising betrayal of the public trust, the Justice Department announced in October 2015 that it was closing its investigation of the IRS, claiming that there was not sufficient evidence to "seek any criminal charges" against Lois Lerner or any other IRS officials. DOJ admitted that it had found "substantial evidence of mismanagement, poor judgment, and institutional inertia" and that the IRS had "mishandled the processing of tax-exempt applications in a manner that disproportionately impacted applicants affiliated with the Tea Party and similar groups, leaving the appearance the IRS's conduct was motivated by political, discriminatory, corrupt, or other inappropriate motive." However, DOJ claimed that "ineffective" or "poor management is not a crime." The letter made no mention of clear violations of the law such as Lerner's transfer of over a million pages of confidential taxpayer information to the FBI and the Justice Department, a *per se* violation of federal law.

Using the IRS to Win an Election

President Obama's IRS was used against his opponents to help him win reelection. So the Obama Justice Department's decision to shut down its IRS abuse investigation with no prosecutions is as unsurprising as it is corrupt. Judicial Watch's independent litigation proved the Obama IRS obstructed justice and destroyed evidence. And we uncovered that the IRS and Lois Lerner conspired with the Justice Department and FBI on a plan to jail the very Americans the IRS was illegally suppressing. In fact, at almost the same time Justice Department lawyers admitted in federal court that the IRS watchdog was still digging through IRS backup tapes, the same Justice Department decided it could shut down its criminal investigation. In other words, it decided there was no criminal case before it had all the evidence. That might pass muster in Chicago, but America deserves better—the IRS is not above the law.

Despite the refusal of the Obama Justice Department to prosecute anyone at the IRS, it is clear that what happened was an epic clampdown on any conservative voices speaking or advocating against the president's disastrous policies and in favor of patriotism and adherence to the Constitution and the rule of law. Over the course of twenty-seven months leading up to the 2012 election, not a single Tea Party–type organization received tax-exempt status. Many were unable to operate; others disbanded because donors refused to fund them without the IRS seal of approval; some organizations and their donors were audited without justification;

and many incurred legal fees and costs fighting the unlawful conduct by Lerner and other IRS employees.

The IRS suppressed the entire Tea Party movement just in
time to help Obama win reelection. And everyone in the administration involved in this outrageous conduct got away with it
without being punished or prosecuted. Was it simply a case of
retribution against the perceived "enemies" of the administration?
No, this was much bigger than political payback. It was a systematic and concerted effort to squash the Tea Party movement—one
of the most organic and powerful political movements in recent
memory—during an election season. [See Appendix for select IRS
documents uncovered by Judicial Watch.]

This was about campaign politics. It was a scandal for the
ages. President Obama obviously wanted this done even if he
gave no direct orders for it. In 2015, he told Jon Stewart on *The
Daily Show* that "you don't want all this money pouring through
non-profits." But there is no law preventing money from "pouring
through non-profits" that they use to achieve their legal purposes
and the objectives of their members. Who didn't want this money
pouring through nonprofits? Barack Obama.

In the subsequent FOIA litigation filed by Judicial Watch, the
IRS obstructed and lied to a federal judge and Judicial Watch in
an effort to hide the truth about what Lois Lerner and other senior
officials had done. The IRS, including its top political appointees
like IRS Commissioner John Koskinen and General Counsel William J. Wilkins, have much to answer for over their contempt of
court and of Congress. And the Department of Justice lawyers and
officials enabling this cover-up in court need to be held accountable as well.

If the Tea Party and other conservative groups had been fully active in the critical months leading up to the 2012 election, would Mitt Romney have been elected president? We will, of course, never know for certain. But we do know that President Obama's Internal Revenue Service targeted right-leaning organizations applying for tax-exempt status and prevented them from entering the fray during that period.

That is how you steal an election in plain sight. Accountability is not something we will get from the Obama administration. But Judicial Watch will continue its independent investigation and certainly any new presidential administration should take a fresh look at this IRS scandal.

7

IMMIGRATION AND BORDER ENFORCEMENT

The Obama administration has shown again and again that it has little interest in enforcing this country's immigration laws and providing real border security. Judicial Watch has found evidence that, in essence, the administration gave the Department of Homeland Security and the Border Patrol a Benghazi-style "stand down" order when it comes to enforcement, and has done everything it can to provide administrative amnesty, as well as government benefits, to millions of illegal aliens.

How bad is the threat along our border? You know that the border security situation has reached a "Code Red" when a decorated and battle-tested Marine general, who led troops in the Iraq combat zone for years, says the situation on the border has become an "existential threat" to the United States—and he asks for help. In January 2016, four-star Marine Corps General John Kelly retired after forty years of experience from Vietnam to Iraq to our southern border, to our nation's great loss.

But in 2014, when he was the commander of the US Southern Command, he said that his task force was flat-out unable to respond to 75 percent of the illicit activity occurring on the border: "I simply sit and watch it go by," said General Kelly, who once led Marines who reduced terrorist activity in Baghdad by 80 percent over a six month period. What's happening on the border today is a "crime-terror convergence," according to Kelly, a gaping hole in our security that creates opportunities for drug cartels and terrorists and leaves US citizens vulnerable. Kelly said that military budget cuts were "severely degrading" the military's ability to defend southern approaches to the US border and his requests for more money, ships, and resources went unanswered by Congress and the administration.[1]

As Kelly warned, "In comparison to other global threats, the near collapse of societies in the hemisphere with the associated drug and [illegal immigrant] flow are frequently viewed to be of low importance. Many argue these threats are not existential and do not challenge our national security. I disagree."[2]

Refusing to Deport Illegal Aliens

As an example of the work Judicial Watch has done on this issue, starting in 2010, Judicial Watch filed FOIA requests with Department of Homeland Security (DHS) seeking records on the administration's policy of suspending the deportation of some illegal aliens. After DHS failed to respond, Judicial Watch was once again forced to file a lawsuit. The agency claimed it did not have to turn over the documents because it was exempt from FOIA and the documents were protected by attorney-client privilege. In 2013, a federal judge ruled in favor of Judicial Watch, chastising the agency for withholding documents, and he specifically ruled against DHS's improper claim of attorney-client privilege.

The documents uncovered by Judicial Watch showed that DHS officials misled Congress and the public about its implementation of a new policy that resulted in the dismissal of multiple deportation cases against illegal alien criminals convicted of violent crimes. The administration decided to halt almost all enforcement actions (on an alleged "case-by-case" basis) against any illegal alien who has not committed any other "serious" crimes. As a result, it is failing to protect citizens from the scourge of rampant illegal immigration and criminal illegal aliens.

In 2014, Judicial Watch filed another FOIA lawsuit to get more information about this issue, after the Center for Immigration Studies (CIS) reported that 36,000 criminal aliens who were awaiting the outcome of deportation proceedings were released by DHS in 2013.[3] This group consisted of aliens convicted of hundreds of serious, often violent crimes, including homicide, sexual assault, kidnapping, and aggravated assault. The 36,000 criminal aliens had nearly 88,000 convictions, including one for willfully killing a public official with a gun. Yet this alien, and tens of thousands of other dangerous thugs, were released by DHS onto an unsuspecting American public.

Former House Judiciary Committee Chairman Lamar Smith (R-TX) called it the "worst prison break in American history" and said the administration's "actions are outrageous." They "willfully and knowingly put the interests of criminal immigrants before the safety and security of the American people." He criticized the administration for trying to persuade the American people that these aliens were guilty of minor, petty offenses. But "the convictions tell a chilling story" of dangerous criminals being released.[4]

• • •

In documents that Judicial Watch finally obtained in 2015 through its lawsuit, we discovered that the 36,000 criminal aliens that CIS discovered were only the tip of the iceberg. As of April 2014, DHS had actually released 165,900 convicted criminal aliens throughout the United States, including murderers, kidnappers, and aliens convicted of aggravated and sexual assault.

Through a second FOIA lawsuit filed in January 2015 on behalf of a former Border Patrol agent, Edward "Bud" Tuffly II, Judicial Watch also discovered that the administration released thousands of illegal aliens in 2013 in anticipation of "sequestration" budget cuts. Hundreds had criminal records. Although the administration claimed that they were only guilty of petty offenses, it turned out that many of the criminals released were guilty of much more serious offenses such as kidnapping, sexual assault, drug trafficking, and homicide.[5]

Sen. John McCain (R-AZ) found it "deeply troubling that [US Immigration and Customs Enforcement] ICE would knowingly release thousands of undocumented immigrant detainees—many with prior criminal records—into our streets, while publicly downplaying the danger they posed." A report by the DHS Inspector General found that many of the aliens with criminal convictions were released despite the fact that their "detention was statutorily required."[6] As former Border Patrol agent Bud Tuffly said, "our government has broken trust with the American people by recklessly releasing criminals onto the streets" and is not providing the "details about the illegal alien jailbreak that could save lives, including those in law enforcement on the border."

Judicial Watch's investigation of this unjustified (and

dangerous) release showed that 260 illegal criminal aliens were released in Arizona alone, including forty who had been incarcerated for violent crimes. What made this even worse was that the administration refused to divulge the names of the released criminals, preventing law enforcement from protecting the public or notifying victims. Local authorities in Arizona such as Pinal County Sheriff Paul Babeu tried unsuccessfully to obtain information about this and other alien releases. The refusal to identify the dangerous criminals released showed that the administration was obsessed with supporting nationwide sanctuary and unlawful amnesty for illegal aliens, even those who have committed violent crimes. This soft-on-crime approach endangered the safety of innocent Americans.

This victimization of Americans is multiplied by the sanctuary policies that have been adopted by cities all over the country. Their refusal to cooperate with DHS even when DHS is actually trying to detain an illegal alien, particularly a criminal alien, provides a sanctuary for criminals that victimizes Americans. A tragic example of that is Judicial Watch's client, Brian McCann, a lifelong Chicago resident. Judicial Watch represented McCann in an ultimately unsuccessful lawsuit against Cook County Sheriff Tom Dart for his refusal to honor Immigration and Customs Enforcement (ICE) immigration detainers or to cooperate with ICE in trying to identify deportable criminal aliens. McCann's brother, William "Denny" McCann, was run over and killed in June 2011 by a criminal alien who had just completed a two-year term of probation for a DUI conviction. The illegal alien was charged with felony aggravated driving under the influence for McCann's death, but Sheriff Dart released him from the Cook County jail despite an ICE immigration detainer. In just the eighteen months prior to the filing of this lawsuit in 2013, Cook County had released over one thousand criminal aliens sought by ICE.

Judicial Watch has been investigating and fighting the sanctuary policies of places like Los Angeles, Houston, and San Francisco for years. Sanctuary policies severely limit or prohibit cooperation between local law enforcement and federal immigration authorities, so that local law enforcement is forbidden from notifying ICE when they arrest an illegal alien, or from holding an illegal alien until ICE can pick him up.

These policies have led directly to the death of innocent Americans like Kate Steinle, who was callously shot and killed on July 1, 2015, as she was walking with her father in downtown San Francisco. The murderer was Juan Francisco Lopez-Sanchez, an illegal alien who had been deported five times and convicted of seven felonies. He was released by federal officials to San Francisco County Sheriff Ross Mirkarimi after serving time in federal prison because San Francisco had an outstanding arrest warrant for selling narcotics. But San Francisco *dismissed* the charges and, in accordance with the city's sanctuary policy, *ignored* the detainer request that ICE officials had filed on Lopez-Sanchez to be held in custody until ICE could pick him up and start deportation proceedings.

Sheriff Mirkarimi released this dangerous criminal back into the city's streets to prey on its people. And that is exactly what Lopez-Sanchez did. In a jailhouse interview, Lopez-Sanchez admitted that he came to San Francisco *specifically* because "he knew San Francisco was a sanctuary city where he would not be pursued by immigration officials."[7]

The sanctuary policy of Los Angeles has been particularly dangerous since the city is the de facto headquarters of the notoriously violent Mara Salvatrucha (M-13) and 18th Street gangs, comprised primarily of illegal aliens from Central America. On March 2, 2008, seventeen-year-old Jamiel Shaw was shot to death by an 18th Street gang member, an illegal alien, who had been released from the L.A. County Jail only one day earlier because of the city's sanctuary policy. He had been held on a gun charge. As Shaw's father, Jamiel Shaw Sr., told the House Oversight and Government Reform Committee in February 2015 in devastating testimony that was critical of both sanctuary policies and Obama's amnesty programs:

> *My son, Jamiel Andre Shaw II, was murdered by a DREAMer, a DACA recipient, a child brought to this country by no fault of his own. My family's peace and freedom was stolen by an illegal alien from Mexico. He was brought here by his illegal alien parents and allowed to grow up as a wild animal. Some people believe that if you are brought over by no fault of your own that it makes you a good person. They want you to believe that DREAM Act kids don't murder. I am here to debunk that myth.*[8]

The Center for Immigration Studies (CIS) estimates that there are 340 jurisdictions with sanctuary policies, located in forty-three states and the District of Columbia. CIS found that in just one eight-month period in 2014, more than 8,100 deportable aliens were released by sanctuary jurisdictions. Three thousand were felons and 62 percent had prior criminal records. Nineteen hundred were later rearrested a total of 4,300 times on 7,500 offenses including assaults, burglaries, sexual assaults, thefts, and even murders—*none of which would have occurred except for these sanctuary policies!*

Such sanctuary policies are illegal under federal immigration law, which specifies that "no State or local government entity may be prohibited, or in any way restricted, from sending to or receiving from the Immigration and Naturalization Service information regarding the immigration status, lawful or unlawful, of any alien in the United States."[9] But in accordance with its nonenforcement policy on immigration, the Obama administration announced in 2010 that it would not sue sanctuary cities for violating federal law.

As Kate Steinle's father, Jim Steinle, told the Senate Judiciary Committee on July 21, 2015:

Everywhere Kate went throughout the world, she shined the light of a good citizen of the United States of America. Unfortunately, due to disjointed laws and basic incompetence at many levels, the U.S. has suffered a self-inflicted wound in the murder of our daughter by the hand of a person who should have never been on the streets of this country.[10]

Kate Steinle's murderer had been deported five times, and kept reentering the country with no consequences. So on July 9, 2015, Rep. Matt Salmon (R-AZ) introduced H.R. 3011—Kate's Law—to impose a five-year mandatory prison sentence on anyone arrested in the United States after having been previously deported. A companion bill was introduced in the Senate by Sen. Ted Cruz (R-TX). But the Obama administration made it clear it would not support such a bill if it passed Congress.

What has made this even worse is the fact that the Obama administration has systematically dismantled the use of detainers by ICE and enabled the ability of sanctuary cities to ignore them. Detainers—requests by the federal government for local authorities to detain an illegal alien until ICE can take custody of the alien—have been used by the federal government since at least 1950. This was codified in federal regulations, which direct local law enforcement "to maintain custody of the alien" for at least forty-eight hours "to permit assumption of custody by the Department."

But in 2010, ICE Director John Morton issued an internal policy directive telling ICE that it could not issue detainers for illegal aliens who had been only "temporarily detained" by local law enforcement, such as a roadside traffic stop. In other words, ICE couldn't issue a detainer unless the alien had been arrested for another, nonimmigration-related crime. In 2011, ICE further weakened law enforcement by revising its detainer policy again, including requiring that illegal aliens be given a hotline to call if they believed their "civil rights" had been violated or they had been the victim of a crime. This set them up to claim a right to a special immigrant visa for illegals who are the supposed victim of criminal activity, providing de facto amnesty to as many illegal aliens as possible who only have to "claim" a problem.

Following this pattern, in 2012 the detainer procedure was changed again, placing additional limitations on which illegal aliens immigration agents could file detainers for. The new procedure imposed highly restrictive conditions such as requiring a prior felony conviction or pending charge, or at least three misdemeanor convictions, among others.

The final administrative assault came in 2014 when Acting ICE Director Dan Ragsdale sent a letter to Congress asserting that complying with federal detainers was "not mandatory as a matter of law" for a local jurisdiction. This was a complete about-face by the Obama administration—it was taking the completely opposite legal position that prior administrations, Republican and Democratic, had uniformly taken for more than sixty years and that was codified into Immigration and Naturalization Service (INS) regulations. Mandatory detainer notification to hold illegal alien criminals was eliminated in favor of voluntary requests.

To make it even more difficult to find or detain illegal aliens, the Obama administration at the same time ended the very successful Secure Communities Program. In effect since 2008, this program facilitated data sharing between local and federal law enforcement agencies that enabled immigration agents to identify, detain, and remove illegal aliens. The Obama administration obviously did not like the success of the Secure Communities Program—data compiled by the Center for Immigration Studies found that a total of 406,411 illegal aliens had been removed over the life of the program.[11] And that had included literally tens of thousands of criminal aliens convicted of aggravated felony offenses, including murder, rape, and the sexual abuse of children.

Coupled with localities refusing to cooperate with ICE, even when it wanted to detain illegal aliens, the Obama administration wanted to stop attempts by states that wanted to help the federal government's enforcement of immigration laws. It filed a lawsuit against Arizona over its precedent-setting law on illegal aliens, SB 1070. This law, among other provisions, allowed Arizona's state and local law enforcement officers to check on the immigration status of individuals they arrested or stopped for questioning whom they suspected were in the United States illegally. In fact, this cooperation is authorized under an existing federal law that mandates that the federal government provide immigration status information to local officials.

When that case reached the US Supreme Court, Judicial Watch filed an amicus brief on behalf of state Senator Russell Pearce,[12] the author and driving force behind the Arizona law. The brief was also joined by twenty-nine legislators from twenty states. While the court in the end struck down some parts of the law, it upheld the main provision directing local officials to verify the immigration status of individuals they suspect are in the United States illegally, an important component of enforcing federal immigration requirements.

This was a victory for the safety and security of Arizona and the nation, and a sensible application of the law giving local law enforcement an additional tool to protect public safety. As Sen. Pearce said in testimony before the Senate Judiciary Subcommittee on Immigration, Refugees, and Border Security on April 24, 2012:

> *The illegal alien problem is a critical issue, not only in Arizona, but across the country. The adverse effects of illegal immigration ripple throughout society . . . The invasion of illegal aliens we face today—convicted felons, drug cartels, gang member, human traffickers, and even terrorists—pose one of the greatest threats to our nation in terms of political, economic, and national security.*

It was clear that the Obama administration's attacks on states like Arizona for trying to help the federal government enforce our immigration law undermined the nation's constitutional order. The administration failed to abide by its mandate to secure the border and as a result, states are left to fend for themselves against a flood of illegal aliens. As Sen. Pearce said, "instead of enforcing the law, the Obama administration does the opposite, by encouraging further lawbreaking."

The Narco-Terror Border Threat

Judicial Watch helped uncover a sophisticated narco-terror ring run by two of the FBI's "most wanted" (Jaber A. Elbaneh and Adnan Gulshair el Shukrijumah) and connections spanning from El Paso to Chicago to New York City. Among the ringleaders is an Islamic State of Iraq and Syria (ISIS) operative arrested in Chicago a few years ago and released months later to serve probation in Illinois for a state crime that secretly drew federal intervention. His name is Emad Karakrah, and the FBI facilitated his release from Cook County Jail. Judicial Watch uncovered Karakrah's terrorism record, which includes a 2009 plot to bomb talk-show host Oprah Winfrey's Chicago studios and the iconic Sears Tower. Among Karakrah's accomplices in the truck bomb plot was Shukrijumah—al-Qaeda's Director of North American Operations, who flew in and out of the United States from Mexico as "Javier Robles." Shukrijumah was eventually killed in a Pakistani Army raid in the northwestern territory of Pakistan.

Karakrah is a logistics and transportation operative for militant Islamists in the United States, according to sources close to the investigation. He moves people, weapons, explosives, drugs, money, and other materiel to terrorist cells operating in Chicago, Brooklyn, NY, and Saddle Brook, NJ—among other locations across the United States. More than a decade ago Karakrah smuggled drugs and weapons for the Juárez drug cartel in Mexico. Before moving to Chicago sometime in 2011, Karakrah lived in Anthony, NM, and a suburb of El Paso, TX. His ex-wife and two children remain in the El Paso area. In 1999, Karakrah pleaded guilty to felony "Criminal Sexual Penetration of a Child, Ages 13–16" as well as a related conspiracy charge, according to public records. Law enforcement sources characterized Karakrah as a "dangerous, crazy thug."

Karakrah's El Paso business associate, Hector Pedroza Huerta, is a forty-six-year-old illegal alien who has been deported twice and arrested three times for drunken driving. In 2015, an El Paso judge, Frank Montalvo, sentenced Huerta to fifteen months after his third DUI with no deportation or supervised release.

Judicial Watch's reporting also uncovered that ISIS is operating a camp just a few miles from El Paso, Texas, and that "coyotes" engaged in human smuggling—and working for the Juárez Cartel—help move ISIS terrorists through the desert and across the border between Santa Teresa and Sunland Park, New Mexico. Sources including a Mexican Army field grade officer and a Mexican Federal Police Inspector reveal that the exact location where the terrorist group has established its base is approximately eight miles from the U.S. border in an area known as "Anapra," situated just west of Ciudad Juárez in the Mexican state of Chihuahua. Another ISIS cell to the west of Ciudad Juárez, in Puerto Palomas, targets the New Mexico towns of Columbus and Deming for easy access to the United States, the same knowledgeable sources confirm.

During the course of a joint operation, Mexican Army and federal law enforcement officials discovered documents in Arabic and Urdu, as well as "plans" of Fort Bliss—the sprawling military installation that houses the US Army's 1st Armored Division. Muslim prayer rugs were recovered with the documents during the operation. Law enforcement and intelligence sources report that the area around Anapra is dominated by the Vicente Carrillo Fuentes Cartel ("Juárez Cartel"), La Línea (the enforcement arm of the cartel), and the Barrio Azteca (a gang originally formed in the jails of El Paso). Cartel control of the Anapra area make it an extremely dangerous and hostile operating environment for Mexican Army and Federal Police operations. The same sources told Judicial Watch that Mexican human and drug smugglers help move ISIS terrorists through the desert into the United States.

Last summer Judicial Watch uncovered a ring involving the smuggling of foreigners from countries with terrorist links into a small rural Texas town near El Paso. The Special Interest Aliens (SIA) were being transported to stash areas in Acala, a rural crossroads located around fifty-four miles from El Paso on a state road—Highway 20. Once in the United States, the SIAs wait for pickup in the area's sand hills just across Highway 20. Terrorists have entered the United States through Mexico for years, and in fact, an internal Texas Department of Public Safety report leaked by the media months ago documents that several members of known Islamist terrorist organizations have been apprehended crossing the southern border in recent years.

Now they're also being smuggled in through border region airfields, according to JW's civilian, law enforcement, and intelligence sources. The notorious Juárez Cartel is using the Horizon Airport (formerly "West Texas Airport") in El Paso's lower valley to smuggle SIAs into the United States from Mexico, say JW's inside sources. The facility is convenient because it's located only eleven miles from El Paso's central business district, yet it's small enough that security is virtually nonexistent.

The crisis at the Mexican border—and the government's lies about the worsening Islamist terror threat—could result in a terrorist attack calamity for the United States. We see debate about building a wall with Mexico, but our reporting suggests the debate ought to focus on more immediate security measures such as the deployment of our military to secure the border. We'll keep on the alert for you. In the meantime, you might want to take action and ask your elected officials why they're AWOL on border security in the face of this potentially catastrophic threat from Islamic terrorists.

The Radicals inside the Government

None of the administration's border security and extreme immigration policies should be a surprise. The administration is filled with radical political appointees like Cecilia Muñoz, who joined the administration as the Director of Intergovernmental Affairs and then moved up to be the director of the White House Domestic Policy Council. Muñoz, who was only able to join the administration after she was granted an ethics waiver from Barack Obama's supposed lobbyist ban, was a senior official at the National Council of La Raza. La Raza openly advocates for illegal alien sanctuary policies and has been linked to the Mexican *Reconquista* movement, which seeks to conquer the American Southwest and return it to Mexico. According to a Judicial Watch investigation, federal funding for La Raza nearly tripled from $4.1 million to $11 million in FY 2010, the year Muñoz joined the Obama administration. This seems to be the story of a left-wing interest group benefiting from White House connections at the expense of taxpayers, an all-too-typical story in Washington.

Another such radical is Thomas Perez, Obama's labor secretary and former assistant attorney general for Civil Rights at the Justice Department. He was the president of the board of CASA de Maryland, an illegal alien advocacy group financially supported by the late Venezuelan dictator Hugo Chávez. Sen. Jeff Sessions

(R-AL) called CASA de Maryland a "fringe advocacy group that has instructed illegal aliens on how to escape detection, and also promoted illegal labor sites and driver's licenses for illegal immigrants."[13] When Hilda Solis, the labor secretary prior to Perez, visited CASA de Maryland on May 20, 2012, Judicial Watch served a FOIA request on the Department of Labor seeking all records pertaining to that visit, as well as information on all federal funding given to the organization. Judicial Watch was forced to sue when DOJ refused to comply with the FOIA request. It was another example of outrageous stonewalling by an administration that wanted to cover up its partnership with a radical organization that openly encourages illegal immigrants to operate outside the law.

Giving Illegals Virtual Amnesty

From almost the first moment President Obama began implementation of administrative amnesty for illegal aliens, Judicial Watch was involved in bringing to light the inside machinations that led to those policies. We filed a FOIA lawsuit in August 2012 over the Deferred Action for Childhood Arrivals (DACA) program the administration implemented on June 15, 2012.

DHS and the Justice Department refused to provide any of the legal research or memoranda that provided a legal opinion authorizing the president to pursue this program. It was no surprise that the administration didn't want to share the legal basis for its unilateral executive action, since Obama and his political appointees were abusing their offices with this new amnesty program and violating federal immigration law and the Constitution. If the administration had been confident about the legality of its actions, it wouldn't have fought our FOIA requests and/or try to keep secret the legal basis for President Obama's extraordinary decision to unilaterally change the law.

Judicial Watch's investigation into the DACA program revealed that DHS abandoned the background check required by federal immigration law, adopting instead a costly "lean and lite" procedure in an effort to keep up with the flood of applications spurred by the DACA program. Acting on a tip from a whistleblower, Judicial Watch obtained documents showing a haphazard process with only cursory review of the backgrounds of aliens. A field director told his staffers he didn't know "when things will revert back to the way they used to be." One email chain showed managerial pressure not to turn any illegal alien applicant away for lack of ID, including an explicit directive in an October 3, 2012, memo that said "processing should not be refused solely because an applicant does not present an acceptable ID."

Chris Crane, president of the National Immigration and Customs Enforcement Council and a veteran ICE agent himself, said that "Officers have been told that there is no burden for the alien to prove anything." Crane added that "At this point we don't even know why DHS has criteria at all, as there is no requirement or burden to prove anything on the part of the alien" as long as they claim to be "dreamers," aliens who came to the United States as children.

The documents also showed that the administration lied, once again, to the American people. Former DHS Secretary Janet Napolitano said that the DACA program applied only to minors who came to this country illegally "through no fault of their own."

However, an internal directive actually created a new avenue of chain migration, whereby immediate relatives of DACA requesters could be approved for amnesty. As a result, according to a June 18, 2012, agency memo from District 15 Director, David Douglas, "some of the districts closer to the U.S./Mexico border have been inundated."

The administration's amnesty program led directly to a huge upswing in unaccompanied minors coming across the border because of its policy of uniting the minors with their illegal parents present in the United States, and then refusing to take any action against the parents. A federal judge in Texas issued a searing indictment of the administration policy in *U.S. v. Nava-Martinez*, accusing the government of "completing the criminal mission" of human traffickers "who are violating the border security of the United States" and assisting a "criminal conspiracy in achieving its illegal goals."

The judge called the administration's behavior "dangerous and unconscionable" and he was especially angry over the fact that in this case, the mother of the child had instigated the illegal crossing by paying a trafficker. Yet DHS delivered the child, who had been caught at the border, to the mother and "did not arrest her. It did not prosecute her. It did not even initiate deportation proceedings for her."

Judicial Watch helped uncover the extent of DHS's malfeasance, filing a FOIA lawsuit against DHS to obtain information about the agency's "escort service" for unaccompanied illegal alien minors that delivers them to their parents who are illegally in the United States. In 2014, that meant that DHS requested bids from contractors to provide escort services for 65,000 minors, with DHS paying for transportation costs, including by charter and commercial air, as well as meals, clothing, and numerous other supplies. DHS agents blamed the "lack of deterrence" for the huge increase in border crossings, since minors and their parents were aware of the lack of consequences if they were apprehended. They knew the minor would be reunited with their U.S.-based family member.

How much was this costing taxpayers? In September 2014, Judicial Watch obtained documents from DHS revealing that the Obama administration paid Baptist Children and Family Services $182,129,786 to provide "residential services" to just 2,400 "unaccompanied alien children" for only four months at Fort Sill, Oklahoma, and Lackland Air Force Base in San Antonio, Texas. According to the documents obtained by Judicial Watch, the cost to the American taxpayer was $86,846.34 per illegal alien child at Fort Sill. The bill included more than $2.6 million in compensation for thirty members of the Baptist Children and Family Services management staff. Among the items listed in the budget as being provided were catered meals, cable television with video screen/projector setup, numerous recreational items, cell phones with international calling services, and laptops.

It was outrageous that the administration was spending nearly $200 million of taxpayer funds to provide illegal alien children with extravagant high-tech equipment and benefits many American families cannot even afford for their own children—instead of immediately returning these alien minors to the countries they came from. The hordes of illegal immigrant minors entering the United States are bringing serious diseases—including swine flu, dengue fever, Ebola virus, and tuberculosis—that present a danger to the American public as well as the Border Patrol agents forced to care for the kids. Barack Obama's response was to ask Congress for $3.7 billion in supplemental funding to address the humanitarian issues, with only 5 percent of that allocated to boots on the ground—a sure sign that he was not interested in stopping this surge across the border.

The length to which the Obama administration went to cater to illegal aliens, including those actually detained by DHS, was demonstrated by another Judicial Watch FOIA lawsuit. We discovered that the US Immigration and Customs Enforcement (ICE) arm of DHS had issued detention standards in 2011 to provide detainees with "advice and consultation about family planning and birth control, and where medically appropriate, prescribe and dispense birth control." ICE would also "assume the costs associated with a female detainee's decision to terminate a pregnancy" in case of rape or incest. Additionally, ICE would pay for "hormone therapy" for transgender detainees, as well as "transgender related health care and medication." It would come as quite a surprise to most Americans to know that illegal alien detainees can receive birth control, sex change procedures, and abortions courtesy of the US taxpayer.

When President Obama expanded the DACA program with the Deferred Action for Parents of Americans and Lawful Permanent Residents (DAPA), Judicial Watch called on Congress to investigate whether the administration was using unappropriated funds for these programs in violation of the federal Antideficiency Act. Unfortunately, Congress failed to take action and even continued to fund the president's unilateral actions.

That left it up to twenty-six states, led by Texas, to file suit in federal court in Texas in December 2014 over President Obama's plan to "unilaterally suspend the immigration laws as applied to 4 million of the 11 million" illegal aliens in the United States, according to the complaint. This lawsuit wasn't even so much about immigration but the rule of law. As the states pointed out, Obama had unilaterally rewritten immigration law. Obama himself said, "What you're not paying attention to is, I just took an action to change the law." The lawsuit had a damning list of other admissions by Obama that the court considered when it issued a preliminary injunction stopping the implementation of the DAPA program.

Judicial Watch became involved in this suit at the district court level, filing an amicus brief against the government when the Obama administration asked the judge for an emergency stay, or suspension, of his preliminary injunction while the government appealed the decision. As we told the court, if the stay was granted, it would give the administration the ability to "cast aside immigration laws passed by Congress and signed by the President. These laws have been in place for almost 30 years . . . [the Obama administration] fail[s] to demonstrate why destroying 30 years of status quo and undermining enacted law is necessary."

Fortunately, the district court refused to stay its injunction. The Justice Department lawyers were basically asking the court to allow President Obama to govern as a king who can rewrite, ignore, and create new law based on personal whim or political needs. The only "emergency" was the threat to public safety caused by President Obama's unconstitutional refusal to obey and enforce the nation's laws against illegal immigration.

When the government appealed this decision to the Fifth Circuit Court of Appeals, Judicial Watch filed another amicus brief urging the court to uphold the injunction. The Obama administration argued with no sense of shame that the injunction against its mass amnesty program "interferes with [its] ability to protect the Homeland and secure our borders." But as Judicial Watch told the court, the amnesty had nothing to do with finding criminal aliens for removal or preventing them from remaining in the country.

Our FOIA investigations had uncovered that DHS was failing to conduct the required, comprehensive background checks on aliens who applied for the DACA program in order to accelerate the processing of the applications. Allowing the new DAPA program to go into effect was not likely to assist DHS to distinguish between criminal and noncriminal aliens. Fortunately, the Fifth Circuit Court of Appeals refused to lift the injunction and confirmed that the district court had acted correctly in granting it. This was a win for the American people.

Encouraging Illegal Immigration

Another example of the administration's giving away of taxpayer dollars to illegal aliens was uncovered by Judicial Watch in April 2013 through a FOIA investigation of the US Department of Agriculture (USDA). Judicial Watch obtained documents showing that the Agriculture Department was working directly with the Mexican government to encourage illegal aliens to apply for the US food stamp program, which is paid for by US taxpayers. The Department of Agriculture sent the Mexican Embassy a Spanish-language flyer advising Mexicans in the United States that they would not need to declare their immigration status in order to get food stamps through the Supplemental Nutrition Assistance Program (SNAP). It contained a statement in boldface and underlined that "**You need not divulge information regarding your immigration status in seeking this benefit for your children**."

The USDA even sought the approval of the Mexican Embassy in drafting a letter addressed to Mexican consulates throughout the country to encourage their staffers to enroll in a webinar to learn how to promote increased enrollment among the Mexicans that the consulates serve. The USDA took a whole series of other actions intended to maximize participation by illegal Mexican aliens, even telling the Mexican Embassy that the Obama State Department and ICE had reached an agreement that the food voucher program would not violate federal immigration law that prohibits immigrants from becoming a "public charge," a denial of basic reality.

These documents obtained by Judicial Watch showed that the USDA was actively working with a foreign government to coordinate evading US immigration laws and to force American taxpayers to subsidize welfare-type payments to illegal aliens. The administration had no interest in restricting aid to, identifying, or apprehending illegal aliens who may be on the food stamp rolls.

While the Mexican government and its embassy and consulates in the United States have been working with the Obama administration to provide US taxpayer benefits to illegal Mexican immigrants, the Mexican government itself has shown that it has little regard for the sovereignty of the United States. For over a decade, Judicial Watch has forced both the Bush and Obama administrations to release documents detailing intentional border incursion by Mexican military and other government personnel. Those documents revealed that there have been three hundred documented incursions since 2004.

That includes a June 26, 2014, attack by a Mexican government helicopter on US Border Patrol agents. It crossed into US airspace and fired two rounds that landed about fifteen yards from the side of an unmarked Border Patrol vehicle that was parked next to two marked Border Patrol vehicles. As Judicial Watch said at the time, this was another sign of how insecure our border is, with the Mexican military and law enforcement personnel of a corrupt Mexican government intentionally and without consequence crossing our border and placing US law enforcement and other innocent Americans at risk.

The Obama administration issued directives to its agents that are shocking in the face of an unsecure border, and tens of thousands of narcotics-related murders attributed to sophisticated and heavily armed Mexican drug cartels competing with each other for trafficking routes into the United States. The Border Patrol union reveals on its website that agents are forced to take lengthy computer courses known as the Virtual Learning Center where they are taught in an Active Shooter course that they are to "run away" and "hide " if they encounter a shooter in a public place. Only if cornered by a shooter, as a last resort, should agents become "aggressive" and "throw things" at the attacker. This is downright insulting considering the US Border Patrol is a law enforcement agency with officers that carry weapons for a reason—one of which is to prevent narcoterrorists and other dangerous criminals from crossing our border.

It All Comes Down to Politics

For those Americans wondering about motives for the misbehavior of the Obama administration, apparently the main reason for the Obama administration's push to legalize millions of illegal aliens may be purely political. In November 2015, Judicial Watch filed a FOIA lawsuit seeking records related to letters sent by DHS to nine million current green card holders (permanent resident aliens) urging them to become naturalized US citizens *before* the 2016 election. We learned that the Citizenship and Immigration Services of DHS was reallocating vast resources away from its "Electronic Immigration System," a computerized system designed to facilitate national security and criminal background checks, to fund the letter campaign.

Naturalizing citizens before the election was part of the White House's strategic plan released by the White House Task Force on New Americans. What made this even more worrisome was that DHS had already abandoned its normal criminal and security background investigation in favor of its "lean and lite" procedures created to keep up with the flood of amnesty applications spurred by the DACA program. This seemed like another plan to use tax money to rush through citizenship for millions of legal and illegal aliens just in time for the 2016 elections, and elections beyond. The bottom line seems to be an effort to import voters and grant unilateral amnesty to help win future elections at the expense and security of American citizens by creating a new, permanent majority that favors one political party.

The callousness of the Obama administration on all of these issues was demonstrated on July 14, 2015, when Department of Homeland Security Secretary Jeh Johnson testified before the House Judiciary Committee. Under questioning by Rep. Steve Chabot (R-OH) about the murder of Kate Steinle by an illegal alien, Johnson made it clear he had no knowledge of the case:

> REP. CHABOT: *Has the administration reached out to the Steinle Family, to your knowledge?*

SEC. JOHNSON: To who?

REP. CHABOT: To the family of the woman who was brutally murdered by this individual who had committed seven different felonies in four different states and to my understanding had been deported, kept coming back, has the administration reached out to that family?

SEC. JOHNSON: I'm sorry, I don't know the answer to that question, sir.

Perhaps no exchange speaks more cogently to the Obama administration's icy indifference to the damages, injuries, deaths, and fallout from its illegal alien policies and its mishandling of immigration over the entire eight years of Barack Obama's presidency.

TERRORISM AND THE RECKLESS ACTIONS OF THE OBAMA ADMINISTRATION

Only a coalition of Marxists and Islamists can destroy the United States.
—ILICH RAMÍREZ SÁNCHEZ, AKA "CARLOS THE
JACKAL," *REVOLUTIONARY ISLAM*, 2003

The future must not belong to those who slander the prophet of Islam.
—PRESIDENT BARACK OBAMA, 67TH SESSION,
UN GENERAL ASSEMBLY, SEPTEMBER 25, 2012

Our job is to change the Constitution of America.
—SAYYID SYEED, PHD, ISLAMIC SOCIETY OF
NORTH AMERICA, 43RD ANNUAL CONFERENCE,
ROSEMONT, IL, LABOR DAY, 2006

The American people deserve complete, accurate, and factual information concerning the threats of subversion and terror posed to our country—particularly by Islamic jihad—and whether the Obama administration has acted forcefully to stop those threats. Unfortunately, Judicial Watch's investigations into Islamist influence and terrorist operations and the actions of federal law enforcement and intelligence agencies have shown that the administration has endangered national security and the safety of Americans because of political correctness and a refusal to recognize the true nature of the threat.

Kneecapping Our Counter-Terrorism Agents

A prime example is a controversial meeting held on February 8, 2012, between FBI Director Robert Mueller and various Islamic organizations including the Council on American Islamic Relations (CAIR) and the Islamic Society of North America (ISNA). Both CAIR and ISNA were named by the government as unindicted coconspirators in the Holy Land Foundation for Relief and Development (HLF) terrorist financing lawsuit in 2007 along with the North American Islamic Trust (NAIT). The FBI and the Justice Department refused to respond to our FOIA request for all records generated by that meeting including any concerning "setting criteria or guidelines for FBI curricula on Islam or records identifying potentially offensive materials within the FBI curricula on Islam." We also sought all communications between the administration and Muslim organizations like the Muslim Brotherhood (MB), ISNA, and CAIR over this issue. We were forced to file a lawsuit in July 2012 because of the administration's failure to provide the records as federal law requires.

The motto of the MB, which was founded in Egypt in 1928, expresses the common ideology of all the jihadist terrorist organizations that are targeting America: "Allah is our objective; the Quran is our law; the Prophet is our leader; Jihad is our way; and dying in the way of Allah is the highest of our aspirations." The English language website of the MB states that it is an "Islamist organization founded for launching Jihad against the infidels in general and Christian West in particular."

In June 2013, as a result of its lawsuit, Judicial Watch obtained hundreds of pages of FBI records revealing that in 2012 the FBI purged its antiterrorism training materials of anything that might be "offensive" to Muslims based on the determinations of a group of unidentified "Subject Matter Experts." The excised material included references linking the Muslim Brotherhood to terrorism; tying al-Qaeda to the 1993 World Trade Center and Khobar Towers bombings; and suggesting that "young male immigrants of Middle Eastern appearance . . . may fit the terrorist profile best."

In the documents obtained by Judicial Watch, the FBI claimed that these types of statements were "highly inflammatory" or "inaccurate." The FBI also removed "references to mosques specifically as a radicalization incubator" despite the overwhelming evidence that this is correct, and even criticized one author because he "seems to conflate 'Islamic Militancy' with 'terrorism,'" as if there is a dime's worth of difference between the two. Ironically, in 2011, FBI Director Mueller had himself described the Muslim Brotherhood as a group that supports terrorism in the United States and overseas; yet in 2012, he ordered their exoneration in order not to offend radical Muslim groups.

We also discovered an FBI policy document, "Guiding Principles: Touchstone Document on Training," which contained an extraordinary statement: "Mere association with organizations that demonstrate both legitimate (advocacy) and illicit (violent extremism) objectives should not automatically result in a determination that the associated individual is acting in furtherance of the organization's illicit objective(s)." Perhaps not "automatically" but it should definitely result in a preliminary inquiry and some fundamental investigative work. Yet the FBI was in essence handicapping its agents to meet the propaganda requirements of Islamic organizations directly or indirectly connected to jihadists who are targeting America.

The FBI should not "outsource" its counter-terrorism training to the terrorists or their agents of influence who have sworn to destroy our country. The Muslim Public Affairs Council (MPAC) has lobbied successfully for years to remove references to Islam, Sharia law, and jihad from the national security dialogue and terminology of law enforcement, intelligence, and defense agencies—even though terrorists from al-Qaeda to Hamas use those terms and Quranic doctrine and quotes to justify their operations and attacks. In 2005, MPAC founder Salam al-Marayati made a public statement at an ISNA conference in Dallas that "counter-terrorism and counter-violence should be defined by us . . . [And] number one, we reject any effort, notion, or suggestion that Muslims should start spying on one another." In other words, he made it clear that he did not want Muslim Americans providing any information on terrorist activities by other Muslims to American law enforcement.

Yet during the notorious February 8, 2012, meeting, FBI Director Mueller reportedly assured the Islamic groups in attendance that the agency had ordered the removal of all presentations and curricula on Islam from FBI offices around the country that were deemed "offensive," including the mention of groups in the meeting who had been tied to terror organizations like Hamas and the Muslim Brotherhood in a federal court decision.

The Obama administration ordered the Department of Defense to engage in the same type of purge of anything offensive about Muslim radicals as the FBI. On April 24, 2012, Joint Chiefs

Chairman Gen. Martin E. Dempsey ordered the entire US military to "review" its education and training classes, files, and rosters of instructors to ensure there was no material "disrespectful of the Islamic religion."

The end result of all this has been to remove from US government law enforcement and intelligence records and training materials terms and phrases rooted in basic Islamic history as well as the language and publications of the terrorists themselves. Why? Whose interests are served by not using accurate language to describe the actions of persons attacking the United States? How does one identify, study, and plan for a defense to a militant Islamist terror threat if one is not permitted to examine (or discuss) the doctrine, organization, history, ideology, and conduct of the opposition? It appears that the US government has elected to deny reality.

Some members of Congress were complicit in encouraging this systematic purge, such as Sen. Dick Durbin (D-IL), and Rep. Jan Schakowsky (D-IL).[1] But then-Rep. Allen West (R-FL), a former Army officer and Iraq combat veteran, objected to allowing radical Muslim organizations the opportunity to dictate US counter-terrorism policy and wanted the material to be reinserted into the documents: "Now you have an environment of political correctness which precludes these [FBI] agents from doing their proper job and due diligence to go after the perceived threat."[2] This started in the Bush administration, but as journalist and author Diana West says:

> *The Obama administration would carry this same see-no-Islam policy to its zealous limits, finally mounting a two-front assault on the few trainers and fact-based training materials that were*

sometimes (sparingly) used by law enforcement agencies and the military to educate personnel about Islam and jihad. What history should remember as the Great Jihad Purges of 2012 began at the Justice Department, affecting domestic law enforcement agencies, and spread to the Pentagon, affecting the entire U.S. military.[3]

"Offending" Islamic Terrorists—and Conservatives

The administration wasn't just afraid of offending Islamic militants in the United States; it was also afraid of offending Islamic terrorists abroad. Judicial Watch engaged in a long, contentious FOIA fight with the administration over access to the details regarding the burial of terrorist mastermind Osama bin Laden after the special operations raid that found and killed him. The administration argued that the information should be kept secret because it might offend terrorists abroad.

According to a sworn statement from a DOD official, bin Laden was given full Islamic burial honors but they were afraid that details of the burial would inflame "al-Qa'ida members or sympathizers, encouraging propaganda by various terrorist group or other entities hostile to the United States, and potentially leading to retaliatory attacks." The administration's logic was absurd—did they really think that bin Laden's burial, as opposed to his killing by a special operations team, is what would lead to "retaliatory attacks"? These jihadists want to destroy America—they don't need an excuse to do it.

The Defense Department went even further than just purging all references to Islamic jihad—it also promulgated educational materials "for training purposes" that depicted conservative organizations as "hate groups." The documents obtained by Judicial Watch through a FOIA request repeatedly cited the left-wing Southern Poverty Law Center as a resource for identifying "hate groups"—an organization that has falsely and maliciously labelled as "hate groups" mainstream conservative organizations like the Family Research Council, the American Family Association, and Concerned Women for America.

These DOD "educational materials" said that US history had many examples of "extremist ideologies and movements" such as the "colonists who sought to free themselves from British rule." In the same section, the 9/11 attack was listed under a category of "Historical events." It advised that "many extremists will talk of individual liberties, states' rights, and how to make the world a better place." It warned that "active participation . . . with regard to extremist organizations is incompatible with military service." Other than a mention of 9/11 and the Sudan, *there was no discussion of Islamic extremism!* This was a stunning example of the Obama administration's nasty habit of equating conservative, constitutionally based values with terrorism. The Defense Department was saying that conservative Americans and anyone who holds the same values as the Founding Fathers would not be welcome in today's military.

Aiding the Fight against Terrorism

Judicial Watch's work on national security matters relating to terrorism began in August 2001 when FBI Special Agent Robert G. Wright contacted us. In a tragic foreshadowing of the massive terrorist attack that occurred on September 11, 2001, Agent Wright needed help dealing with FBI efforts to silence him about Islamist money laundering and financial support to terrorist organizations.

Only nine days after 9/11, we filed a "Complaint Concerning Certain Tax Exempt and Other Organizations Reportedly Used As Money Laundering Front Operations for Terrorist Activities in The United States and Abroad" with the IRS. Our report listed the activities of twenty terrorist front organizations, including the Holy Land Foundation for Relief and Development, which was convicted in 2008 of supporting and funding terrorism.

In another case, we obtained more than five thousand pages of records, many of which were previously classified. These concerned Anwar al-Awlaki,[4] an American citizen and militant imam of the Dar al-Hijrah mosque in Falls Church, Virginia. He was eventually killed by a Hellfire missile strike in Yemen fired from a Predator drone on September 30, 2011, which was authorized by President Obama.

Al-Awlaki presented himself publicly as the face of moderate Islam in America. He gave a number of media interviews and appeared on the National Geographic Channel, National Public Radio, and in the *New York Times*. In 2002, he even had lunch in the dining room of the secretary of defense and made a presentation to Pentagon brass, as part of the military's outreach to the Muslim community. Yet he was described as the "spiritual leader" and inspiration of the 9/11 hijackers; the Fort Hood murderer, US Army Major Nidal Hasan; the 2009 Christmas Day (attempted) airline bomber, Umar Farouk Abdulmutallab of Nigeria; and others.[5]

In fact, Judicial Watch obtained documents showing that the FBI had trailed al-Awlaki to his presentation at the Pentagon because of his suspected ties to terrorists (the FBI was also aware that he was a regular patron of prostitutes in Washington). According to records and surveillance logs obtained through our FOIA lawsuit against the FBI, the bureau actually issue a bulletin at 10:40 a.m. *the day before the Pentagon luncheon* (February 2, 2002) that declared al-Awlaki to be a terrorist. The warning reads: "Warning—approach with caution. . . . Do not alert the individual to the FBI's interest and contact your local FBI field office at the earliest opportunity."

Yet his telephone number had been found by German police in the Hamburg apartment of 9/11 hijacker Ramzi bin al-Shibh. He had been investigated by the FBI in 1999 and 2000 for his contacts with operatives associated with Omar Abdel-Rahman (the "Blind Sheikh" and mastermind of the 1993 World Trade Center bombings) and the terror group Hamas.[6] Documents suggest that the FBI was aware as far back as September 27, 2001, that al-Awlaki may have purchased airplane tickets for three of the 9/11 terrorist hijackers, including mastermind Mohamed Atta, and had numerous other contacts with them. Within six days of 9/11, he suggested on an Islamist website that Israeli agents might have been responsible for the attacks.

There is even evidence that al-Awlaki may have been used as an intelligence asset by the FBI *despite* his obviously radical Islamist beliefs and aid to terrorists. Within days of the Pentagon luncheon, al-Awlaki left the United States. Eight months later, he returned under mysterious circumstances. He was stopped and detained by Customs officers at John F. Kennedy International Airport because of an outstanding warrant for his arrest, until FBI Special Agent Wade Ammerman ordered al-Awlaki's *release!*

The records obtained by Judicial Watch show that then–FBI Director Robert Mueller may have been deeply involved in the post-9/11 handling of al-Awlaki. One memo from Mueller to then–Attorney General John Ashcroft on October 3, 2002—seven days before al-Awlaki reentered the United States and was temporarily detained at JFK—is marked "Secret." The substance of the memo is redacted in full, but the memo is one of at least three FBI reports, whose primary subject is al-Awlaki, in the nine days leading up to his return to the United States in October 2002. Another FBI memo marked "Secret" on October 22, 2002, twelve days after the terrorist cleric's return, includes the subject line "Anwar Nasser Aulaqi" and "Synopsis: Asset reporting."

Other records Judicial Watch uncovered show that on October 1, 2002—before al-Awlaki returned to the United States—a memo marked "Secret" and "Priority" was faxed from the FBI's Washington Field Office to FBI headquarters. On October 3, the FBI director's memo was sent to Ashcroft. On October 10, the day al-Awlaki entered the United States, there was a heavily redacted fax from the FBI resident office at John F. Kennedy International Airport that included copies of his plane ticket, customs form, passport, and Social Security card.

Al-Awlaki seems to be the perfect example of an active measures operative, someone who uses covert and deceptive tactics to carry out his objectives. By means of deception, he conducted himself publicly as a supposedly "moderate" Muslim cleric, while engaged in clandestine operations supporting the 9/11 hijackers. He lectured Pentagon officials on their need to be "sensitive" to the Muslim community, despite the FBI's knowing that he was a terrorist! Based on the records obtained by Judicial Watch, he may have even been used as an intelligence asset or agent by the US government. But it seems that al-Awlaki was actually successfully manipulating the US government to achieve his own radical goals.

When he fled the country at the end of 2002, after the FBI refused to enforce the arrest warrant against him, he dropped the charade and openly advocated for jihadist attacks against his country of birth. Yet records obtained by Judicial Watch still showed him emailing and leaving voice messages with an FBI agent in 2003. In one October 2, 2003, email, an FBI agent whose name is redacted writes to a colleague regarding a voice mail: "Holy crap, [redacted] isn't this your guy? The aman (imam) with the prostitutes?" Three weeks later, after he left another voice mail message, al-Awlaki sent an email to an FBI agent complaining about a news account alleging his connection to the 9/11 terrorists: "I'm amazed at how absurd the media could be and I hope that the US authorities know better and realize that what was mentioned about me was nothing but lies." Another email showed an FBI agent's annoyance at the attempts of the 9/11 investigating commission trying to locate al-Awlaki to interview him.

Al-Awlaki radicalized, inspired, and directed terror attacks as the chief of external operations for al-Qaeda in the Arabian Peninsula until his death. Al-Awlaki pioneered the digital jihad, now being capitalized on by the Islamic State of Iraq and Syria (ISIS). If he had been kept in custody instead of let go at the insistence of the FBI, there might have been much slower development of the Internet as a terrorist weapon and recruitment device that we are all now facing.

Al-Awlaki's passport was not even revoked until approximately six months before his death by drone strike on September 30, 2011. There seems little doubt, however, that President Obama authorized the assassination of a terrorist who, for a long period of time, was an asset of the US government.

Ignoring the al-Qaeda Threat

In May 2002, we sought information regarding al-Qaeda as part of Judicial Watch's Terrorism Research and Analysis Project. It took the government eleven years to furnish the records we requested. One of the surprising discoveries we made was that at the end of the Clinton administration, the United States disregarded an intelligence report about an al-Qaeda plot to hijack a commercial airliner departing Frankfurt Airport between March and August 2000 because, according to the intelligence documents, "nobody believed that Usama bin Laden's organization or the Taliban could carry out such an operation."

This belief came despite an intelligence report remarkably rich in operational details, including the names, addresses, telephone numbers, assignments, and duties of the terrorist operatives (an Arab, a Pakistani, and a Chechen). Al-Qaeda had actually penetrated the consular section of the German Embassy in Islamabad, Pakistan, to obtain European Union (EU) visas for use in the forged Pakistani passports for the terrorists. The only reason the hijack plot was not carried out was because the Chechen terrorist withdrew from the operation after the EU condemned Russian actions in Chechnya.

Leaking to Hollywood

It is interesting to contrast the Obama administration's constant resistance to transparency and refusal to grant FOIA requests from Judicial Watch for national security information like the death photographs of Osama bin Laden to its cooperation in providing sensitive and classified information and access to Hollywood. It seems that helping its public image or winning an election is more important.

Judicial Watch launched an investigation in 2011 following press reports that the Obama administration may have leaked classified information to Kathryn Bigelow and Mark Boal, the director and screenwriter of *Zero Dark Thirty*, a movie about the successful May 2, 2011, mission by Navy SEAL Team Six to find and kill Osama bin Laden. Maureen Dowd of the *New York Times* wrote that the information leak was designed to help the Obama 2012 presidential reelection campaign:

> *The White House is also counting on the Kathryn Bigelow and Mark Boal big-screen version of the killing of Bin Laden to counter Obama's growing reputation as ineffectual. The Sony film by the Oscar-winning pair who made 'The Hurt Locker' will no doubt reflect the president's cool, gutsy decision against shaky odds. Just as Obamaland was hoping, the movie is scheduled to open on Oct. 12, 2012—perfectly timed to give a home-stretch boost to a campaign that has grown tougher.*[7]

Judicial Watch was once again forced to file a lawsuit after the administration failed to respond to our FOIA request for all information and communications between government agencies and Bigelow, Boal, and their Hollywood cohorts. As Dowd also ironically pointed out, these "moviemakers are getting top-level access to the most classified mission in history from an administration that has tried to throw more people in jail for leaking classified information than the Bush administration."

We eventually obtained almost three hundred pages of records from DOJ and the CIA. These documents indicated that in violation of protocols designed to zealously protect the identities of special forces teams like SEAL Team Six, the Obama administration provided Bigelow with the identity of a "planner, SEAL Team 6 Operator and Commander," although his name was blacked out in what Judicial Watch received. CIA Director Leon Panetta himself revealed classified information at a June 24, 2011, bin Laden assault awards ceremony at the CIA attended by Boal. Boal and Bigelow were also given access to other personnel, such as the translator who was on the raid.

What was even more shocking was that in sworn declarations, DOD and CIA officials admitted that publicly releasing the names of the military and CIA officers involved in the bin Laden raid could be dangerous and provide an "unnecessary security and counterintelligence risk." Yet they conceded that this information had been given to Bigelow and Boal. The administration claimed that they had asked them not to share the information, yet the filmmakers were not required to sign a nondisclosure agreement nor did they undergo any background checks or receive security clearances before being given the information.

Bigelow and Boal not only had meetings at the Defense Department where they were briefed on this highly secret operation, they also went to the White House twice to meet with John Brennan, the chief counter-terrorism adviser to Obama, and Denis McDonough, his deputy national security adviser. They were even granted access to "the Vault" at the CIA, the building where some of the tactical planning for the bin Laden raid took place, and Boal was given an internal, formerly classified CIA memo called a "deep dive" into the operation. At least one email from June 2011 suggested that the request from Bigelow and Boal to meet with defense officials came via the White House press office and another email said that the administration wanted to have "high visibility" into any bin Laden–related projects.

The DOD inspector general eventually sent a criminal referral to the Justice Department for Michael Vickers, the undersecretary of defense for intelligence, for providing the filmmakers with the name of the special operations command officer who helped plan the raid.[8] It should not surprise anyone that the highly politicized Obama Justice Department refused to do anything about it.

These documents about *Zero Dark Thirty* took nine months and a federal lawsuit to disgorge. They show politically connected filmmakers being given extraordinary and secret access to bin Laden raid information. It is both ironic and hypocritical that the Obama administration stonewalled Judicial Watch's pursuit of the bin Laden death photos and burial details, citing national security concerns, yet seemed willing to share intimate details regarding the raid to help Hollywood filmmakers release a movie timed to give a homestretch boost to the Obama campaign. They must have been very disappointed when the movie's release was delayed until December 2012.

A final note: because of the aggressive efforts of Judicial Watch to obtain images of the bin Laden raid, Admiral William McRaven, the commander of US Special Operations, eventually issued an order to purge *all* of DOD's systems of any records about the Navy SEAL raid on Osama bin Laden's compound, and transfer them to the CIA, where they could be shielded from FOIA requests. Of course, that didn't stop the administration from giving Hollywood access to classified details about the raid.

Opening the Border to Terrorists

As if all of these security lapses weren't enough, Judicial Watch also discovered that the Obama administration's lax security on our southern border with Mexico has given not just Islamic terrorists, but also narcoterrorists, a porous border they can cross to enter the United States. A State Department report recently exposed a "dramatic increase in violence" along the Mexican border and warned of "violent attacks and persistent security concerns" in the area. It lists tens of thousands of narcotics-related murders attributed to sophisticated and heavily armed drug cartels competing with each other for trafficking routes into the United States.

In Texas, the situation is so bad that state officials created a website to track Mexican drug-cartel violence that has transformed chunks of the southern border into a war zone. The Texas Department of Agriculture started the website to keep farmers and residents informed about the growing danger created by Mexican drug cartels illegally crossing into the state. It is occurring at an "increasingly alarming rate" according to Texas Agriculture Commissioners Todd Staples, and Washington is ignoring the crisis.

A Judicial Watch source inside the Department of Homeland Security told us that some of the most dangerous gangs involved in the drug trade and other criminal violence are actively recruiting new soldiers inside DHS detention facilities, including in particular illegal immigrant minors in US shelters. The source told Judicial Watch that Mara Salvatrucha (MS-13) and the 18th Street gangs are on a recruiting frenzy, and they're using cell phones supplied to these minors by the Red Cross.

MS-13 is a feared street gang of mostly Central American illegal immigrants that has spread throughout the United States and is infamous for drug distribution, murder, rape, robbery, home invasions, kidnappings, vandalism, and other violent crimes. The 18th Street gang is considered the largest organized gang in Los Angeles County with about 15,000 members. As the president of the Tucson Border Patrol Union, Art Del Cueto, told Judicial Watch, many of the unaccompanied minors coming across the border are in their late teens and have possible ties to gang members.

But it is not just dangerous criminal gangs that are pouring across a virtually undefended border. In 2014, high level federal law enforcement, intelligence, and other sources confirmed to Judicial Watch that a warning bulletin was issued to Homeland Security and the Justice and Defense Departments about Islamic terrorist groups, including ISIS, operating in the Mexican border city of Ciudad Juárez, an infamously crime-infested narcotics hotbed situated across from El Paso, Texas. Fears of a terrorist attack on the border were so high that the commanding general at Fort Bliss, the US Army Post in El Paso, was briefed on the problem, leading to increased security measures. For too long, "experts" have discounted the level of cooperation between Mexican drug cartels and Islamist militants. Meanwhile, terrorists, weapons, drugs, and money cross back and forth over the border virtually undetected.

This included an al-Qaeda terrorist on the FBI's most wanted list who for years crossed back and forth into the United States from Mexico to meet fellow militant Islamists in Texas and piloted an aircraft into the Cielo Dorado airfield in Anthony, New Mexico, according to law enforcement sources. Adnan G. el Shukrijumah (Javier Robles) was eventually killed in Pakistan in December 2014. But in 2010 he was indicted in a federal court in New York for his role in a terrorist plot to attack targets in the

United States—including New York City's subway system—and in the United Kingdom, according to the FBI.

In the first two months of fiscal year 2016 alone, at least three ports of entry—Boquillas and El Paso, Texas, and Yuma, Arizona—saw a mind-boggling 500 percent increase in illegal immigrants according to US Border Patrol records. El Paso and Yuma are notoriously busy crossings, but Boquillas is in the remote Big Bend National Park vicinity of Texas and has been open for only a few years. Other entry ports that saw larges hikes in Central American illegal immigrants during the two months include Del Rio, Texas (269 percent), El Centro, California (216 percent), and Rio Grande Valley, Texas (154 percent). During this period the Border Patrol reported 35,234 apprehensions in the regions of foreigners labeled by the government as "Other Than Mexican" or OTM. This is a term used by federal authorities to refer to nationals of countries that represent a terrorist threat to the United States.

This is just more evidence of how susceptible the long, porous Mexican border is. In the fall of 2014, Homeland Security sources told Judicial Watch that four ISIS terrorists, who had infiltrated the United States through Mexico, were arrested in McAllen and Pharr, Texas. Over the summer of 2015, Judicial Watch uncovered evidence that Mexican drug cartels were smuggling foreigners from countries with terrorist links into a rural Texas town near El Paso.

In December 2015, Judicial Watch reported that five young Middle Eastern men were apprehended by the Border Patrol in an Arizona town (Amado) just thirty miles from the Mexican border, carrying stainless steel cylinders in their backpacks. This came just days after six men—one from Afghanistan, five from Pakistan—were arrested in nearby Patagonia, a quaint ranch town that sits twenty miles north of the Mexican border city of Nogales. At almost the same time, a Middle Eastern woman was caught surveilling a US port of entry in Nogales, Arizona, with a sketchbook with Arabic writing and drawings of the facility and its security system.

The FBI has nearly one thousand active probes involving ISIS inside the United States. Mexican sources, including a Mexican Army field grade officer and a Federal Police Inspector, confirmed to Judicial Watch that ISIS has established a base just south of the US border in an area known as Anapra situated just west of Ciudad Juárez that targets the New Mexico towns of Columbus and Deming for easy access into the United States, with another ISIS cell to the west of Ciudad Juárez in Puerto Palomas. This area is an extremely dangerous and hostile operating environment for Mexican law enforcement because it is controlled by the Juárez Cartel and the Barrio Azteca gang. These same sources told Judicial Watch that coyotes engaged in human smuggling working for the Juárez Cartel are helping move ISIS terrorists through the desert and into New Mexico.

These problems are not just at the southern border. In 2015 Judicial Watch filed a FOIA lawsuit against the Department of Homeland Security to obtain information about a "hands off list" used by the Obama administration to allow individuals to enter the United States who had been barred because of terrorist ties.

One email cited by Sen. Chuck Grassley (R-IA) from an Immigration and Customs Enforcement official to an official at Customs and Border Protection indicated his puzzlement that "someone could be a member of the Muslim Brotherhood and unindicted coconspirator in the Holy Land Foundation trial, be an associate of [redacted], say that the US is staging car bombings in

Iraq and that [it] is ok for men to beat their wives, question who was behind the 9/11 attacks, and be afforded the luxury of a visitor visa and de-watchlisted."

The Obama administration's immigration policies are so lax that they have allowed too many terrorists with documented ties to ISIS and other radical Islamic groups into the United States, including individuals from Yemen, Saudi Arabia, Somalia, and Uzbekistan who have been criminally charged in recent years.

Examples include a "refugee" from Uzbekistan (Fazliddin Kurbanov) convicted of conspiring and attempting to provide material support to a designated foreign terrorist organization and procuring bomb-making materials; an Iraqi immigrant (Omar Faraj Saeed Al Hardan) charged with attempting to provide material support to ISIS; an Iraqi refuge (Aws Mohammed Younis Al-Jayab) suspected of travelling to Syria to fight with the Al-Nusra Front and charged with lying to federal agents conducting a terrorism investigation; and San Bernardino attacker Tashfeen Malik, a Pakistani.

For decades, Judicial Watch has been actively at work informing the American people about the threat that Islamic terrorists pose to our national security and bringing to light information that the federal government—and particularly the Obama administration—is unwilling to share with the American people. Unfortunately, the administration's reaction to this threat has been to refuse to secure the border, to handicap the efforts of federal law enforcement and counter-intelligence agents, while denying, or attempting to discredit, reports on its lax security efforts. Rather than allowing terrorism to triumph by causing us to live in fear, all of us must be vigilant in defense of the nation—and the federal government in particular bears that heavy burden.

CONCLUSION

JUDICIAL WATCH'S MISSION

Since 1994, Judicial Watch has been on the front lines fighting against political corruption in the nation's capital. Founded as a watchdog group during the ethical excesses of the Clinton administration, we have since developed a reputation as a non-partisan crusader for good government, relentlessly dogging the George W. Bush administration during its eight years in office. No matter who succeeds Barack Obama, we will stand watch in the fight against officials who abuse the powers entrusted to them by the American people. Our motto is "Because no one is above the law!"

When it comes to the Obama administration, we have observed how it has operated by implementing the "Chicago Way," an approach to government Obama learned in his days serving the Daley Machine in Chicago. It's a "my way or the highway" style that combines unaccountability and illegal secrecy with brazen favoritism toward allies and the punishment of political enemies.

Despite the idealism with which he promised he would govern, President Obama has proven quite comfortable operating in the morally bankrupt idiom of the urban politico. We have detailed shady dealings with cronies, clear and present dangers to our national security, cozy relationships with union bosses, ethically questionable appointments, abuse of power in the use of executive orders, double talk on ethics reform, politicization of government agencies such as the Internal Revenue Service, and, of course, the widespread practice of "crony capitalism," which rewards friends of the president and the Democratic Party.

These accounts suggest that we might have entered something of a new Gilded Age. As the country limps through a weak economic recovery, politicians take advantage of weak ethics laws to line their own pockets, strong-arm their opponents, and reward their supporters.

With the "Chicago way" dominating the political process for the past seven years, let us hope that in the next administration we won't see the out-of-control and lawless ways of the Obama administration.

Why Oversight Isn't Enough

One thing is for certain. Relying on Congress alone to police its own ethics or expose wrongdoing and incompetence in the executive branch is unrealistic and shortsighted.

Sen. Ben Sasse (R-NE), a historian and former university president who was elected in 2014, bemoans the failure of Congress to engage in legislative oversight.

"We have massive overreach in large part because we have had legislative under reach for so long, as Congress has surrendered the power of the purse to unelected bureaucrats," he says. "Real oversight of the executive branch would exercise some kind of counterbalance but the imbalance is so great it will take massive efforts to get there." Sasse tells the story of Congress's investigation of Lois Lerner, the Obama IRS official accused of targeting conservative nonprofits for political punishment: "There was a subcommittee with jurisdiction over the IRS that wanted to hire one temporary high-quality lawyer to get some answers. It was an impossible tangle to get that done, while at the same time the IRS commissioner had up to two hundred lawyers in his office to play defense and frustrate the search for answers."

Sasse says that in the current environment, private groups such as Judicial Watch fill a needed role. "The Freedom of Information Act and other transparency tools are some of the few ways we can get to the bottom of a lot of bad or unaccountable behavior," he says. "Watchdog groups can serve the role of citizen sentinels making sure there are some checks on the power of the central government, even when Congress fails to exercise proper oversight."

Judicial Watch fills the yawning gap between what official investigations can accomplish given bureaucratic and other barriers and the need for honest accountable government that is operated with integrity and within the rule of law. We promote high standards of ethics and morality in our nation's public life. We stand watch to ensure that our elected officials and judicial officials don't abuse their public offices.

In my previous book, *The Corruption Chronicles*, I detailed how Judicial Watch fulfills its mission through litigation, investigations, and public outreach. We don't take no for an answer, and we will sue whomever and whatever necessary to enforce the rule of law.

That means we sometimes stand out alone on the battlements—but we don't mind, since that's what we're here to do. But we never sue just for the sake of suing. We often sue to gain access to information that can educate the American people about the operations of our government. And we sometimes even sue politicians directly to hold them accountable. All of our lawsuits, whether they are against the government or to protect innocents, are designed to uphold the rule of law.

Our chief methods of pursuing our mission are via open records and Freedom of Information Act laws. Litigation and the civil discovery process not only uncover information for the education of the American people on anticorruption issues, but can also put a stop to corruption by public officials and government agencies. In other words, we're doing the work that the government will not do itself. We provide the information and the impetus to enforcement of law designed to promote honest and open government.

That need has never been greater.

During the Watergate era of Richard Nixon, delaying tactics by government officials were dubbed "stonewalling."

"Transparency and the rule of law will be the touchstones of this administration," President Obama declared back in 2009. Rarely has there been a greater gap between what a politician said and what he did. Indeed, in the mold of Richard Nixon, the White House asserted dubious claims of executive privilege to avoid scrutiny in the Fast and Furious scandal.

But Obama is publicly oblivious to the contradictions. At a media awards dinner in March 2016, President Obama scolded the press for enabling a candidate like Donald Trump and suggested it had a greater responsibility than to hand someone a microphone.

But as far as Jake Tapper on CNN was concerned "the messenger was a curious one." He succinctly reviewed the Obama administration's deplorable record on transparency and openness and concluded:

"Maybe, just maybe, your lecturing would be better delivered to your own administration."

Speaking with some passion, Tapper told his viewers: "Many believe that Obama's call for us to probe and dig deeper and find out more has been made far more difficult by his administration than any in recent decades. A far cry from the assurances he offered when he first took office." Tapper noted that Obama promised to run the "most transparent administration in history."

"Obama hasn't delivered," ProPublica reporter Justin Elliott wrote in the *Washington Post* in March 2016. "In fact, FOIA has been a disaster under his watch." Elliott went on to write:

> *Newly uncovered documents (made public only through a FOIA lawsuit) show the Obama administration aggressively lobbying against reforms proposed in Congress. The Associated Press found last year that the administration had set a record for censoring or denying access to information requested under FOIA, and that the backlog of unanswered requests across the government had risen by 55 percent, to more than 200,000. A recent analysis found the Obama administration set a record of failing nearly 130,000 times to respond to public records requests under the Freedom of Information Act.*[1]

Tapper closed his broadcast by quoting former *Washington Post* executive editor Leonard Downie, who helped break the Watergate scandal and said in 2013 that Obama had the "most aggressive" administration toward the press since Richard Nixon.

Watching the Courts

And, yes, Judicial Watch "watches" the judiciary. We take on the important job of ensuring high ethical standards in the judiciary itself. Unfortunately, our judiciary is plagued by many of the same problems as the rest of our federal government—it requires constant oversight, just like everything else government does. By monitoring judges and using the judicial ethics process to hold judges to account, we can make sure that the third branch of government does its important job untainted by corruption or even the appearance of corruption. In fact, Judicial Watch took up the work of posting the financial disclosure forms of all federal judges on the Internet, because the judges running the administrative arm of the federal judiciary simply refuse to do so.

Our investigative, legal, and judicial activities provide the basis for our educational outreach, which includes speeches, op-eds, publications, educational conferences, media outreach, radio and news television appearances, and direct radio outreach through informational commercials and public service announcements. Judicial Watch is a long-standing member of the media. Our investigative reports educate the public about abuses and misconduct by political and judicial officials, and advocate for the need for an ethical, law-abiding, and moral civic culture. Our website, www.judicialwatch.org, is specifically designed to make our open records documents, legal filings, and other educational materials accessible to the public and the media. We consider ourselves the "wiki" of government corruption. We know that the media drives the American public debate, and we have no intention of allowing that debate to be defined by the apologists for corrupt politicians and corrupted government in the media establishment.

We also provide legal services to other conservatives (and train "regular" citizen-activists) so they can use the Freedom of Information Act (FOIA) and other open records laws to obtain information and accountability on various issues. FOIA and the Privacy Act deserve more detailed explanation. FOIA especially is a tool that Judicial Watch uses regularly, and one that you, too, can use to help carry through the vision of the Founders and protect your government from corrupt insiders.

Think of Judicial Watch as your anticorruption watchdog in Washington, D.C., and in any state where we can leverage our investigatory and legal expertise to hold corrupt politicians and governments accountable to the rule of law.

We are America's largest and most effective government watchdog group, and we are both proudly conservative and proudly nonpartisan—which means that neither Democratic nor Republican corruption escapes our scrutiny.

The Most Valuable Lesson

The most valuable lesson Judicial Watch has learned is a simple one: watch what politicians do, not what they say. There can be no better illustration of this than Obama's summit meeting with African leaders in 2014. He used the meeting as an opportunity to tout the positive role inspectors general can play in fighting corruption in government agencies; at the same time that he was speechifying about this, some two-thirds of President Obama's own inspectors general wrote a scathing letter to Congress complaining that his administration was placing "serious limitations" on their ability to do their jobs.

Vice President Joe Biden told the African leaders that there is "a need to have in every government agency what we in the United States call, and it could be different in every country; we call it an inspector general." He went on to describe how the office of the IG was created by Congress as a reaction to the Watergate era, during which delaying tactics that came to be known as "stonewalling," so angered the Congress that it passed, in 1978, the original Inspector General Act.

Biden described an IG as "someone who is able to roam through every department, like here in the United States, the Defense Department, the IRS, the Treasury Department writ large, the Department of Interior, to be able to look at the books, to be able to look at everything that's transpired with independent eyes—people who cannot be fired." He concluded that "widespread corruption is an affront to the dignity of people and a direct threat to each of your nations' stability."[2]

Stirring words, but equally stirring were the words of the forty-seven out of seventy-three independent inspectors general who wrote to Congress just the day after Biden's speech to emphasize the importance of "the principle that an Inspector General must have complete, unfiltered, and timely access to all information and materials available to the agency that relate to that Inspector General's oversight activities, without unreasonable administrative burdens."[3] Referring to current IG investigations, they issued a stark warning:

> *Without timely and unfettered access to all necessary information, Inspectors General cannot ensure that all government programs and operations are subject to exacting and independent scrutiny. Refusing, restricting, or delaying an Inspector General's*

independent access may lead to incomplete, inaccurate, or signifi-
cantly delayed findings and recommendations. . . . It also may im-
pede or otherwise inhibit investigations and prosecutions related to
agency programs and operations.

Representative John Conyers, a Michigan Democrat and former chairman of the House Judiciary Committee, agrees that the Justice rule is a clear violation of the Inspector General Act of 1978 in that it would allow an agency to completely withhold information from the IG.

What made the IGs' letter to Congress all the more troubling is that most of them were appointed by President Obama and confirmed by a Democratic Senate: it's impossible to characterize them as wild-eyed partisans.

The IG letter to Congress cited several specific examples and was signed by IGs for the Treasury Department, the Justice Department, the Homeland Security Department, the Internal Revenue Service, and the National Security Agency. Many of the IGs who did not sign oversee very small agencies or congressional branch agencies that seldom have document-access needs of their own. It's not as if the IGs are a clique of obsessive, conservative Inspector Javerts. President Obama appointed most of the IGs in office today, and with a very few exceptions those who were appointed by him have been confirmed by a Democratic Senate.

That makes the complaints raised in the IGs' letter all the more serious. More and more agencies are setting documents off-limits by declaring them "privileged." The Peace Corps is said to have refused to provide documents for a probe into whether its administrators were properly handling charges of sexual abuse. The Environmental Protection Agency withheld documents by

claiming they might fall under an attorney-client privilege, though
the IGs' letter makes clear that such privilege shouldn't prevent another executive-branch official from reviewing them. Eric Holder's
Department of Justice withheld FBI records that had been previously produced to investigators in past administrations. FBI Director James Comey told Congress in 2015 that the DOJ's Office
of Legal Counsel was still reviewing what "was a difference of view
as to what the law permitted here." A similar "difference of view"
prompted the US House to hold Attorney General Holder in contempt in 2012 for refusing to turn over documents related to the
Fast and Furious gunrunning scandal that resulted in the death of
US Border Patrol Agent Brian Terry.

The IGs' concerns aren't just parochial. Their problems are
"not unique" and other investigators had "faced similar obstacles
to their work." Indeed, in 2014 Darrell Issa, the then chairman
of the House Oversight and Government Reform Committee,
noted that more than twenty witnesses in the Obama administration have lost or deleted emails without notifying the National
Archives or Congress, in violation of federal law. Lois Lerner, now
notorious for having supposedly "lost" her emails, is far from a
unique character.

All this led Sen. Chuck Grassley (R-IA), the then–ranking
Republican on the Judiciary Committee, to note: "These nonpartisan, independent-agency watchdogs say they are getting
stonewalled. How are the watchdogs supposed to be able to do
their jobs without agency cooperation?" Thomas Carper (D-DE),
the Democratic ranking member on the Senate Government Reform Committee, agreed that the IG letter "outlines serious concerns that are unacceptable." He added that he will "continue to
work closely with the inspectors general to address their concerns."

It is time for both Republicans and independent Democrats to recognize the horrible precedent the Obama administration is setting for future White Houses. From the very beginning, the Obama team has been hostile to IG independence. We broke open the IG crisis in our first book in 2012. But it got even worse. As columnist Michele Malkin wrote: "It's transparently clear: President Obama loathes and fears independent watchdogs."[4]

Consider just some of the ways, President Obama and his appointees have stifled their own internal watchdogs, making the role of Judicial Watch all the more vital:

While defanging Washington's most effective guardians of the public's trust and tax dollars, the Obama administration has stocked the government with whitewash puppies who've compromised the independence of IG offices at the Department of Homeland Security, the Interior Department, and Department of Justice.

Obama appointees have distorted and destroyed the plain meaning of "all records" to sabotage the IGs' access to damning agency documents relevant to their probes. In congressional testimony in 2015, DOJ IG Michael Horowitz exposed the Obama administration's "continued refusal by the Department to recognize that Section 6(a) of the Inspector General Act authorizes the DOJ OIG to obtain access to all records in the Department's possession that we need in order to perform our oversight responsibilities" as the office investigates the IRS witch hunts, the Fast and Furious scandal, and systemic public-disclosure evasions. The FBI has repeatedly run out the clock to thwart IG document-production requests and unilaterally claimed power to pre-screen and limit records disclosures.

In 2015, the White House arrogantly announced that IGs

needed to secure permission from the heads of agencies they were investigating to gain access to grand jury, wiretap, and fair-credit information. Horowitz noted that "pending legislation in the Senate, S. 579, and the House, H.R. 2395, would restore IG independence and empower IGs to conduct the kind of rigorous, independent and thorough oversight that taxpayers expect."

Obama's compromised and shackled IGs show the dire need for the independent oversight of groups like Judicial Watch.

The Media Wakes Up to Obama "Stonewalling"

Another group that can hardly be accused of membership in a vast, right-wing conspiracy is the coalition of fifty-three press and open-government organizations that in 2015 "once again" urged President Obama "to stop practices in federal agencies that prevent important information from getting to the public."

In their letter they cite examples such as "refusing to allow reporters to speak to staff at all or delaying interviews past the point they would be useful." Another tactic used by Obama officials is "monitoring interviews and speaking only on the condition that the official not be identified, even when he or she has the title of spokesperson.[5]

Not surprisingly, Hillary Clinton has set the gold standard for concealment during the Obama era. She used a "private" server and email account to conduct all her government business and surrendered the server only after months of stonewalling. When she did hand over some of her emails in December 2014, she did it on paper, to make it as difficult as possible to read them, and so metadata associated with them wouldn't be included.

Of course, Team Obama isn't the first White House to avoid transparency. In 2007, it was revealed that some Bush White House officials had used private email accounts set up on a server through the Republican National Committee and that some of the emails were likely not recoverable. While the RNC servers were supposed to be used only for political matters, not official business, it's likely there were violations of that policy. But what have been off-and-on attempts at avoiding transparency in previous administrations has become a type of official policy in the Obama era.

Tom Coburn (R-OK), who served as the GOP ranking member on the Senate Government Reform Committee until his retirement in 2014, once partnered with then-Senator Barack Obama to sponsor a transparency-in-government bill. He recently reflected on how deeply disappointed he is in the anti-transparency precedents set by this president: "If the next administration is allowed to pursue the same policies, what will become of us when so much of what government does can be hidden from all of us?" Coburn is worried about the precedent the Obama administration has established: "This is an extremely dangerous place to be for a government established to be of the people, by the people, for the people."

A CALL FOR ACTION

Extending FOIA to Congress and the Judiciary

The biggest issue with transparency—or more precisely, the lack of transparency—is the fact that the Freedom of Information Act only applies to the executive branch. Congress and legislative branch agencies like the Congressional Research Service are not subject to FOIA. Neither are the federal courts. It is fundamentally unfair that neither the legislative nor the judicial branches are subject to the same transparency law that presidents must follow. And it is hard to ensure "good government" when two-thirds of the federal government is exempt from open records requirements.

Finally, as Judicial Watch knows from its long experience, FOIA litigation against recalcitrant agencies can be very expensive and requires knowledgeable lawyers who know how to fight back against an administration with experienced government attorneys bent on resisting compliance with the law. Because of the generous support of its members, Judicial Watch has had the resources to fight these extended battles in the courts. But individual taxpayers and other watchdogs often do not have the time, money, or access to experienced attorneys to wage such fights against the government.

A Freedom of Information Act IG

The federal government has an Inspector General system with independent IGs at many different federal agencies. But what it doesn't have is a FOIA inspector general. A possible solution to this problem would be for Congress to establish a FOIA IG. Individuals and organizations who have been denied documents or who are having problems getting a particular agency to respond could be given the right to file an administrative appeal with the FOIA IG. That IG would have the authority to overrule decisions by the agencies to withhold records or redact documents, or to force agencies to respond. FOIA requestors would still have the ability to go directly to court as Judicial Watch has in a countless number of cases without going to the FOIA IG; but this would provide an administrative alternative. That IG could also be given the authority to impose civil fines on agencies and individual federal employees who fail to abide by decisions and directives from the IG.

Securing the Integrity of Elections

In addition to fostering transparency in our government, the processes by which we elect our representatives must be completely above board if we want to preserve our republic. The most fundamental and basic standard for all elections must be to ensure that everyone who is eligible is able to vote, and that no one's vote is stolen or diluted. The integrity and security of our elections should be our number one concern. Unfortunately, we know through our work with the Election Integrity Project that our elections—and the individual votes of citizens—are vulnerable to incompetence, errors, oversights, fraud, and blatant corruption that can happen at any point in the process, from the registration of voters to the casting and counting of ballots.

Judicial Watch has done a great deal of work in this area, from suing states to force them to clean up their voters rolls, to supporting state efforts to implement common sense security requirements like showing a government-issued, photo ID when you vote and providing proof-of-citizenship when you register to vote. But the average American citizen can also do a lot. The first line of defense in preventing corruption and election fraud is not Judicial Watch, it is the American public—people who volunteer their time and services to ensure clean and fair elections, a process that encompasses events before, during, and after Election Day.

You might ask: "What can I do? I don't work for the city or town; I'm not on an election board; I don't even work for a candidate." The answer may surprise you. In fact, there is a great deal you can do, and it mostly involves being present, being watchful, and being willing to question and speak out as permitted by state law.

Become a Poll Worker

First and foremost, you can become a poll worker. Poll workers are usually volunteers who are hired and trained by county election officials and typically work at a local precinct throughout Election Day. As a poll worker, your primary focus will be to help prepare the precinct by setting up the voting equipment and distributing election supplies, greeting voters and helping them sign in, checking voter registrations and IDs (in states that require it), and handing out ballots to voters. You may also be called upon to provide instructions to voters on how to use voting machines, and once the polls are closed, you may be involved in shutting down the precinct and counting the ballots.

A disadvantage of serving as a poll worker is that while you can help ensure that the election process under your control is honest, fair, and in compliance with the law, you may have limited ability to observe the actions of others: voters, other poll workers, election board members, and people who may or may not have a legitimate reason for being there. A position that will enable you to also make a significant contribution to ensuring the accuracy and fairness of elections is being a poll watcher.

Become a Poll Watcher

Poll watchers—called "poll observers" in Massachusetts and California, and "challengers" or "checkers" in Illinois—have certain rights and obligations, and must adhere to prescribed rules that depend on state laws, which vary. For example, the state of New York allows each candidate on the ballot to have up to three poll watchers per precinct, one of whom can stand or sit next to the table with election officials; while Massachusetts permits one per candidate, and one within six feet of the check-in or check-out station.

In Illinois, on the other hand, the number is unspecified, but in the case where a polling place becomes overcrowded with poll watchers, the election officials ("poll judges" in Illinois) may decide to limit the number by drawing lots, but to no less that one for each candidate (as well as one for each of the other permitted groups such as political parties). Poll watchers in Illinois are allowed to be near enough to election officials to be able to compare voter signatures with registration records.

All states permit poll watchers in all precincts, and what you can and can't do is regulated by state law. Guides for poll watchers are published by most states and you should be able to obtain a copy through your state election board or from the secretary of state, who is the chief election official in many states. Poll watchers normally require signed credentials appointing them, and at a minimum must be registered voters in the state (and in the specific precinct in some states).

Poll watchers are permitted to be present before the polls open, during voting hours, and after the polling place is closed to observe the counting of ballots. You can volunteer to be a poll watcher with candidates, local political parties, and other organizations like True the Vote, depending again on the state's rules. Poll watchers are there to observe everything going on in the precinct, and to see if all of the applicable rules and laws (like checking voter ID) are being followed. They cannot campaign in the polling place or interfere in any way in the voting process but they can report any irregularities they see.

Depending on the state, a poll watcher may be able to issue a challenge to the eligibility of a particular voter. Under such circumstances, the voter is usually allowed to vote a provisional ballot, which is not counted until the validity of the challenge is determined by election officials after Election Day is over.

Perform Voter Registration Research

Without question, one of the keys to ensuring voter integrity during an election is being able to verify that the names and addresses on the voter registration list are legitimate and up-to-date. In each state, voter registration lists can be obtained ahead of the election. Checking these lists against other available data is a laborious, time-consuming—but essential—job for which your help would definitely be welcomed.

While voter registration lists can be purchased from an online service and directly from some of the states (either of which can be expensive), you should be able to get a copy of the list for your precinct from the state or county headquarters of your candidate or political party. You can also file an "open records" request in some states. Perhaps the best thing to do, however, is to contact True the Vote, which maintains an extensive database of voter registrations for each state, or other state-based citizen groups that have organized in recent years to protect the integrity of the vote and clean up voter registration rolls.

The process of checking voter registration lists against other available resources such as property tax information or www .tributes.com (which has obituaries) requires a degree of patience and creativity. But it is an extremely important function, as it is the foundation of ensuring voter integrity on Election Day.

Legislation

Another important objective of citizens should be to convince states to implement election reform. Through phone calls, meetings with state legislators, letters, emails, and working with other conservative grassroots organizations, you can work on getting the election laws of your state improved to increase the security and integrity of your elections.

There are a series of recommended changes to state election laws that have been made by Judicial Watch and nationally recognized election experts like Hans von Spakovsky of The Heritage Foundation and John Fund of *National Review*. These include requiring:

- A government-issued, photographic identification for all individuals voting in-person, as well as those casting absentee ballots. States like Georgia and Indiana have passed such legislation requiring IDs for in-person voting and states like Kansas and Alabama have passed such legislation for absentee ballots that can serve as models for other states.

- Anyone registering to vote to provide proof that they are US citizens—such legislation has been passed by states such as Arizona, Kansas, and Georgia.

- All state court clerks to notify local election officials when individuals called for jury duty from the voter registration rolls are excused because they are not US citizens.

- State election officials to run monthly comparisons with other available in-state and federal databases, such as driver's license records, corrections records of criminal convictions, vital records of deaths, etc., in order to keep voter rolls accurate and deleting individuals who have died, moved, or become ineligible to vote due to a felony conviction.

- State election officials to participate in projects like the Kansas Interstate Crosscheck program that compares the voter registration rolls of all of the states participating in the program to catch individuals registering in more than one state.

The Public Information War

There are a number of other actions ordinary Americans can take. Opponents of election integrity and measures like voter ID and verification of the accuracy of voter registration lists are extremely vocal in their false claims of "voter suppression" and "racism." They make their voices heard at meetings and hearings of county and state election boards. Those meetings are an excellent opportunity for you to find out what's going on and what issues are not being addressed by election officials, as well as to express your opinions on such issues. It is your right to both ask questions when the opportunity presents itself at such hearings and to voice your views. Discussions about dead people voting, registration clean-ups, and precautions to prevent ballot tampering should come up; if not, you can raise these important issues.

Helping support election reform can also be accomplished through letters to the editor and opinion editorials. These are an extremely important tool for grassroots activists in election reform. Letters to the editor allow you to comment on articles and editorials in local and national papers. While such letters may not seem ineffective, many legislators and policymakers keep an eye on letters to the editor, so they can find out what the public is thinking about a particular issue.

Many newspapers also have guidelines for guest editorials. Such an opinion editorial is similar to a letter to the editor, but is generally longer and provides more in-depth analysis and commentary. You need to be concise, honest, and relevant. Be sure your facts are correct and include your contact information so the editors of the paper can get in touch with you.

You should also call in to radio talk shows. Millions of people tune in to listen every day at home, at the office, and during their commutes. You can reach thousands of people at a time by calling in to local and regional shows. Those are the best places to talk about election fraud and other problems in your states. Write down concisely what you want to say before you call in, so you can clearly voice your points. Remember, you may have only a short time to get your message across and every radio talk show has call screeners who will want to know who you are and what you want to talk about.

Create your own blog or blog on other websites about these issues, and take advantage of social media like Twitter to link to articles on elections and voter fraud. Today, there are millions of blogs on the Internet ranging in topics from politics to personal lives. Election fraud is a sensitive issue and you should have no trouble getting people to respond to your opinions, commentaries, Tweets, and Facebook postings. Be sure to be well informed by staying on top of relevant events and what the media is saying in your state and region.

The bottom line is that you can make a difference, the way Judicial Watch has made a difference, in securing the integrity of the election process.

The Mission of Judicial Watch

For more than two decades, Judicial Watch has stood in the barricades, fighting official corruption and working to ensure transparency and a government that is accountable to the citizens of the United States. When the federal government and state governments have failed to comply with the law, we have gone to court to fight them. While we are a conservative organization that believes in the Constitution and the rule of law, we are strictly nonpartisan—and our record shows it. We have battled with, and sued, both Democratic and Republican administrations. Our only interest is stopping government corruption by exposing it, and protecting the sanctity of the democratic process that allows us to choose who our representatives are in that government.

We are in Washington working on behalf of the American people. Our motto is "Because no one is above the law," and we have worked hard to ensure that everyone in Washington and in state capitals is forced to live up to that motto. With your help, we hope to continue to do that for a long time to come.

ACKNOWLEDGMENTS

Through this book, I am honored to present the work of my Judicial Watch colleagues, whose diligence, persistence, and commitment have built our organization into one of the most remarkable public policy organizations in our nation. Paul Orfanedes, our Director of Litigation, and Chris Farrell, our Director of Research and Investigations, have helped lead our team to truly historic accomplishments for the rule of law. Judicial Watch is truly an American success story, because as a non-profit educational foundation, we owe all our achievements through the years to the generous and *voluntary* financial support of more than a million Judicial Watch members. Of course, the families of our staff deserve a special note of thanks, as their steadfast support is essential to our success. And for those of you who helped me directly on *Clean House*, thank you for ensuring the success of this massive educational project.

And thank you to everyone who helped directly on *Clean House* at Threshold Editions/Simon & Schuster, including Louise Burke (President & Publisher), Mitchell Ivers (Vice-President & Editorial Director), Natasha Simons (Associate Editor), Al Madocs (Production Editor), Liz Psaltis (Marketing Director), Jean Anne Rose (Director of Publicity), and the entire sales and production team, whose work is indispensable and much appreciated.

APPENDIX

IRS SCANDAL DOCUMENTS

FRA/DOJ EVIDENCE

The emails I attached to our press release that we acquired from the IRA as a result of our lawsuit are the most egregious.

They prove that the corrupt Obama Justice Department reached out to Lois Lerner — and together they conspired about possibly subjecting "certain groups" (and you can be sure they meant conservative and Tea Party groups only) to criminal prosecution.

This is nothing less than a full-scale attack by government on opponents of the current administration and on Americans' right to political free speech.

Every American should be outraged by this conspiracy between the Justice Department and the IRA to subvert the U.S. Constitution.

Tom

erta B; Kindell Judith E; Biss Meghan R; Light Sharon

didn't know!

eghan R; Light Sharon P

around the corner. This is obviously a
u can tell him, unless you want to tell him that

ony from our Legislative Affairs folks.
en you spoke.

FOR IMMEDIATE RELEASE
April 16, 2014

Judicial Watch Obtains Internal IRS Documents Showing Lerner in Contact With DOJ about Potential Prosecution of Tax-Exempt Groups

May 9, 2013, email reveals IRS plans to meet with Department of Justice over whether to prosecute groups that "lied" about plans for political activity

(Washington, DC) – Judicial Watch today released a new batch of internal IRS documents revealing that former IRS official Lois Lerner communicated with the Department of Justice (DOJ) about whether it was possible to criminally prosecute certain tax-exempt entities. The documents were obtained as a result of an October 2013 Judicial Watch Freedom of Information Act (FOIA) lawsuit filed against the Internal Revenue Service (IRS) after the agency refused to respond to four FOIA requests dating back to May 2013.

The newly released IRS documents contain an email exchange between Lerner and Nikole C. Flax, then-Chief of Staff to then-Acting IRS Commissioner Steven T. Miller discussing plans to work with the DOJ to prosecute nonprofit groups that "lied" (Lerner's quotation marks) about political activities. The exchange includes the following:

- <u>May 8, 2013</u>: Lerner to Flax

I got a call today from Richard Pilger Director Elections Crimes Branch at DOJ ... He wanted to know who at IRS the DOJ folk s [sic] could talk to about Sen. Whitehouse idea at the hearing that DOJ could piece together false statement cases about applicants who "lied" on their 1024s -- saying they weren't planning on doing political activity, and then turning around and making large visible political expenditures. DOJ is feeling like it needs to respond, but want to talk to the right folks at IRS to see whether there are impediments from our side and what, if any damage this might do to IRS programs.

I told him that sounded like we might need several folks from IRS…

- <u>May 9, 2013</u>: Flax to Lerner

I think we should do it – also need to include CI [Criminal Investigation Division], which we can help coordinate. Also, we need to reach out to FEC. Does it make sense to consider including them in this or keep it separate?

Lerner then "handed off" scheduling the issue to Senior Technical Adviser, Attorney Nancy Marks, who was then supposed to set up the meeting with the DOJ. Lerner also decided that it would be DOJ's decision as to whether representatives from the Federal Election Commission would attend.

Democratic Rhode Island Senator Sheldon Whitehouse had held a hearing on April 9 during which, "in questioning the witnesses from DOJ and IRS, Whitehouse asked why they have not prosecuted 501(c)(4) groups that have seemingly made false statements about their political activities." Lerner described the impetus for this hearing in a March 27, 2013, email to top IRS staff:

As I mentioned yesterday -- there are several groups of folks from the FEC world that are pushing tax fraud prosecution for c4s who report they are not conducting political activity when they are (or these folks think they are). One is my ex-boss Larry Noble (former General Counsel at the FEC), who is now president of Americans for Campaign Reform. This is their latest push to shut these down. One IRS prosecution would make an impact and they wouldn't feel so comfortable doing the stuff.

So, don't be fooled about how this is being articulated – it is ALL about 501(c)(4) orgs and political activity

But in an email sent a few minutes earlier, Lerner acknowledged prosecutions would evidently be at odds with the law:

Whether there was a false statement or fraud regarding an [sic] description of an alleged political expenditure that doesn't say vote for or vote against is not realistic under current law. Everyone is looking for a magic bullet or scapegoat -- there isn't one. The law in this area is just hard.

You bet it is!!

The documents also include email exchanges showing that before Lerner's May 10, 2013, speech to the American Bar Association blaming "low-level" employees in Cincinnati for targeting tax-exempt organizations, the IRS Exempt Organizations division was scrambling to defuse the emerging targeting scandal:

- May 1, 2013: After receiving an email from an assistant showing that 501(c)(4) applications had increased from 1591 in 2010 to 3398 in 2012 , Lerner wrote back, "Looks to me like 2010-2012 doubled too. Oh well – thanks."

- May 2, 2013: Discussing an upcoming conference call with approximately 100 congressional staffers on May 22, Lerner cautions aides, "Need to be careful not to mention sequester/furlough unless asked although can allude to budget and resources restraints."

- May 2, 2013: In response to an email reminding her about the upcoming conference call with congressional staffers, Lerner responded, "Arrgh – I just saw it. Sharon [White] could skate, but Cindy [Thomas] is the person who could answer that stuff. We need to give them some type of language in the event that type of question comes up" [apparently in reference to earlier email referencing "sensitive issues"].

The new documents obtained by Judicial Watch also include emails exchanged after Lerner's May 10 ABA speech:

- May 10, 2013: In an email to an aide responding to a request for information from a *Washington Post* reporter, Lerner admits that she "can't confirm that there was anyone on the other side of the political spectrum" who had been targeted by the IRS. She then adds that "The one with the names used were only know [sic] because they have been very loud in the press."

- May 10, 2013: An email from former Cincinnati program manager Cindy Thomas excoriates Lerner for her comments blaming "low-level" employees in its Cincinnati office for targeting tax-exempt organizations that had "Tea Party" or "Patriots" in their names during the 2012 election. Highlighting the words "low-level workers" in bold-face type each of the seven times she used it in short, pungent email, Thomas asked, "How am I supposed to keep the **low-level workers** motivated when the public believes they are nothing more than **low-level workers** and now will have no respect for how they are working cases?" Lerner's response nearly an hour later was a terse, "I will be back shortly and give you a call."

- May 15, 2013: In an email from an aide to Lerner, the aide specifically mentions "Tea Party Organizations, the "Tea Party movement," and "Tea Party Patriots" as organizations targeted by the IRS.

The Judicial Watch FOIA requests came on the heels of an explosive May 14, 2013, Treasury Inspector General report revealing that the IRS had singled out groups with conservative-sounding terms such as "patriot" and "Tea Party" in their titles when applying for tax-exempt status. The IG probe determined that "Early in Calendar Year 2010, the IRS began using inappropriate criteria to identify organizations applying for tax-exempt status to (e.g., lists of past and future donors)." According to the report, the illegal IRS reviews continued for more than 18 months and "delayed processing of targeted groups' applications" preparing for the 2012 presidential election.

Lerner, who headed the IRS division that handles applications for tax-exempt status, refused to testify at a May 2013 hearing before Rep. Darrell Issa's (R-CA) House Oversight Committee, demanding immunity concerning her role in the targeting scandal. Lerner retired from the IRS with full benefits on September 23 after an internal investigation found she was guilty of "neglect of duties" and was going to call for her ouster, according to news reports. On April 9, 2014, the Ways and Means Committee referred Lois Lerner to the DOJ for criminal prosecution. On April 10, 2014, the House Oversight Committee voted to hold Lerner in contempt of Congress.

"These new emails show that the day before she broke the news of the IRS scandal, Lois Lerner was talking to a top Obama Justice Department official about whether the DOJ could prosecute the very same organizations that the IRS had already improperly targeted," said Judicial Watch President Tom Fitton. "The IRS emails show Eric Holder's Department of Justice is now implicated and conflicted in the IRS scandal. No wonder we had to sue in federal court to get these documents."

From: Flax Nikole C
Sent: Thursday, May 09, 2013 8:04 AM
To: Lerner Lois G
Cc: Grant Joseph H; Marks Nancy J; Vozne Jennifer L
Subject: RE: DOJ Call

I think we should do it – also need to include CI, which we can help coordinate.   Also, we need to reach out to FEC.   Does it make sense to consider including them in this or keep it separate?

From: Lerner Lois G
Sent: Wednesday, May 08, 2013 5:30 PM
To: Flax Nikole C
Cc: Grant Joseph H; Marks Nancy J
Subject: DOJ Call
Importance: High

— liberal Sen. Sheldon Whitehouse <D-RI>

I got a call today from Richard Pilger Director Elections Crimes Branch at DOJ. I know him from contacts from my days there. He wanted to know who at IRS the DOJ folk s could talk to about **Sen. Whitehouse** idea at the hearing that DOJ could piece together false statement cases about applicants who "lied" on their 1024s --saying they weren't planning on doing political activity, and then turning around and making large vis ible political expenditures. DOJ is feeling like it needs to respond, but want to talk to the right folks at IRS to see whether there are impediments from our side and what, if any damage this might do to IRS programs.

I told him that sounded like we mi ght need several folks from IRS. I am out of town all next week, so wanted to reach out and see who you think would be right for such a meeting and also hand this off to Nan as contact person if things need to happen while I am gone --

Thanks

Lois G. Lerner
Director of Exempt Organizations

From:	Lerner Lois G
Sent:	Wednesday, March 27, 2013 12:39 PM
To:	Flax Nikole C; Sinno Suzanne; Barre Catherine M; Landes Scott S; Amato Amy; Vozne Jennifer L
Subject:	RE: UPDATE - FW: Hearing

As I mentioned yesterday --there are several groups of folks from the FEC world that are pushing tax fraud prosecution for c4s who report they are not conducting political activity when they are(or these folks think they are). One is my ex-boss Larry Noble(former General Counsel at the FEC), who is now president of Americans for Campaign Reform. This is their latest push to shut these down. One IRS prosecution would make an impact and they wouldn't feel so comfortable doing the stuff.

So, don't be fooled about how this is being articulated --it is ALL about 501(c)(4) orgs and political activity

Lois G. Lerner
Director of Exempt Organizations

It's all about abusing the law to advance a left-wing political agenda.

From: Griffin, Ayo (Judiciary-Dem) [mailto:Ayo_Griffin@judiciary-dem.senate.gov]
Sent: Tuesday, March 26, 2013 7:44 PM
To: Sinno Suzanne
Subject: Hearing

Hi Suzanne,

I hope you're well. You may recall we met last summer during a couple of very helpful IRS briefings that you put together for staff for several Senators relating to political spending by 501(c)(4) groups.

I wanted to get in touch because Sen. Whitehouse is convening a hearing in the Judiciary Subcommittee on Crime and Terrorism on criminal enforcement of campaign finance law on April 9, which I think you may have already have heard about from Bill Erb at DoJ. One of the topics actually involves enforcement of tax law. Specifically, Sen. Whitehouse is interested in the investigation and prosecution of material false statements to the IRS regarding political activity by 501(c)(4) groups on forms 990 and 1024 under 26 U.S.C. § 7206.

This is Orwellian!

Sen. Whitehouse would like to invite an IRS witness to testify on these issues. Could you please let me know if it would be possible for you to provide a witness?

I sincerely apologize for the late notice. We had been hoping that a DoJ witness could discuss all of the topics that Sen. Whitehouse was interested in covering at this hearing, but we were recently informed that they would not be able to speak about enforcement of § 7206 in this context.

I have attached an official invitation in case you require one two weeks prior to the hearing date (as D oJ does).

Perhaps we can discuss all of this on the phone tomorrow if you have time.

Thanks very much,

Ayo

Ayo Griffin
Counsel
Subcommittee on Crime and Terrorism
Senator Sheldon Whitehouse, Chair
U.S. Senate Committee on the Judiciary
(202) 224-5168

From:	Lerner Lois G
Sent:	Wednesday, March 27, 2013 12:31 PM
To:	Sinno Suzanne; Flax Nikole C; Barre Catherine M; Landes Scott S; Amato Amy
Subject:	RE: UPDATE - FW: Hearing

In looking at their testimony though, it's all about criminal prosecution of federal campaign laws--so we're all talking apples and oranges. At the bottom line. in both instances, the issue is whether a particular expenditure was political intervention. Whether there was a false statement or fraud regarding an description of an alleged political expenditure that doesn't say vote for or vote against is not realistic under current law. Everyone is looking for a magic bullet or scapegoat--there isn't one. The law in this area is just hard.

Lois G. Lerner
Director of Exempt Organizations

But they kept trying.

From: Sinno Suzanne
Sent: Wednesday, March 27, 2013 1:19 PM
To: Flax Nikole C; Lerner Lois G; Barre Catherine M; Landes Scott S; Amato Amy
Subject: UPDATE - FW: Hearing

I just spoke with Ayo. He told me that DOJ said the IRS does the initial investigations into violations of IRC section 7206 (fraud and false statements) and DOJ prosecutes IRS referrals.   DOJ said they have not gotten any referrals from the IRS.

The Subcommittee is interested in an IRS witness to testify on:
- the process of an investigation before a case is turned over to DOJ
- how a determination is made
- how different elements of the offense are interpreted under IRC section 7206

Please let me know your thoughts.

Thanks,
Suzie

Feel free to call me directly at 927-6922 if you would like to discuss over the phone.

Thank you,
Suzie

Suzanne R. Sinno, J.D., LL.M. (Tax)
Legislative Counsel
Office of Legislative Affairs
Internal Revenue Service
202-927-6922
202-622-5247 (fax)
Suzanne.R.Sinno@irs.gov

From:	Lerner Lois G
Sent:	Wednesday, May 01, 2013 8:33 PM
To:	Paz Holly O
Subject:	Re: Revised response

Looks to me like 2010-2012 doubled too. Oh well --thanks Lois G. Lerner ----------------------- Sent from my BlackBerry Wireless Handheld

----- Original Message -----
From: Paz Holly O
Sent: Monday, April 29, 2013 01:05 PM Eastern Standard Time
To: Lerner Lois G
Subject: RE: Revised response

Lois,

We do have numbers on c4 apps from 2010 -2012 ███████████████ *(b)(5)* ███████████████

Increase in section 501c4 applications
2008 - 1410
2009 - 1571
2010 - 1591
2011 - 2242
2012 - 3398
2013 - 2,092 (through March 26, 2013)

A "smoking gun" — Lerner was tracking the growth of Tea Party groups.

-----Original Message-----
From: Lerner Lois G
Sent: Monday, April 29, 2013 1:01 PM
To: Daly Richard M; Grant Joseph H; Paz Holly O; Marks Nancy J
Cc: Flax Nikole C
Subject: RE: Revised response

We've had this conversation before --we don't have stats for the 20010 -12 period. Everyone is aware --it was in "our" draft also.

I agree ████████████████████████ ██████████████

Lois G. Lerner
Director of Exempt Organizations

-----Original Message-----
From: Daly Richard M
Sent: Monday, April 29, 2013 12:33 PM

This is what "transparency" looks like to the IRS!

To: Grant Joseph H; Lerner Lois G; Paz Holly O; Marks Nancy J
Cc: Flax Nikole C
Subject: FW: Revised response

More Obama FRA transparency!

I have four comments:

1. ██

2. ██
   ██
   b(5)\deliberative process ████████████████
   ██

3. ██

4. ██
   ██
   b(5)\deliberative process ████████████████
   ██

There are a few other personal-preference nits, but I'm suppressing them.

Mike

-----Original Message-----
From: Lerner Lois G
Sent: Monday, April 29, 2013 11:50 AM
To: Flax Nikole C; Grant Joseph H; Daly Richard M
Subject: RE: Revised response

I think the response looks really good. Admits some flaws, but lays out the context and what we did to correct. Good job! Holly and I will work on dates --some easier to shorten up than others --stay tuned

Lois G. Lerner
Director of Exempt Organizations

-----Original Message-----
From: Flax Nikole C
Sent: Sunday, April 28, 2013 9:34 AM
To: Grant Joseph H; Lerner Lois G; Daly Richard M
Cc: Flax Nikole C
Subject: Revised response

Please take a look and let me know of any suggested edits. Steve needs to see any changes before we submit so please send back to me. Also, ██
████████████ Thanks

From:	Lerner Lois G
Sent:	Thursday, May 02, 2013 4:09 PM
To:	Light Sharon P; Partner Melaney J; Paz Holly O
Cc:	White Shirley A; Thomas Cindy M
Subject:	RE: Reminder about 5/22 phone forum for congressional staff

I am out of the country for that one, so Holly and you all should figure out what you plan to say about why things take forever. Need to be careful not to mention sequester/furlough unless asked although can allude to budget and resource constraints.

Lois G. Lerner
Director of Exempt Organizations

From: Light Sharon P
Sent: Thursday, May 02, 2013 5:05 PM
To: Lerner Lois G; Partner Melaney J
Cc: White Shirley A; Thomas Cindy M
Subject: RE: Reminder about 5/22 phone forum for congressional staff

Cheryl, Cindy and I have a call scheduled on the 16 th from 11-12 to discuss the forum in advance.

We have gotten a couple of messages that the questions submitted in advance are complaints that the Determs process takes too long.

It would be good to have the "sensitivity training" conversation on that 5/16 call.

They knew trouble was brewing! (handwritten)

From: Lerner Lois G
Sent: Thursday, May 02, 2013 4:57 PM
To: Partner Melaney J
Cc: White Shirley A; Light Sharon P; Thomas Cindy M
Subject: RE: Reminder about 5/22 phone forum for congressional staff

Arrgh--I just saw it. Sharon could skate, but Cindy is the person who could answer that stuff. We need to give them some language in the event that type question comes up.

Lois G. Lerner
Director of Exempt Organizations

Hunkering down. (handwritten)

From: Partner Melaney J
Sent: Thursday, May 02, 2013 3:34 PM
To: Lerner Lois G
Cc: White Shirley A
Subject: Reminder about 5/22 phone forum for congressional staff

Lois,

That's code for embarrassing media attention!

With all the sensitive issues lately, I just wanted to make sure that you remembered EO's upcoming phone forum for congressional staff. We have about 100 signed up so far. It is scheduled for Wednesda y, May 22 from 2 to 3:30, and the promotional materials say:

Experts from IRS Exempt Organizations will present an overview and updates for congressional staff on the following topics:

- *Applying for tax-exempt status*
- *Automatic revocation of tax-exempt status*
- *IRS Exempt Organizations products & resources*

If you have specific questions related to these topics that you would like the forum to address, please submit them in advance through your IRS Governmental Liaison.

We are working directly with Eric Hall (who is working with GL and TAS as they share the congressional staff). Our speakers are Cheryl, Sharon, and Cindy T. TAS and GL folks are listening, but asked not to engage during the forum as it is for the congressional s taffers.

. . .

From: Lerner Lois G
Sent: Friday, May 10, 2013 3:21 PM
To: Flax Nikole C; Eldridge Michelle L; Lemons Terry L; Marks Nancy J
Subject: RE: Proposed answers: Washington Post Editorial Board

It isn't the balance I am focused on --it's the idea that we know--that sounds like we track it and we don't. Doesn't look good if it looks like we check to see what side of the aisle an org is on.

Lois G. Lerner
Director of Exempt Organizations

Which is exactly what they did!

From: Flax Nikole C
Sent: Friday, May 10, 2013 4:17 PM
To: Lerner Lois G; Eldridge Michelle L; Lemons Terry L; Marks Nancy J
Subject: RE: Proposed answers: Washington Post Editorial Board

---

From: Lerner Lois G
Sent: Friday, May 10, 2013 4:09 PM
To: Flax Nikole C; Eldridge Michelle L; Lemons Terry L
Subject: RE: Proposed answers: Washington Post Editorial Board

Because there weren't!

I can't confirm that there was anyone on the other side of the political spectrum --I think that sentence presumes we keep track of which side of the aisle an or falls --we don't. The one with names used were only know because that have been very loud in the press. I think that line is dangerous

Lois G. Lerner
Director of Exempt Organizations

From: Flax Nikole C
Sent: Friday, May 10, 2013 3:44 PM
To: Lerner Lois G; Eldridge Michelle L; Lemons Terry L
Subject: FW: Proposed answers: Washington Post Editorial Board

(b)(5)

From: Flax Nikole C
Sent: Friday, May 10, 2013 3:35 PM
To: Eldridge Michelle L; Vozne Jennifer L; Lemons Terry L; Miller Steven T
Cc: Patterson Dean J
Subject: RE: Proposed answers: Washington Post Editorial Board

(b)(5)

From: Eldridge Michelle L
Sent: Friday, May 10, 2013 3:15 PM
To: Flax Nikole C; Vozne Jennifer L; Lemons Terry L
Cc: Patterson Dean J
Subject: Proposed answers: Washington Post Editorial Board

Here is the proposed answer based on our discussion. Comments or concerns?

Proposed answer:

Here is our full statement. I have also answered your questions below.   *More IRS transparency!*

IRS Statement

(b)(5)

From: Stromberg, Stephen W [mailto:stephen.stromberg@wpost.com]
Sent: Friday, May 10, 2013 1:46 PM
To: Burke Anthony
Subject: From Washington Post Editorial Board

Hi –

I am writing an on-deadline editorial on the Tea Party/IRS issue, filing by 4:30 p.m. at the latest. At the moment, I have three questions:

Why weren't there protections in place to ens ure that selecting out groups of a particular political stripe was not possible?   What procedures are in place now to prevent this, both in the tax -exempt office and elsewhere in the IRS?

Who has led the investigation into this episode? Is someone else inside or outside of the IRS going to investigate further?

Thanks in advance.

Best,
Steve Stromberg

Steve Stromberg
Editorial Writer
The Washington Post
Office: 202.334.6370
Cell: 310.770.6646

From: Thomas Cindy M
Sent: Friday, May 10, 2013 1:48 PM
To: Lerner Lois G
Subject: RE: Low-Level Workers thrown under the Bus

I am working from home. My number is: _[redacted]_

From: Lerner Lois G
Sent: Friday, May 10, 2013 2:43 PM
To: Thomas Cindy M
Subject: Re: Low-Level Workers thrown under the Bus

I will be back shortly and will give you a call.
Lois G. Lerner----------------------
Sent from my BlackBerry Wireless Handheld

[handwritten: Evidently not something she was willing to put in an email!]

From: Thomas Cindy M
Sent: Friday, May 10, 2013 01:58 PM Eastern Standard Time
To: Lerner Lois G
Cc: Paz Holly O
Subject: Low-Level Workers thrown under the Bus

As you can imagine, employees and managers in EO Determinations are furious. I've been receiving comments about the use of your words from all parts of TEGE and from IRS employees outside of TEGE (as far away as Seattle, WA).

I wasn't at the conference and obviously don't know what was stated and what wasn't. I realize that sometimes words are taken out of context. However, based on what is in print in the articles, it appears as though all the blame is being placed on Cincinnati. Joseph Grant and others who came to Cincinnati last year specially told the **low-level workers** in Cincinnati that no one would be "thrown under the bus." Based on the articles, Cincinnati wasn't publicly "thrown under the bus" instead was hit by a convoy of mack trucks.

Was it also communicated at that conference in Washington that the **low-level workers** in Cincinnati asked the Washington Office for assistance and the Washington Office took no action to provide guidance to the **low-level workers?**

One of the **low-level workers** in Cincinnati received a voice mail message this morning from the POA for one of his advocacy cases asking if the status would be changing per "Lois Lerner's comments." What would you like for us to tell the POA?

How am I supposed to keep the **low-level workers** motivated when the public believes they are nothing more than **low-level** and now will have no respect for how they are working cases? The attitude/morale of employees is the lowest it has ever been. We have employees leaving for the day and making comments to managers that "this low -level worker is leaving for the day." Other employees are making sarcastic comments about not being thrown under the bus. And still other employees are upset about how their family and friends are going to react to these comments and how it portrays the quality of their work.

The past year and a half has been miserable enough because of all of the auto revocation issues and the lack of insight from Executives to see a need for strategic planning that included having anyone from EO Determinations involved in the upfront planning of this work. Now, our leader is publicly referring to employees who are the ones producing all of this work with fewer resources than ever as **low-level workers!**

[handwritten: She was right — JW discovered more documents proving IRS HQ. in Washington ran this illegal program!]

If reference to **low-level workers** wasn't made and/or blame wasn't placed on Cincinnati, please let me know ASAP and indicate what exactly was stated so that I can communicate that message to employees.

http://www.washingtonpost.com/business/irs-apologizes-for-inappropriately-targeting-conservative-political-groups-in-2012-election/2013/05/10/5afcf7b8-b980-11e2-b568-6917f6ac6d9d_story.html?wpisrc=al_comboPNE_p

http://www.usatoday.com/story/news/politics/2013/05/10/irs-apology-conservative-groups-2012-election/2149939/

http://www.wlwt.com/news/local-news/cincinnati/irs-cincinnati-workers-singled-out-conservative-groups-for-review/-/13549970/20096270/-/xcujae/-/index.html

---

From:	Marks Nancy J
Sent:	Wednesday, May 15, 2013 11:28 AM
To:	Lerner Lois G
Subject:	RE:

Yes indeed in fact let me know if you want it at the house I could always do a drop off.

-----Original Message-----
From: Lerner Lois G
Sent: Wednesday, May 15, 2013 12:25 PM
To: Marks Nancy J
Subject: Re:

Once I get back, I assume I can get the entire thing --unredacted and the letters?
Lois G. Lerner-------------------------- Sent from my BlackBerry Wireless Handheld

-----Original Message-----
From: Nancy Marks
To: Lois Call in Number
Subject: FW:
Sent: May 15, 2013 12:21 PM

The actual language on bolo changes so you can annotate the redacted version (sorry could only send that)

Will also send you the full TIGTA report and timeline electronically for further background.

-----Original Message-----
From: Light Sharon P
Sent: Tuesday, May 14, 2013 1:11 PM
To: Marks Nancy J; Paz Holly O
Subject: RE: What is the third bolo change?

Here is holly's email:

6/2012-present   Current Political Issues - 501(c)(3), 501(c)(4),
501(c)(5), and 501(c)(6) organizations with indicators of significant amounts of political campaign intervention (raising questions as to exempt purpose and/or excess private benefit). Note: advocacy action type issues (e.g., lobbying) that are currently listed on the Case Assignment Guide
(CAG) do not meet this criteria.

01/2012-6/2012   Current Political Issues - Political action type
organizations involved in limiting/expanding government, educating on the constitution and bill of rights, $oci al economic reform / movement. Note:
typical advocacy type issues that are currently listed on the Case Assignment Guide (CAG) do not meet these criteria unless they are also involved in activities described above.

7/2011-1/2012   Advocacy Orgs - Organizations involved with
political, lobbying, or advocacy for exemption under 501(c)(3) or 501(c)(4).

2/2011-7/2011   Tea Party - Organizations involved with the Tea
Party movement applying for exemption under 501(c)(3) or 501(c)(4). [EO Determinations specialists indicated that they
interpreted this as including organizations meeting any of the following criteria: 1. 'Tea Party', 'Patriots' or '9/12 Projec t'
is referenced in the case file. 2. Issues include government spending, governmen t debt and taxes. 3. Educate the public
through advocacy/legislative activities to make America a better place to live. 4. Statements in the case file that are
critical of the how the country is being run.]

08/2010-2/2011   Tea Party - These case involve various local
organizations in the Tea Party movement are applying for exemption under
501(c)(3) or 501(c)(4). [EO Determinations specialists indicated that they interpreted this as including organizations
meeting any of the following
criteria: 1. 'Tea Party', 'Patriots' or '9/12 Project' is referenced in the case file. 2. Issues include government spending,
government debt and taxes. 3. Educate the public through advocacy/legislative activities to make America a better
place to live. 4. Stat ements in the case file that are critical of the how the country is being run.]

-----Original Message-----
From: Marks Nancy J
Sent: Tuesday, May 14, 2013 1:10 PM
To: Paz Holly O; Light Sharon P
Subject: Re: What is the third bolo change?

I was using ti gta report which has two problem change points
----
Sent using BlackBerry

------Original Message------
To: Holly Paz
Subject: What is the third bolo change?
Sent: May 14, 2013 1:08 PM

Sent using BlackBerry

NOTES

Introduction: Why Judicial Watch?

1. Melissa Quinn, "Most of Government's Own Watchdogs Say They're Stonewalled," *Daily Signal*, August 7, 2014.
2. Hans von Spakovsky and John-Michael Seibler, "The Obama Administration's Defiance of Inspectors General," Heritage Foundation Legal Memorandum No. 169, December 11, 2015.
3. *McGrain v. Daugherty*, 273 U.S. 135, 174–75 (1927); see also *Anderson v. Dunn*, 19 U.S. 6 Wheat. 204 (1821).
4. Todd Garvey and Alissa M. Dolan, "Congress's Contempt Power," Congressional Research Service, May 8, 2014, 3.
5. U.S.C. 552(b) (1).
6. U.S.C. 552(b) (4).
7. U.S.C. 552(b) (5).
8. U.S.C. 552(b) (6).
9. U.S.C. 552(b) (7).
10. U.S.C. 552(b) (8) .

Chapter 1: Peeling Back the Benghazi Cover-up

1. Judicial Watch press release of April 19, 2014.
2. Judicial Watch press release of December 3, 2015.
3. Sarah Westwood, "Emails Suggest Pentagon Had Troops Ready During Benghazi Siege," *Washington Examiner*, December 8, 2015.
4. Judicial Watch press release of December 11, 2014.
5. Judicial Watch press release of May 18, 2015.
6. A reference to the death of al-Qaeda's second-in-command, Libyan national Abu Yahya al-Libi.
7. Judicial Watch press release of May 26, 2015.
8. Judicial Watch press release of December 8, 2015.
9. Judicial Watch press release of April 19, 2014.
10. Judicial Watch press release of October 20, 2015.
11. Judicial Watch press release of February 26, 2015.

12. Judicial Watch press release of May 26, 2015.
13. Judicial Watch press release of November 13, 2015.
14. Judicial Watch press release of June 29, 2015.
15. Judicial Watch press release of October 20, 2015.
16. Judicial Watch press release of February 26, 2015.
17. Judicial Watch press release of June 29, 2015.
18. Judicial Watch press release of May 19, 2015.
19. Judicial Watch press release of June 29, 2015.
20. Judicial Watch press release of April 19, 2014.
21. Judicial Watch press release of February 19, 2015.

Chapter 2: Hillary Clinton's Private Email Cover-up

1. Judicial Watch press release of March 5, 2015.
2. Judicial Watch press release of March 9, 2015.
3. Judicial Watch press release of April 30, 2015.
4. Judicial Watch press release of May 6, 2015.
5. Judicial Watch press release of July 7, 2015.
6. Judicial Watch press release of July 20, 2015.
7. Judicial Watch press release of August 6, 2015.
8. Judicial Watch press release of August 10, 2015.
9. Judicial Watch press release August 10, 2015.
10. Judicial Watch press release of August 13, 2015.
11. Judicial Watch press release of August 19, 2015.
12. Judicial Watch press release of August 26, 2015.
13. Judicial Watch press release of August 26, 2015.
14. Judicial Watch press release of September 14, 2015.
15. Judicial Watch press release of October 29, 2015.
16. Deputy Director of Office of Secretary of State Internal Memorandum at https://www.judicialwatch.org/wp-content/uploads/2015/11/2015-Clinton -memoir-documents-pg-12.pdf.
17. http://www.breitbart.com/big-government/2016/03/28/147-fbi-agents-work ing-on-hillary-clintons-email-investigation/.
18. Judicial Watch press release of December 18, 2015.
19. Judicial Watch press release of December 18, 2015.
20. Judicial Watch press release of February 1, 2016.
21. Judicial Watch press release of July 28, 2014.
22. Judicial Watch press release of July 28, 2014.
23. This was for two speeches.
24. Sam Callahan, "Bill's Libido Threatens to Derail Hillary Again," *New York Post*, February 14, 2015.

Chapter 3: Fast and Furious

1. Frank Miniter, "Fast and Furious Just Might Be President Obama's Watergate," Forbes.com, September 28, 2011.
2. Judicial Watch press release of July 8, 2012.
3. John Dodson, *The Unarmed Truth: My Fight to Blow the Whistle and Expose Fast and Furious* (New York: Threshold Editions, 2013), 41.
4. Letter from Senator Chuck Grassley to Justice Department, October 16, 2011.
5. Katie Pavlich, *Fast & Furious: Barack Obama's Bloodiest Scandal and Its Shameless Cover-up* (New York: Regnery Books, 2014), 27.
6. Ryan Mauro, "Where Drug Cartels Really Get Their Arms," Frontpagemag .com, October 11, 2011.
7. Letter from Senator Chuck Grassley to Justice Department, January 27, 2011.
8. CBS News, "Agent Was Ordered to Let U.S. Guns into Mexico," March 3, 2011.
9. Matthew Boyle, "Issa on Terry Murder Anniversary," Breitbart.com, December 15, 2013.

Chapter 4: Voter Fraud

1. Tom Fitton, *The Corruption Chronicles: Obama's Big Secrecy, Big Corruption, and Big Government* (New York: Threshold Editions, 2014).
2. John Fund and Hans von Spakovsky, *Who's Counting? How Fraudsters and Bureaucrats Put Your Vote at Risk* (New York: Encounter Books, 2012).
3. heritage.org/issues/legal.elections; rnla.org/votefraud.asp.
4. Robert Popper, "Political Fraud About Voter Fraud," *Wall Street Journal*, April 27, 2014.
5. "Literally a Toss-up: Coin Tosses Helped Give Clinton Edge in Tight Iowa Race," Fox News, February 2, 2016.
6. Interview with Robert Popper, January 30, 2016.
7. For a fuller description of how Chris Coates was mistreated by the Obama administration, see John Fund and Hans von Spakovsky, *Obama's Enforcer: Eric Holder's Justice Department* (New York: Harper Collins/Broadside Books, 2014).
8. "Inaccurate, Costly and Inefficient—Evidence That America's Voter Registration System Needs an Upgrade," Pew Center on the States, issue brief, February 2012.
9. "With USJF Support, Defend the Vote Testifies to Illinois Election Board," United States Justice Foundation online report (February 23, 2012).
10. *Davis v. Hargett*, Case No. 2: 12-cv-00023 (M.D. Tenn., September 24, 2012).
11. Jesse Richman, Gulshan Chattha, and David Earnest, "Do Non-Citizens Vote in U.S. Elections?" *Electoral Studies*, Vol. 36, page 153, December 2014.
12. Noah Rothman, "Al Sharpton Reveals Details of His Meeting with Obama, Holder, on Plan to Go After Voter ID States," Mediaite.com, July 30, 2013.

13. "Maryland Redistricting Maps Are Comic and Controversial," *Washington Post*, October 29, 2011.

Chapter 5: Obamacare: Congress Exempts Itself

1. Brendan Bordelon, "How Five Republicans Let Congress Keep Its Fraudulent Obamacare Subsidies," *National Review*, May 7, 2015.
2. Ibid.
3. Judicial Watch press release of April 22, 2014.
4. Judicial Watch press release of March 25, 2014.
5. Judicial Watch press release of September 25, 2014.
6. Judicial Watch press release of March 25, 2015.
7. Robert Pear, "Official Who Led Medicare Through Insurance Shakeup Is Resigning," *New York Times*, January 16, 2015.
8. Judicial Watch press release of January 19, 2016.

Chapter 6: Using the IRS as a Political Tool

1. "Inappropriate Criteria Were Used to Identify Tax-Exempt Applications for Review," Treasury Inspector General for Tax Administration Ref. No. 2013-10-053, May 14, 2013.
2. "IRS's Lois Lerner Had Database of Tax-Exempt Organizations Sent to FBI Weeks Before 2010 Midterm Elections," House of Representatives, Committee on Oversight, press release, June 9, 2014.
3. Letter of January 8, 2014, from House Committee on Oversight to Attorney General Eric Holder, U.S. Department of Justice.
4. Eliana Johnson, "Who Is Toby Miles?" *National Review*, August 25, 2015.

Chapter 7: Immigration and Border Enforcement

1. Caroline May, "Top General: Border Crisis 'Existential' National Security Crisis," Breitbart.com, July 7, 2014.
2. Molly O'Toole, "Top General: Says Mexico Border Security Now 'Existential' Threat to the U.S.," Defenseone.com, July 5, 2014.
3. Jessica Vaughn, "Catch and Release," Center for Immigration Studies, March 2014.
4. "Smith: ICE Authorizes Worst 'Prison Break' in History," press release, Representative Lamar Smith, May 12, 2014.
5. Brad Heath, "U.S. Misinformed Congress, Public, on Immigrant Release," *USA Today*, October 22, 2014.
6. "ICE's Release of Immigration Detainees," Office of Inspector General, Department of Homeland Security, OIG-14=116, August 2014.
7. Michelle Moons, "Murderer: I Chose SF Because It Is a 'Sanctuary City,' " Breitbart.com, July 6, 2015.

8. Jason Howerton, "You Could Hear a Pin Drop During Father's Devastating Testimony," TheBlaze.com, February 25, 2015.

9. 8 U.S.C. 1644. See also U.S.C. 1373.

10. "Father of Kate Steinle Blasts 'Legal Loopholes' that Helped Daughter's Alleged Killer," Fox News, July 21, 2015.

11. Caroline May, "Center of Immigration Studies Unveils Interactive Map of Immigrant Removals by County," Breitbart.com, May 6, 2015.

12. Judicial Watch press release of August 26, 2010.

13. "Sessions Comments on Nomination of Thomas Perez," press release, Senator Jeff Sessions, March 18, 2013.

Chapter 8: Terrorism and the Reckless Actions of the Obama Administration

1. Senator Richard Durbin, letter to FBI Director Robert Mueller, March 27, 2012.

2. Jonathan Easley, "West Says Muslim Brotherhood Being Allowed to Influence Strategy," *The Hill*, April 23, 2012.

3. Diana West, *American Betrayal: The Secret Assault on Our Nation's Character* (New York: St. Martin's Press, 2013).

4. His last name is also spelled "al-Awlaki" in some reports.

5. Scott Shane and Souad Medkhennet, "Imam's Path from Condemning Terror to Practicing Jihad," *New York Times*, May 8, 2010.

6. Susan Schmidt, "Imam from Va. Mosque Now Thought to Have Aided Al-Qaeda," *Washington Post*, February 27, 2008.

7. Maureen Dowd, "Downgrade Blues," *New York Times*, August 6, 2011.

8. Marisa Taylor and Jonathan Landay, "Bin Laden Film Leak Was Referred to Justice," McClatchy Newspapers, December 17, 2012,

Conclusion: Judicial Watch's Mission

1. Justin Elliott, "Federal Government No Longer Cares About Disclosing Public Information," *Washington Post*, March 11, 2016.

2. John Fund, "Stonewaller-in-Chief," *National Review*, August 10, 2014.

3. "Dozens of Inspectors General Say Federal Agencies Hindering Their Work," *Washington Post*, August 6, 2014.

4. Michelle Malkin, "Stop Obama's war on watchdogs," October 21, 2015, http://michellemalkin.com/2015/10/21/stop-obamas-war-on-watchdogs/.

5. John Fund, "How Obama Officials Dodge the Freedom of Information Act," *National Review*, August 28, 2015.

INDEX